UNDER THE GUNS OF THE
GERMAN ACES

IMMELMANN, VOSS, GÖRING, LOTHAR VON RICHTHOFEN
THE COMPLETE RECORD OF THEIR VICTORIES AND VICTIMS

UNDER THE GUNS OF THE GERMAN ACES

IMMELMANN, VOSS, GÖRING, LOTHAR VON RICHTHOFEN
THE COMPLETE RECORD OF THEIR VICTORIES AND VICTIMS

NORMAN FRANKS
AND HAL GIBLIN

GRUB STREET · LONDON

TO STEWART K TAYLOR,CANADA, WITH GRATITUDE AND RESPECT

Published by Grub Street
The Basement,
10 Chivalry Road,
London SWll lHT

British Library Cataloguing-in-Publication Data
Franks, Norman L.R.
Under the Guns of the German Aces: Immelmann, Voss, Göring, Lothar Von Richthofen. The Complete Record of their Victories and Victims
I. Title
940.44943092
ISBN 1-898697-72-8

Printed and bound in Italy by Vallardi grafiche SpA

ACKNOWLEDGEMENTS

The large amount of research distilled into these pages came to us from all quarters of the world. The authors would like to record their appreciation to the following for many kindnesses received, as well as for the valuable help and assistance freely given:

Mark Abbott, Ormskirk, Lancs;
All Staff at the Commonwealth War Graves Commission, Maidenhead, Berks;
All Staff at the Central and Reference Libraries, Liverpool;
Armée de L'Air, Service Historique, France;
The Lord Bagot, Llithfaen, Gwynedd;
Frank W Bailey, USA;
R G M M Baily, Assistant Archivist, Wellington College, Berks;
A H U Bain, London;
Desmond D U Bain, London;
David Baldwin, Stafford, Staffs;
Mike Blackburn, St Helens, Lancs;
R L Bland, Archivist, Clifton College, Bristol;
Cliff Blood, Prestwich Manchester;
Steve Bury, Nelson, Lancs;
Hugh Casement, Munich, Germany;
Frank Cheesman, Margate, Kent;
Neil Clark, Southport, Lancs;
Liz Clarke, Somerset Studies Library, Taunton;
Geoff Coles, Kimbolton School, Huntingdon, Cambs;
Jean M Cook, The Librarian, Smythe Library, Tonbridge School, Kent;
Mike Cooper, Birkdale, Lancs;
Gaby Crolla, Greasby, Wirral;
D P M Daly, Tarpoley, Cheshire;
Jeff Day, Chard, Somerset;
Department of Documents, Imperial War Museum, London;
Liz Deverell, Local Studies, Central Library, Kingston upon Hull;
Joe Devereux, Cheltenham, Gloucestershire;
Chris Dixon, Bridlington, Yorkshire;
Robin S Don, Dereham, Norfolk;
George Donnison, Greasby, Wirral;
David Dutton, Formby, Merseyside;
Peter Elliott, RAF Museum;
David Empson, Ipswich, Suffolk;
Julie Evans, Wallasey, Cheshire;
Major David Evans TD, Hon Sec, Liverpool Scottish Museum;
Andrew Farthing, Crosby Reference Library;
Nick Forder, Curator, Air & Space, The Museum of Science & Industry in Manchester;
M R M Foster, London;
Russell Guest, Writer and Historian, Melbourne, Australia;
Jan Hayzlett, Fort Collins, Colorado, USA;
Vernon Henstridge, Wareham, Dorset and Boscombe, Hampshire;
Nicholas Hinde, Archivist, Felsted School, Dunmow, Essex;
Simon Jones, Liverpool Museums and Galleries;
Keeper and Staff, Public Records Office, Kew;
Kevin Kelly, Sunderland, Tyne & Wear;
Iain Kerr, Edinburgh and Windsor;
Paul Leaman, Cross & Cockade Society;
Ian Livesley, Southport, Lancs;
Graham Maddocks, Birkenhead, Wirral;
Miss J Marsh, Reference Library, Bournemouth;
Jane Maxwell, Assistant Librarian (College Archives), Trinity College Library, University of Dublin;
Nigel McCrery, Nottingham;
Malcolm McGregor, Esher, Surrey;
Mrs McMahon, Worthing Reference Library;
Paul Morris, Blackpool, Lancs;
Humphrey W Osmond, The Archivist, Dean Close School, Cheltenham, Gloucestershire;
Dave Parry, Imperial War Museum, London;
Sally Parsons, Eastbourne Library;
Simon Pile, Haydock, Lancs;
Moira Reid, Local Studies, Central Library, Paisley;
Keith Rennles, Sutton, Surrey;
Alex Revell, Cornwall;
Bob Rogers Jnr, Viet Nam Veteran (USMC) and WW1 Historian, Stone Mountain, Georgia, USA;
Neil Rose, Birkdale, Lancs;
Norman Rosser, Archivist, Malvern College, Worcs;
Wing Commander Jim Routledge, Morpeth, Northumberland;
Harry Rudd, Hightown, Merseyside;
Graham Sacker, Cheltenham, Gloucs;

Dr D A Scales, St Lawrence College, Ramsgate, Kent;
Mike Schoeman, Vlaeberg, South Africa;
Patricia Sheldon, Local Studies, Central Library, Newcastle upon Tyne;
David Slade, Billinghurst, Kent;
Gordon Smith, Bonnyrigg, Midlothian;
Phillip T I Smith, The Registrar, The Old Denstonian Club, Denstone College, Uttoxeter, Staffs;
Robert Smith, Cowling, Nr Keighley, Yorkshire;
Steve Snelling, *Eastern Daily Press*, Norwich, Norfolk;
Catherine Spackman, Reference Library, Bournemouth;
Peter Stott, Hon Secretary, Old Lerpoolian Society, Liverpool;
Stuart Tamblin, Moulton, Northants;
Gordon Taylor, Edinburgh;
Jeff Taylor, Rubery, Rednall, Birmingham;
Roy Thorniley, Warrington, Cheshire;
Brian J Turner, Leigh on Sea, Essex;
Miss Chris Watkins, Local Studies Library, Rochdale, Lancs;
David R C West OBE, TD, MA, Hon Archivist, Marlborough College, Wiltshire;
Margery West, Ballaragh, Isle of Man;
Mrs A C Wheeler, The Library, Charterhouse, Godalming, Surrey;
Hugh Winkler, Abingdon, Oxs;
Dianne Yeadon, Norfolk and Norwich Central Library.

CONTENTS

INTRODUCTION

As with the previous book in the series, *Under the Guns of the Red Baron*, we have attempted not just to identify the victims of the aces but, wherever possible, to 'flesh out' the cold impersonal list of names into personalities – to understand something about the lives and backgrounds of the many young men whose bright futures were, in most cases, violently and brutally curtailed. The courage and steadfastness of the fliers – often mere boys – never fails to elicit a mixture of admiration and astonishment. The extent of the waste of their very considerable potential talent is, paradoxically, most graphically demonstrated when contrasted with the success made of subsequent lives and careers by those who did, fortunately, survive.

The approach adopted in the Red Baron book was so well received that it was felt it could be extended to others of the German aces, but which?

Max Immelmann was, along with Oswald Boelcke, the first of the famous German Aces of World War I. His total of seventeen victories proved modest by later standards but was, at the time, considered nothing short of phenomenal. He and his contemporaries were the innovators, literally the pioneers, of aerial combat. They had no text books to consult, no precedents to draw upon, they learnt their lessons in the most difficult and dangerous way possible – their success or failure truly a matter of life or death.

We looked next at Hermann Göring, later to become Reichmarshal and leader of the German Luftwaffe, not because he was in the very forefront of the aces in terms of victories gained, but simply because we thought it would be interesting to do so – for the obvious reasons! And interesting it proved – but not in the way we had anticipated. We can honestly say that we approached the assessment of his claims with open minds, thinking that we would be presented with only the usual problems but, in the event, what we found both surprised and puzzled us. There are, of course, many difficulties encountered in the untangling of often conflicting pieces of incomplete, eighty-odd-year-old 'evidence' surrounding the aerial conflicts on both sides but in the case of Hermann Göring the anomalies and inconsistencies were staggering. Despite expending a disproportionate amount of time and effort in researching, unravelling, checking and cross-checking the Göring 'victory' claims, we were forced to the conclusion that 'something is amiss'! In the end we decided to present the facts in so far as they could be ascertained and to let readers come to their own conclusions!

Moving forward chronologically, we next chose the mercurial Werner Voss. A pilot of exceptional ability, his forty-eight victories were achieved in a relatively short period. By the time of his death in one of the greatest aerial combats ever, he was second only to Manfred von Richthofen, the eponymous 'Red Baron'. The evidence suggests that Voss was ruthless in the execution of his work as a fighter pilot. Often, he relentlessly and mercilessly pursued his victims down to ground level, regardless of the state of helplessness he had already reduced them to. And, when his own time came, Voss in turn asked no quarter, fighting impossible and overwhelming odds to the end.

The fourth subject chosen was, almost inevitably, Lothar von Richthofen, the Red Baron's younger brother. Although a highly successful ace with forty victories in only seventy-seven days of actual combat flying, his achievements seem forever to be overshadowed by the deeds of his famous brother. Their 'styles' contrasted sharply – Manfred describing his brother as a 'butcher'. If Manfred's approach was rapier-like, Lothar's was bludgeoning!

Having chosen the subjects, we have to say that not all the questions have been answered – indeed, some new ones have been posed – but we hope that this book will stand as another memorial to those brave men who fought in the very first aerial war.

Norman Franks, Morden, Surrey
Hal Giblin, Hightown, Liverpool

CHAPTER 1

OBERLEUTNANT MAX IMMELMANN

Max Immelmann – 'The Eagle of Lille'.

Manfred von Richthofen apart, probably the next best known of the German aces of the Great War, Immelmann was born on 21 September 1890, the son of, and named after, a prosperous Dresden factory owner, Max Immelmann. His father died whilst Max was a child but still the family could afford to indulge the adolescent's wishes and so, in his fifteenth year, he was sent to the Cadet School in Dresden. By 1912 he held the rank of Ensign, having joined the prosaically named 2nd Railway Regiment the previous year. Altogether a less than glamorous start for a man who, in a few short years, would be a household name not only in Germany but around the world. Immelmann spent the next two years studying at the War Academy, only returning to his regiment upon the outbreak of war in August 1914. By this time, however, he had become interested in military aviation, a new and exciting arm of service. November 1914 saw him attending the flying school at Johannistal, Berlin before, in February 1915, going on to continue his training at nearby Adlerdhof.

After successfully graduating as a pilot, he was sent to Aircraft Park No. 3 outside Rethal, to await a posting to a front-line unit. Never idle, he used the waiting time to fly mail and airmen to various front-line abteilung, even piloting a long-range test-flight to Brussels. His first combat posting came in early April when he was ordered to report to FFA10 at Vrizy, behind the Champagne Sector of the front lines.

Like most pilots in WWI, Immelmann's first experience of war flying was in a two-seater aeroplane designed to undertake a variety of tasks besides observation (the primary purpose) including reconnaissance, photography and the ranging of artillery. He remained at FFA10 for less than two weeks

Pilots of FA62: back L to R : Max von Muzler; von Schilling; Max von Cossel; Fromme; von Gusnar. front L to R: Salffener; Meding; Albert Oesterreicher; Oswald Boelcke; Hptm Erich Kastner; Immelmann; von Krause and Hess.

at the end of which he was assigned to Feldflieger Abteilung No. 62 (FFA62 – literally field flying section 62) then in the process of formation. Another of the pilots joining the new unit was Leutnant Oswald Boelcke, a name which would forever be linked with that of Immelmann.

FFA62, commanded by Hauptmann Hermann Kastner, was another 'two-seater' unit, flying LVG C-type machines. The unit was based at Brayelles, an airfield just south-east of Douai – to all intents and purposes the present-day site of the Renault Works. In the spring of 1917 it would also be the home of Manfred von Richthofen's Jasta 11.

Immelmann arrived on 28 April 1915 with the rank of Fahnrich (Ensign) just at the time when, after a comparative lull, events at the battle front were 'warming up'. Some units began to receive one or two of the new, small and handy, single-engined monoplanes designed and built by the Dutch genius, Anthony Fokker. Fokker, a national of neutral Holland, had first offered his services to the British and the French – both countries, to the delight of the Germans, turning him down. The nimble Fokker Eindekker ('one wing' or monoplane) was designed to be used to protect the slower, vulnerable two-seaters. Protection that was becoming imperative as the French with their Nieuport Scouts, and the British with their Bristol Scouts and Vickers FB5 'Gunbuses', were successfully opposing the cumbersome German two-seaters and badly disrupting their intelligence-gathering reconnaissance flights.

Some pilots were content to remain two-seater airmen but for others, like Immelmann and Boelcke, the chance of flying and fighting in these new single-seaters (or 'Scouts', as they had lately become known) proved an irresistible challenge. Already there was an aura – a certain *je ne sais quoi* – building up around these men. The term 'fighter pilot' remains as potent today as it was in those early days, conjuring up images of single-handed combat and deeds of derring-do redolent of the age of chivalry and the gallant knights of old. Despite the risks and dangers, never was there a lack of volunteers ready and willing to join this élite fraternity.

Anthony Fokker himself, personally flew-in the first of his monoplanes to the base of FFA62 in June 1915, the harbinger of the 'Fokker Scourge' soon to be unleashed upon the unsuspecting Allied airmen on the Western Front. In the meantime, however, the airmen of FFA62 continued with their plodding LVG two-seaters. Immelmann, who had already received the Iron Cross 2nd Class and the Saxon Friedrich August Medal in Bronze and Silver, was further heartened on 20 July by a formal commission. By this time Boelcke was flying the Fokker Eindekkers every day, making himself familiar with their handling characteristics and generally learning to use them effectively. Immelmann's first opportunity to fly a Fokker came on 30 July. Despite helpful briefings from Boelcke, virtually everything had to be learnt from scratch. There were no books to refer to; air fighting was entirely new and had to be self-taught. However, the Fokker had one major and telling advantage over the British and French machines - it carried a machine gun that enabled the pilot to shoot directly at an opponent.

Frenchman Roland Garros was among the first to appreciate the advantages that would accrue to the combat pilot who could point his machine at the target and, with direct line of sight, fire through the propeller. Garros, bravely if somewhat rashly, used metal deflector plates to protect the wooden propeller against the inevitable, if small, percentage of self-inflicted strikes. Unfortunately, shortly after implementation of his innovation Garros was forced down behind German lines and the secret was out! Fokker was asked to copy the Garros design but the inherent dangers were so obvious that he bent his inventive mind to coming up with an alternative. The result was as brilliant as it was simple – an 'interrupter gear' which would not allow the machine gun to fire when a propeller blade was directly in front of its muzzle. Air fighting took a giant step forward and the Fokker menace was spawned. Now the German scout pilots could not only protect their vulnerable two-seater brethren but

One of Immelmann's Fokker Eindekker fighters (EIV No. 127/16) with his ground crew.

could also fly hunting sorties themselves, aggressively seeking out and bringing down the Allied aircraft engaged on the Corps work of reconnaissance, photography and artillery co-operation.

By the end of July Boelcke, in an Eindekker, had brought down his first opponent whilst Immelmann, desperate to emulate his mentor, was still routinely flying two-seaters. Despite it being high summer, the weather was poor on the first day of August and Immelmann's scheduled flight was cancelled. However, adverse weather or not, the British were up and over the front! Immelmann's longed-for moment arrived when Boelcke invited him to join him in opposing the intruders. The two Fokker Eindekkers took off, climbing hard into the western sky.

Said to be Immelmann flying an Eindekker – on this occasion as an escort to a Roland CII.

VICTORY NO 1

1 August 1915 BE2c (No. 2003) 2 Squadron 06.15 hours

The German Scouts had been ordered to take off as yet another formation of ten hostile aeroplanes were reported crossing the lines. The British machines – their target pre-selected sites at Douai – were intercepted at 05.15 (German time was one hour ahead of the British equivalent and would remain so until 25 March 1917). Immelmann caught up with the British planes just as some were turning for home, their bombs already dropped. Three of the BEs had dispensed with the services of an observer so as to increase their bomb-carrying capacity and now all were flat out in the rush for home, their formation open and loose. Immelmann closed on the BE that had arrived last over the target area. Boelcke, in the meantime, suffered a gun stoppage and had broken away. Armed only with two automatic pistols, Immelmann's intended victim was Lieutenant William Reid of 2 Squadron, RFC. Immelmann fired burst after burst, expending 450 to 500 bullets, and before long the unequal contest was over with Reid wounded and forced down near Brebières, just past Vitry. Setting down his Fokker nearby, Immelmann actually helped Reid to climb out of his cockpit and saw to it that he was sent off to the nearest medical unit, the 1st Bavarian Reserve Corps Field Hospital.

Following his return from captivity in March 1918, Reid reported the details of his last fight. He stated that on the Saturday evening of 31 July 1915, Major Blake, the Squadron CO, called five pilots into the orderly room and gave them instructions for a bombing raid that was to take place the following morning. The five were Captain J G Hearson (RE/RFC), Captain T W Smith and Lieutenants Leather, C R Gallie (R. Scots Fus.) and, of course, Reid himself. They were to rendezvous over Arras at 06.00 (British time) and fly to a German airfield between Douai and Vitry. Hearson and Gallie were to carry machine guns and an observer but no bombs, and would offer protection to the others. Smith would carry a machine gun, an observer and three bombs while Leather and Reid, *sans* both observers and machine guns, would each carry six bombs.

Arriving over Arras on time, Reid counted only two other machines and while circling and waiting for the remainder, glimpsed, in the distance, the two errant machines already on their way and heading for the lines. Reid signalled to his neighbours and soon all five BEs, albeit strung out, were en route for the target. Reid saw Leather release his bombs before he, too, dropped his six on some sheds. As he did so he was disappointed to see, in the distance, the two so-called 'escort' BEs already heading back for the lines. Seconds later he looked back to see a Fokker about 50 yards behind him. Reid immediately pulled out one of his pistols with his right hand and with his left hand on the controls, started to turn towards the German. Immelmann opened fire and bullets thudded into Reid's left arm, breaking it in four places.

Reid put his nose down and steered for the lines, hoping that the escort machines might see his plight and return to offer him assistance. His adversary, however, remained just 50 yards astern of him and after yet another burst smashed into the BE's gravity tank, the engine stopped. Reid glided into a landing which, despite Immelmann's continuing attentions, he executed effectively. Immelmann put down about 30 seconds later and coming over to the BE, helped the wounded Reid from the machine. The British machine had taken some 40 hits and most of the instruments had been smashed.

Reid said that he had been told later that Immelmann flew over the British lines and dropped a letter saying that he had been shot up, wounded in the left arm but was otherwise safe. This was indeed the case; Immelmann had taken a LVG two-seater to St Pol to drop the message. Reid was sent to Douai Hospital, operated upon and then transferred to a military hospital in Münster where he remained for the next five months.

Immelmann's accomplishments to date were recognised with the award of the Iron Cross, First Class.

LIEUTENANT
WILLIAM REID,
6TH BATTALION, KING'S LIVERPOOL REGIMENT (TF) (LIVERPOOL RIFLES) AND 2 SQUADRON, ROYAL FLYING CORPS

Reid was commissioned into the second line of the élite 6th Battalion, King's Liverpool Regiment (Territorial Force) – the 'Liverpool Rifles' – on 24 December 1914. On 6 February 1915, he was transferred to the 1/6th King's but was obviously already contemplating a switch to flying. Reid was awarded his Royal Aero Club Aviators Certificate (No. 1128) on 16 March 1915 and was, shortly afterwards, accepted on attachment to the Royal Flying Corps. Because of the severity of his wounds, Reid was exchanged into Switzerland on 30 May 1916 where he continued to receive medical treatment. There was, however, still some considerable time to elapse before he was finally repatriated to Britain on 11 March 1918.

VICTORY NO 2

26 August 1915 Biplane

Boelcke and Immelmann were both out hunting on this summer's evening and had already forced two artillery fliers down into their own lines. There were a number of French machines in the vicinity, indeed both men had been chasing nothing but French aeroplanes over the previous few evenings! Now as they attacked, Boelcke's gun jammed but Immelmann was able to fire 300 rounds and saw the French pilot throw up his arms as if he was hit. The Frenchman appeared to discard his flying helmet as his machine began to spiral down from a height of 2,200 metres before plunging into the ground close to Souchez. By the time Immelmann found his way back to his airfield, it was dark and flares had to be deployed to guide him in.

There were no RFC losses on this evening and so his victim must, indeed, have been French – probably a single-seater as Immelmann only made reference to the pilot being hit.

Soon after this, Immelmann was awarded the Albrecht Knight's Cross Order.

VICTORY NO 3

21 September 1915 BE2c(No.2004) 10 Squadron c10.00 hours

On this, his 25th birthday, Immelmann was escorting German artillery observation machines when, approaching the front lines, he spotted a British aeroplane which he lost no time in attacking. The British machine was a BE from 10 Squadron RFC on a reconnaissance mission and had reached a position east of Neuville at 09.00 (British time) when Immelmann closed in. Its occupants, Second Lieutenant S W Caws and Lieutenant W A Sugden-Wilson, made a good fight of it and at one stage Immelmann was forced to break away with a gun jam. Clearing the problem, the German attacked again, this time hitting and wounding both airmen and forcing the machine down between Acheville and Willerval, the BE bursting into flames as it hit the ground.

Immelmann once again chose to land near his victims, finding that the observer, Sugden-Wilson, although wounded, had been thrown clear. The pilot, Caws, had obviously been killed in the air and his body was still in the burning wreckage. Sugden-Wilson was wounded in several places, his back badly injured but still he was fortunate to have been thrown out and away from the conflagration. He was carried away to hospital and captivity.

SECOND LIEUTENANT
STANLEY WINTHER CAWS,
1ST CANADIAN CONTINGENT AND 10 SQUADRON, ROYAL FLYING CORPS

Immelmann poses alongside the wreck of his third victory – a BE2c from 10 Squadron.

Born on 22 March 1879, the only son of Douglas and Harriet Caws of Saint Catherine's, Sea View, Isle of Wight, Stanley was educated at Portsmouth Grammar School and Christ's College, Blackheath. He served in the South Africa War as a trooper in Paget's Horse for which he was awarded the Queen's Medal and clasps. From South Africa he went to Canada and in August 1914 when the Great War broke out, was engaged in an important and remunerative expedition in the north-west region of that country. He gladly relinquished his part in the expedition, immediately volunteered for service and was with the 1st Canadian Contingent when it arrived in England. Caws learnt to fly at his own expense and was awarded the Royal Aero Club's Aviators Certificate (No.1097) and gazetted Second Lieutenant in the Royal Flying Corps on the same day, 25 February 1915. Although buried with full military honours by the German Air Service, his grave site was subsequently lost in ensuing battles and he is now commemorated on the Arras Memorial to the Missing, France. He was, at thirty-six years of age, the oldest of Immelmann's victims.

LIEUTENANT WILLIAM HODGSON SUGDEN-WILSON, WEST SOMERSET YEOMANRY AND 10 SQUADRON, ROYAL FLYING CORPS

The son of Mr and Mrs W H Wilson of Hexgreave Park, Southwell, Nottinghamshire, Bill Wilson (later to adopt the name, Sugden-Wilson) was educated at Harrow (1903-1906). After the completion of his education, he became a Land Agent in the county of Somerset. Given his ability as a horseman, it was not surprising that, pre-war, he volunteered for and was commissioned into, the West Somerset Yeomanry (3 April 1913). After the outbreak of war, he successfully applied for transfer to the RFC and, following training, was sent to join 10 Squadron in France on 23 July 1915. Although acting as observer on the day he and his pilot Caws met Immelmann, he had already been awarded the Royal Aero Club's Aviators Certificate (No. 1218) on 22 April 1915. After his capture, Sugden-Wilson wrote to his parents with a graphic description of his last flight; a letter that was reproduced in the Times of 25 October 1915: *"We were attacked by hostile machines and had a great fight lasting 15 minutes during which we expended all our ammunition. My pilot, Lieutenant Caws, was shot dead when we were 11,000 foot up, a bullet passing through his neck down to his heart, through the instrument board, and hitting my leg!"* As well as the wounds he received in the air, he broke a bone at the base of his spine in the ensuing crash. Sugden-Wilson was exchanged into neutral Holland on 10 April 1918 and finally repatriated on 25 November 1918.

Two days later, at around 14.00 hours on 23 September 1915, Immelmann was on the receiving end of an air fight over Ham when he engaged a Vickers FB5 Gunbus of 11 Squadron (No.5456) crewed by Second Lieutenant R E A W Hughes-Chamberlain and Captain C W Lane. Lane, in the front cockpit of the 'pusher' machine, saw his bullets splatter about the Fokker's cockpit and later Immelmann, who had to dive away rapidly, admitted to being 'shot about'.

VICTORY NO 4

10 October 1915 BE2c (No. 2033) 16 Squadron 15.00 hours

Second Lieutenant J Gay and Lieutenant D Leeson of 16 Squadron were flying an afternoon sortie over Lille in order to photograph the defences in the area. Immelmann had taken off to patrol between La Bassée and Lens and spotted the BE amongst the tell-tale bursts of AA shells over Lille. Closing in, he fired 400 rounds into the British machine whereupon the BE began to plunge earthwards, spiralling down before landing and trundling into some trees near the village of Verlinghem. The BE was badly smashed, the pilot killed, the Canadian observer Leeson wounded but alive, his gun knocked out in the initial attack. Leeson, who was taken into captivity, later reported that there had been two Fokkers and that his machine gun had been shot away in the burst that had killed Gay. Leeson had been extremely fortunate to survive the crash landing without the hand of the pilot to guide them down.

SECOND LIEUTENANT JOHN GAY, 16 SQUADRON, ROYAL FLYING CORPS

Born in 1893, John (Jock) Gay was the only son of Doctor John and Mrs Catherine Elizabeth Gay of 137 Upper Richmond Road, Putney, London. He was educated at Felsted School (1905-1911) and later became a medical student at St Bart's Hospital. Pre-war, he had joined the City of London Yeomanry and so was mobilised immediately upon the outbreak of war. He learnt to fly and was awarded the Royal Aero Club Aviators Certificate (No. 1135) on 30 March 1915, receiving a Special Reserve commission in the Royal Flying Corps on the same day. He had been in France for four months. Jock Gay is buried in Cabaret-Rouge British Cemetery, Souchez, France (Fr.924). He was twenty-two years old.

LIEUTENANT DAVID LEESON, MID, BRITISH COLUMBIA REGIMENT AND 16 SQUADRON, ROYAL FLYING CORPS

Leeson, an Englishman, had only been in Canada for a short time when the war broke out. He volunteered immediately and after a period of service in the ranks, he was commissioned into the British Columbia Regiment on 30 April 1915. Soon after his arrival in England with the Canadian Infantry, Leeson successfully applied for transfer to the RFC. Following the usual training, he was sent out to join 16 Squadron as a probationary observer. After nearly three years in captivity, he was exchanged into neutral Holland on 19 April 1918.

Immelmann's 4th– the mangled remains of a 16 Squadron BE2c (J Gay/D Leeson).

Strangely, Leeson was incorrectly reported as 'killed' on 26 September 1918 – presumably during the period he was interned in Holland and, intriguingly, he was later Mentioned in Despatches for *'valuable services while in captivity'* – the announcement being made in the *London Gazette* of 16 December 1919. We have been unable to establish if these two significant events were in any way connected. Leeson was finally repatriated on 18 November 1918 and again intriguingly, relinquished his commission the following day.

On 13 October 1915, Leutnant Max Immelmann was awarded the Knight's Cross of Saxon Military St Henry Order, Commander, 2nd Class.

VICTORY NO 5

26 October 1915 VFB5 (No. 5464) 11 Squadron 10.05 hours

Immelmann's next encounter with an 11 Squadron Vickers Gunbus was more successful than on the last occasion he had clashed with one. The British machine, piloted by 'C' Flight commander, Captain C C Darley, with Second Lieutenant R L Slade in the front cockpit, was on a patrol flight in the direction of Cambrai from the Squadron's base at Villers Bretonneux. Just after midnight on 26 October, Darley had received orders to the effect that his Flight was to fly four patrols and recce sorties later that morning. Only two observers were available from his own Flight and so Darley was obliged to 'borrow' two from the other Flight Commanders. As the Squadron was in the process of moving to a new landing ground, the two borrowed men were only partially trained - naturally and responsibly, Darley took one of the tyros himself, Second Lieutenant R J Slade.

He took off at around 07.30 to patrol an area between Cambrai and Péronne. The Gunbus's engine was not running well as he climbed slowly north towards Arras, crossing the lines at 6,000 feet just south of the town. Following the long straight road towards Cambrai, Darley gained a little more height but was still low enough to attract the keen attention of the German AA gunners, with shrapnel hitting the Gunbus on several occasions. The anti-aircraft fire was soon left behind and as there were no enemy machines in sight, Darley steered for the German airfield at Cambrai to, as he later said, *"challenge them!"*

More AA fire greeted them as they neared Cambrai but, ominously, stopped abruptly and unexpectedly. The reason for the cessation of fire became clear as, moments later, a Fokker Eindekker appeared on their tail, its machine gun blazing. The inexperienced RFC observer had been taken completely by surprise. The Gunbus's engine promptly stopped, with the inevitable consequence. Darley, almost fainting from the pain of the wounds he had received, saw that the pressure gauge was not registering and knew that the petrol supply had been cut. As they glided down, Darley banked and urgently signalled Slade to fire at the Fokker but by this time Immelmann had climbed above and behind them again and was lining up another attacking run. Manoeuvring the powerless machine in the best way he could – the whole time harassed with a steady rate of fire from the pursuing Immelmann – Darley attempted to glide the full 20 miles to the lines but only got half way before being forced to put down in a field near Ecoust St Mein. Jumping out of his badly shot-about machine, Darley fired his pistol six times into the fuel tank but without effect. The fuel in the tank had already drained away through the bullet holes put there by Immelmann. Next, he tore off strips of wing fabric and made another unsuccessful attempt to set the machine alight with matches. Darley's wounds were painful and disabling, a bullet had passed through his right upper arm, another had almost severed his right thumb. Both wounds severely hampered his efforts to set the Gunbus alight and forced him to work with one hand. Perhaps significantly, he made no mention of any assistance received from his observer.
Moments later, German cavalry rode up to the crashed machine and took both airmen captive. Shortly afterwards – and predictably – the Fokker landed nearby; Immelmann strolled over to introduce himself to the vanquished crew and saw to it that Darley's wounds received attention before arranging for him to be driven to hospital in a car. The following day a message was dropped over the lines of the French Xth Armée, reporting both men safe.

CAPTAIN (LATER AIR COMMODORE)

CHARLES CURTIS DARLEY,

CBE (1931) AM (1922), MID, SILVER MEDAL OF THE SOCIETY FOR THE PROTECTION OF LIFE FROM FIRE, ROYAL FIELD ARTILLERY AND 11 SQUADRON, ROYAL FLYING CORPS

A pioneer of aerial photography, Charles Darley was born on 31 July 1890, the son of Captain Charles Edward and Mrs Darley of Caynton Manor, Newport, Salop. He was educated at Dulwich College (1903-1908) where, at various times, he captained the

Right: How the inhabitants of a small Lancashire market town were exhorted to help in the fight against 'the Hun' – albeit from a safe distance!

boxing, fencing and athletic teams. He passed into the Royal Military Academy, Woolwich in 1909 from whence he was gazetted Second Lieutenant into the Royal Field Artillery on 23 July 1910. He was in India from 1910 to 1914, only returning home briefly to qualify as a pilot – Royal Aero Club Aviators Certificate No.532 (15 August 1913). When he finally returned to England in 1914, Darley was seconded to the Royal Flying Corps, and shortly afterwards sent to join 3 Squadron at the front, thus qualifying for the 1914 Star. Foreseeing the military value of aerial photography, Darley took and developed his own photographs. Interest in the fuzzy black and white images grew and he began to be invited to headquarters to interpret them for the Staff. Eventually, by the end of January 1915, he had collected enough prints to produce a panorama of the whole of the front covered by his Squadron. Impressed, Major Salmond, his Squadron Commander, took the composite 'photo' map to Corps HQ where it created quite a stir. Early in February 1915 Darley, with Lieutenant W H V Wadham acting as observer, was entrusted with securing photographs of "some troublesome brick-stacks" south of the La Bassée canal. From the intelligence gathered by the Darley and Wadham reconnaissance, a greatly modified plan of attack from that which had been originally formulated was carried out with great success by the Allies. Darley received a Mention in Sir John French's Despatches for his services (*London Gazette* 1 January 1916). After being brought down by Immelmann, Darley was taken prisoner but because of his crippling injuries he was exchanged into neutral Switzerland on 30 May 1916; finally being repatriated via a circuitous route on 4 June 1917. Following a period of convalescence, and despite his physical handicaps, the remarkable Charles Darley was appointed to command 88 Squadron in 1919.

A brilliant all-round sportsman, some of his many sporting achievements included the heavyweight championship of the RMA where, in 1910, he also won the Physical Training Prize. He won both the middle and

heavy weight boxing championships at the Durbar Tournament (India) of 1911. In his fight with Immelmann, Darley lost part of his thumb and partial use of one arm and so, after the war, took up a sport that required the full use of only one arm – fencing! That he was successful is evidenced by the fact that he was the RAF Foil and Epée representative in 1923 and the Foil again in 1925.

In later life, Air Commodore CC Darley CBE AM, Royal Air Force.

In the late summer of 1919, Darley joined forces with his brother, Captain Cecil Hill Darley, DSC and Bar, DFC, Diploma of Military Merit 2nd Class (Spain), to pioneer routes across Europe to the Middle East. The words of the citation for the award of the Albert Medal (*London Gazette*, 25 July 1922, page 5511) best sum up what happened next: *"The King has been pleased to award the Albert Medal to Squadron Leader Charles Curtis Darley of the R.A.F., in recognition of his gallantry in endeavouring to save life. On the night of 27 September 1919, a Vickers-Vimy aeroplane piloted by Captain Cecil Hill Darley, brother of the Squadron Leader (then Flight Lieutenant) Darley, who was acting as Navigation Officer, made a forced landing by Lake Bracciano, some 20 miles north of Rome, when on a flight from England to Egypt. On the following morning, on taking off, the aeroplane failed to clear a telegraph pole and crashed, immediately bursting into flames. Squadron Leader Darley was thrown clear, but at once rushed to the blazing wreckage and displayed very conspicuous bravery and devotion in persistent, but unavailing, attempts to rescue his brother, who was pinned in the driver's seat. His efforts to release his brother were only brought to an end by his collapse. He sustained such severe burns that he was a patient in hospital for over eighteen months."*

Cecil Darley, a former RNAS pilot, had won one of his DSCs when, famously, he bombed the dockgates during the Zeebrugge Raid on 23 April 1918.

After his long spell in hospital, the durable Charles Darley resumed his RAF career and, on St Valentine's Day in 1925, he married Hilda Stephenson. He attended and passed RAF Staff College, Quetta, 1926-27, before going on to command RAF Kohat from 1929 to 1932, where he enjoyed almost unlimited big game hunting. His services were recognised by the award of the CBE in 1931. Darley was responsible for organising the opening of No. 10 Flying Training School at Tern Hill, Shropshire, becoming the school's first Commanding Officer. Returning to India, he commanded No.1 (India) Group, Peshawar, in 1938. In September 1939, as a result of a flying accident, he was invalided out of the RAF – ironically just at the time when the Second World War broke out. However, the undoubted value of his considerable and invaluable experience was recognised by a civilian appointment to the Air Ministry, where he remained for the rest of the war. His marriage to his first wife being dissolved in 1949, he married secondly, Mary Betty. In his last years he lived at 'Fiveways', 149 Broad Street, Birmingham. He died on 10 June 1962, just a few weeks short of his seventy-second birthday.

SECOND LIEUTENANT
REGINALD JAMES SLADE,
ARMY CYCLIST CORPS AND 11 SQUADRON, ROYAL FLYING CORPS

Born in 1890, from Chingford, Essex, Slade was gazetted Second Lieutenant in the Army

Cyclist Corps on 20 October 1914. He subsequently successfully applied for transfer to the RFC which occurred during the summer of 1915. He was still a probationary observer undergoing training when Captain Darley chose him to accompany him on 26 October 1915. Slade remained in captivity in Germany until 19 April 1918 when he was exchanged into neutral Holland. He was repatriated one week after the war ended whereupon he was immediately sent for unspecified treatment to the Eaton Hospital, 82 Eaton Square, London. Slade was finally discharged from active service on 27 May 1919.

VICTORY NO 6

7 November 1915 BE2c (No. 1715) 10 Squadron 15.45 hours

On patrol near Douai, Immelmann looked down from his cockpit to spot a BE below him. Cautiously edging towards it, he soon saw that it was escorted by a single-seat Bristol Scout. This latter (No. 4675) was flown by Captain C Gordon Bell also of 10 Squadron who would later report a fight with a Fokker and an Aviatik. Bell was something of a veteran flyer, having qualified in 1911 and was to be become one of RFC's first aces, gaining five 'victories' in 1915. Later, he became a distinguished instructor, numbering amongst his pupils James McCudden VC, one of the very great aces of WW1. Despite the escort, Max Immelmann was still able successfully to attack the two-seater which spiralled down to crash near Quíevy-la-Motta, just west of Douai, at 14.45 (British time) – both crewmen being killed. In the meantime, Gordon Bell had engaged the Aviatik but was forced to break off because of engine trouble. As he spun away, heading for home and a forced landing, he noticed the Fokker circling above the crashed BE. Immelmann continued with his habit of landing near to his 'kill' – a particularly appropriate word on this occasion as both occupants were beyond his help.

LIEUTENANT

OWEN VINCENT LE BAS,

1/ROYAL WEST SURREY REGIMENT (THE QUEEN'S) AND 10 SQUADRON, ROYAL FLYING CORPS

The younger son of barrister Reginald Vincent Le Bas and his wife, Florence H Le Bas of 38 Hornton Court, Kensington, London and Winsford, Dulverton, Somerset, Owen was born in 1894. He was educated at Wellingborough; at Charterhouse and at West Wrattling Park, Cambridge. Commissioned into the 1st Battalion, Royal West Surreys on 31 July 1914, he was considered too young to accompany his battalion to France in August 1914. However, the 1st Queen's suffered such enormous casualties in the early days of the war that, despite his youthfulness, he was sent to Flanders with

Above: Owen LeBas's Battalion of the Royal West Surreys drawn up on parade before their departure for France in August 1914.

Right: The remnants of the same Battalion three months later on 9 November 1914.

other replacements in September. He was wounded at Langemarck on 21 October 1914 during the first Battle of Ypres and came home for medical treatment. Recovering quickly, he was returned to the front on Christmas eve. An application to join the Royal Flying Corps was granted in January 1915 when he was sent for training as an observer. He also learnt to fly and was awarded the Royal Aero Club Aviators Certificate (No. 1252) on 29 April 1915, travelling back to England on that very day to commence formal pilot training. On 17 August following, he flew across the

Channel to join 10 Squadron. Ironically, Owen Le Bas, the scion of a Huguenot family that had fled France in fear of their lives generations before, lies buried in Brown's Copse Cemetery, Roeux, France (Fr.604). He was 21 years of age.

CAPTAIN

THEODORE DAWSON ADAMS,

1ST LANCS BRIGADE, ROYAL FIELD ARTILLERY AND 10 SQUADRON, ROYAL FLYING CORPS

The younger son of the Reverend William James Adams VD and Mrs Adams of 5 Grosvenor Terrace, Princes Park, Liverpool. Reverend Adams was the Senior Chaplain of 57th (West Lancs) Division (Territorial Force) and Vicar of St Augustine's, Everton, Liverpool. Theodore was educated at Liverpool College (1898-1905). After completing his education, he went into business in Liverpool and, emulating his father, joined the Territorial Force, being gazetted Second Lieutenant to the 1st Lancs Brigade, RFA. A keen and able volunteer, he enjoyed quite rapid progress being promoted to Captain on 18 April 1914, shortly after passing the School of Instruction Artillery examinations. He developed an interest in aviation and successfully sought transfer to the RFC. In fact, he had only been with his Squadron for a matter of days when he was killed. He and his pilot, Owen le Bas, are buried side-by-side in Brown's Copse Cemetery, Roeux,France (Fr.604). He was 26 years old.

Immelmann now received the Knight's Cross, with Swords, of the Royal Hohenzollern House Order, only the second Saxon officer to be so honoured.

VICTORY NO 7

15 December 1915 Morane Parasol (No. 5087) 3 Squadron am

A morning reconnaissance mission for the British 1st Army came to an abrupt end when the machine carrying it out was intercepted by Immelmann and the deadly Fokker. Contact was first made over Valenciennes, Immelmann making a series of attacks as he chased the intruding two-seater back towards its own lines. Finally the German's fire took effect and the Morane fell. The observer and his machine gun being seen to drop out of the shattered aircraft, both falling into a clump of trees whilst the machine itself crunched into the ground, finally coming to rest against the garden wall of a house in Raismes.

LIEUTENANT

ALAN VICTOR HOBBS,

ROYAL SUSSEX REGIMENT AND 3 SQUADRON, ROYAL FLYING CORPS

A V Hobbs was the eldest son of chemist Alfred Ernest Hobbs and Mrs Hobbs of 20 St John's Road, Tunbridge Wells. He was a day boy at Tonbridge (1909-13) having gained a scholarship from Skinners' School, Tunbridge Wells. A clever boy and a member of the OTC he had done extremely well, gaining the Essay Prize and the Leaving Exhibition for Mathematics. He won a Kent County higher scholarship and a scholarship for mathematics at St John's College,

Cambridge. When war broke out, he had just completed his first year at university and was still accumulating scholastic prizes. Volunteering immediately, he joined the ranks of the Special Reserve Battalion of the Queen's Own Royal West Kent Regiment. On 23 October 1914 he was granted a commission, being gazetted Second Lieutenant to the 10th Battalion of the Royal Sussex Regiment. Immediately applying for transfer to the RFC, he was seconded at the end of January 1915, first to Shoreham before going on to Gosport. He was awarded the Royal Aero Club Aviators Certificate (No. 1155) on 2 April 1915, receiving his 'Wings' on 26 May following. Hobbs was first sent to France to join 8 Squadron in July 1915 but shortly afterwards was transferred to 3 Squadron. In a letter to his parents, his Squadron Commander wrote, *".......that the Germans appreciated their bravery and noble self-sacrifice........is shown by the honours they accorded them at their funeral. ....the whole garrison of the town in which their machine fell attended the funeral and both officers were buried with full military honours. The German Flying Corps sent a few wreaths, which they laid on the graves"*. A brother officer also wrote to the Hobbs family explaining that because Alan's machine had been badly strafed the day before, he had been obliged to take out a replacement machine on 15 December. Two escorting machines returned safely but reported that Alan's Morane, *"was seen lying on the house-tops"*. A communiqué, dated 16 December 1915, issued by German Main Headquarters stated: *"Leutnant Immelmann yesterday caused his seventh enemy aeroplane, an English monoplane, to fall down over Valenciennes after an aerial battle"*. A report of Immelmann's latest victory was carried in a German newspaper dropped into the British lines by an enemy pilot. The newspaper included an account of the fight given by a man who was a spectator to it all from a position close to where Hobbs and Tudor-Jones fell. He had never seen, he said, a pluckier fight than that put up by the two young English officers. Alan Hobbs is buried in Raismes Communal Cemetery, France (Fr.1144). He was 21 years old.

SECOND LIEUTENANT

CHARLES EDWARD TUDOR TUDOR-JONES,

EAST LANCASHIRE REGIMENT AND 3 SQUADRON, ROYAL FLYING CORPS

The second son of solicitor Edward Tudor-Jones and his wife, Maria Glynne Tudor-Jones of Swindon, Charles was born on 23 June 1895. He was educated at the Preparatory School, Mill Mead, Shrewsbury and at King William's College, Isle of Man. After leaving school he was articled to H Michelmore, Solicitor, of Exeter. He volunteered into the 7th (Cyclist) Battalion, Devonshire Regiment (TF) and by the time the war came, had been appointed to the temporary rank of Captain, having proved himself a more than capable officer. Deciding to make the Army his career, he resigned his Territorial Force captaincy in May 1915 in order to undertake a course at the Royal Military College, Sandhurst. In September 1915, he was given a Regular Commission and was gazetted Second Lieutenant in the East Lancashire Regiment, attached Royal Flying Corps. Days later, on 23rd of the same month, he was sent to join 3 Squadron in France as an observing officer. Charles Tudor-Jones is buried in Raismes Communal Cemetery, France (Fr.1144). He was 20 years old.

Right: The wreck of the Hobbs/ Tudor-Jones Morane Parasol at the original crash site.

Below: Max Immelmann poses alongside the collected remains of his 7th victory.

VICTORY NO 8

12 January 1916 VFB5 (No. 5460) 11 Squadron 08.30 hours

Once again the tell-tale charcoal puffs of bursting AA fire in the cold morning air above Cambrai, attracted the attention of the patrolling Immelmann who was, today, in company with another FA 62 Fokker flown by Unteroffizier Albert Oesterreicher. Closing in on a Gunbus, Immelmann opened fire and almost immediately his prey began to go down in a right-handed spiral. Following the Gunbus down, Immelmann

11 Squadron's Vickers FB5s.

fired another burst which set the British machine's engine ablaze. With flames all around him, the pilot of the stricken machine was forced into an even more precipitous landing than might otherwise have been necessary. The Gunbus came down north-east of Turcoing with Immelmann landing nearby to discover the observer dead and the pilot wounded and under guard. In his debriefing report following his return from captivity in November 1918 Kemp, the Gunbus pilot, recalled the disastrous circumstances of the recce sortie to Cambrai and district and the two-pronged Fokker attack. He relates how bullets from Immelmann's gun pierced the Vicker's petrol tank, setting the machine on fire at a height of 8,000 feet. Kemp himself was caught a glancing blow on the head by a ricochet off the engine and flames from the same source inflicted yet further injuries. His observer, he added, was killed in the air. Finally, he was careful to note that they came down at Beaumetz-le-Cambrai.

SECOND LIEUTENANT

HERBERT THOMAS KEMP,

CHESHIRE REGIMENT AND 11 SQUADRON, ROYAL FLYING CORPS

Born on 29 October 1892, Herbert Kemp was the son of Mr and Mrs Kemp of 19a Stratford Place, London. Initially gazetted Second Lieutenant to the Cheshires on 17 March 1915, Kemp immediately sought transfer to the Royal Flying Corps. He was awarded the Royal Aero Club Aviators Certificate (No.1231) on 11 May 1915, whereupon he was seconded to the RFC for formal training before being sent to 11 Squadron on 16 July 1915. Following his capture, Kemp was incarcerated until 19 April 1918 when he was exchanged into neutral Holland before finally being repatriated; arriving in Hull aboard the SS *Willocra* on 18 November 1918. Able, at last, to return to his home at 1 Linzee Road, Hornsey.

SECOND LIEUTENANT

SIDNEY CORNELIUS HATHAWAY,

11 SQUADRON, ROYAL FLYING CORPS

Born on 23 March 1898, the son of the works manager of the Triumph Company, C W Hathaway and his wife Kate, of 28 Spencer Avenue, Coventry. He was educated locally and, after leaving school, followed in his by now late father's foot-steps by becoming an engineer's pupil. Sidney volunteered early in the war and was enlisted into a Motorised

Machine-gun Battery of the Royal Field Artillery in October 1914, obviously having successfully lied about his age! Despite his extreme youth, he served at the front with his Battery for most of 1915 before being commissioned into the Royal Flying Corps on 27 December 1915. After receiving his initial training as an observer, he enjoyed a short leave at home before joining 11 Squadron at the front where he had been only three days before that fateful meeting with Max Immelmann. Sidney Hathaway is buried at Achiet-le-Grand Communal Cemetery Extension, France (Fr. 518). He was not yet eighteen years old.

Both Boelcke and Immelmann were, on 12 January 1916, awarded Imperial Germany's highest accolade, the Ordern Pour le Mérite – the first two German airmen so honoured.

VICTORY NO 9

2 March 1916 Morane BB(No. 5137) 3 Squadron am

Immelmann was patrolling more than sixty kilometres behind the front and saw what he initially thought was a British machine being pursued by a Fokker. Closer inspection revealed both the machines as British – a Morane two-seater under the protection of a Morane N. The 3 Squadron machines had taken off at 07.40 with Sergeant T P H Bayetto, flying the single-seater, charged with the responsibility of escorting and protecting the slower machine on a long reconnaissance to Lille, Valenciennes, Donay, Pont-à-Marcq and Mons-en-Pévèle. Bayetto later reported seeing the first Fokker (Immelmann's) then four more. As the sergeant pilot dived to engage one of the enemy machines, Immelmann took the opportunity to come down on the two-seater, quickly despatching it to destruction near to Somain, 14 kilometres west of Valenciennes. The observer was killed but the pilot, although severely wounded in the foot, got down safely. Taken into captivity and hospitalised, he survived until the 29th of the month when, following the amputation of his foot he died, like so many other wounded in the Great War, of septicaemia.

In the meantime, Bayetto had managed to extricate himself from the other Fokkers, even claiming to have downed one in the process, reporting that he saw it go down into a wood on fire near Valenciennes. Whatever the validity of his claim, he was obliged to return home without his original charge.

LIEUTENANT CHARLES WALTER PALMER,

9/BATTALION, LEICESTERSHIRE REGIMENT AND 3 SQUADRON, ROYAL FLYING CORPS

The eldest son of poultry breeder George Alfred Palmer and his wife, Annie, of 'Wykin', Hinckley, Leicestershire, Charles obtained a commission in the 9th Battalion of his county regiment on 28 December 1914, before subsequently being gazetted to the RFC. Palmer was awarded the Royal Aero Club Aviators Certificate (No. 1497) on 24 July 1915, later going on to complete formal pilot training. The day after his amputation and on the very day he died, he wrote a cheerful letter home to his parents saying that he hoped soon to be well and was looking forward to being exchanged and returned home. Palmer is buried at Douai Communal Cemetery, France (Fr. 1276). He was twenty-four years old.

LIEUTENANT
HERBERT FREDERICK BIRDWOOD,
1/20 TH (COUNTY OF LONDON) BATTALION (BLACKHEATH AND WOOLWICH) THE LONDON REGIMENT (TF) AND 3 SQUADRON, ROYAL FLYING CORPS

Born in Bombay on 11 February 1894, the only son of Dr Roger Alan Birdwood MA (Cantab) MD, MRCS and his wife Agnes, of 309 Richmond Road, Twickenham, Middlesex, Herbert was educated at Mount St Mary's, Chesterfield; at the City of London School, Blackfriars and at Peterhouse, Cambridge. When war broke out, he was still reading Law at Peterhouse. Volunteering immediately, he was gazetted Second Lieutenant from the Cambridge University OTC to the 20th London Regiment on 26 August 1914. He was sent to France in March 1915, where he served with the bombing and trench mortar sections of his battalion. Promoted to Lieutenant on 19 May 1915, he was present at the Battle of Loos in September of the same year. In December 1915 he was attached to the RFC and, following training, gained his observer 'Wing'. After his death, his Squadron Commander wrote to his parents: *"He was unfortunate to have encountered several hostile machines, amongst which, we now know, was Immelmann, one of Germany's most daring pilots........We have lost one of our best observers, one who was always ready and willing to go anywhere and do anything"*. Herbert was the fourth nephew of General Sir George Birdwood to be killed in the war. He is buried in Somain Communal Cemetery, France (Fr.1308) – the only Commonwealth War Grave in the cemetery. He was 22 years old.

VICTORY NO 10
13 March 1916 Bristol Scout C (No. 4678) 4 Squadron 12.55 hours

An experienced and aggressive airman, 4 Squadron's Commanding Officer, Major Barrington-Kennett, was flying a probing patrol hoping to meet and engage German aircraft operating beyond the front lines. He was just in the act of engaging one such when Immelmann, in company with Leutnant Max von Mulzer, another of the

The Barrington-Kennetts at home, left to right: Godwin, Basil (killed in action 8.5.1915), Victor (killed in action 13.3.1916), Cousin Guy, and Father. (*via Nigel Wood*)

successful FA62 pilots, arrived on the scene. Immelmann lost no time in picking off Barrington-Kennett's machine and it fell over Serre, near to the front lines, at 11.55 hours. Immelmann later reported that his victim had been a two-seater but the machine had crashed too near to the front lines to allow for studied scrutiny, especially as the wreck was immediately fired upon by British artillery. To add to the confusion, front line observers reported the machine as having been brought down by anti-aircraft fire. There can be little doubt, however, that the Bristol Scout was Immelmann's.

MAJOR VICTOR ANNESLEY BARRINGTON-KENNETT

MID, 2/GRENADIER GUARDS AND 4 SQUADRON, ROYAL FLYING CORPS

Victor, born on 16 June 1887, was the third son of Colonel B H Barrington-Kennett of Her Majesty's Bodyguard and Mrs Barrington-Kennett of 19 Cheyne Gardens, Chelsea, London. He was educated at Ludgrove School; at Eton – where he was a contempory of the poet Julian Grenfell and the diplomat Charles Lister – and at Balliol College, Oxford. A big man, he was a good oar and he became Captain of the Boat Club at Oxford and rowed at Henley. He completed his degree in History in 1910. Whilst at Oxford, he had tried his hand at ballooning and later developed this interest further by becoming a Second Lieutenant in the London Balloon Company, Royal Engineers (Territorial Force). From ballooning he moved on to flying, becoming only the second Territorial to be awarded the Aviators Certificate (No. 190) of the Royal

Aero Club on 5 March 1912 (Sergeant H D Cutler, Royal Engineers No. 189 was the first). The London Balloon Company was disbanded in 1913 and, consequently, Victor transferred to the RFC Special Reserve. By then a member of No. 1 Squadron RFC, Victor crossed to France for the first time on 7 March 1915. He was promoted to Captain and Flight Commander later in 1915, was Mentioned in Despatches (*London Gazette* 1 January 1916) and, in the spring of 1916, was promoted Major and Squadron Commander. Two of his three brothers were also killed in the Great War, one (Aubrey) with the Oxs and Bucks Light Infantry on the Aisne in September 1914, the other (Basil) a Brevet Major in the Grenadier Guards, when leading a charge at Festubert on 18 May 1915. Indeed, Basil, Victor's eldest brother (RAeC Aviators Certificate No. 43, 31 December 1910) became the newly formed RFC's first Adjutant in 1912 before, following a bout of ill health, reverting to his old regiment, the Grenadier Guards. A third brother (Godwin), serving in East Africa, survived the war.

During the early months of 1916, Victor became an accomplished Bristol Scout pilot (single-seaters were something of a rarity in those days), responsible for flying the Squadron's 'Hostile Aircraft Patrols'. 'B-K', as he was affectionately known, is buried in Miraumont Communal Cemetery, France (Fr. 1504). He was twenty-nine years old.

VICTORY NO 11

13 March 1916 BE2c (No. 4197) 8 Squadron 17.40 hours

On this day and for the first time, Immelmann scored a double victory, something he was to achieve only once more – on the day of his death. He took off for the second time shortly after 17.00 hours with the intention of engaging a formation of five British machines of 8 Squadron, over Arras. Once in the area, he found a second group of four 8 Squadron machines and singling one out, attacked with a burst of 300 rounds which sent the BE over onto its right wing. Following up, Immelmann dived to fire a further 200 rounds into the stricken machine and watched as it crashed near Pelves, to the east of Arras, both crewman being killed. Again, observers on the British side mistakenly thought the BE had been hit by AA fire.

LIEUTENANT
GILBERT DENNIS JAMES GRUNE,
4TH HOME COUNTIES HOWITZER COLUMN, ROYAL FIELD ARTILLERY (TF) AND 8 SQUADRON, ROYAL FLYING CORPS

The son of Dr Edward Ferdinand Grune and Mrs Grune of 'The Hall', 49 The Green, Southwick, Brighton, Sussex, Gilbert was educated at South Lodge, Lowestoft and at Steyning Grammar School. After leaving school, he became an engineering pupil with Messrs Vickers at Erith and had just completed his three-year pupilage and was about to embark on a BSc degree at London University, when war broke out. He had, for some time, been a member of the Territorial Force and his unit was one of the first to be mobilised. Grune accompanied his battery to France in November 1914 and was present at a number of major engagements. He learnt to fly, being awarded the Aviators Certificate of the Royal Aero Club (No.1387) on 3 July

1915, and successfully applied for detachment to the RFC. His training completed, he was given his 'Wings' on 2 September 1915 and posted to 8 Squadron in France two months later. The Grune family had something of a military tradition, Gilbert's father serving as a Captain in the Royal Army Medical Corps and his maternal grandfather, Captain E H Chawnor of the 77th Regiment, was a veteran of the Crimean War, having been awarded the French Légion d'Honneur for his part in the taking of the Redan at Sebastopol in 1856. It was a sad irony that the grandfather should go on to outlive the grandson fully sixty years later. Gilbert Grune is buried in Vis-en-Artois British Cemetery, Haucourt, France (Fr. 421). He was 22 years of age.

SECOND LIEUTENANT

BRIAN EDWARD GLOVER,

DCM, MÉDAILLE MILITAIRE (FRANCE), 8 SQUADRON, ROYAL FLYING CORPS

The son of Edward Arthur and Mrs Glover of 'Ringmer', Lewes, Sussex, Brian was born on 4 September 1894. On leaving school he became an employee of civil engineer F J Wood and was formally admitted as a student member of the Institution of Civil Engineers in December 1913. Volunteering immediately upon the outbreak of war, he was enlisted into the Royal Engineers and was sent to France for the first time on 8 November 1914, thus becoming entitled to the award of the 1914 Star. The *London Gazette* of 16 November 1915 (Page 11419) announced the award of the Distinguished Conduct Medal: *"29640 Corporal B E Glover, 47th Signal Company, R.E. For conspicuous gallantry from 21st September to 1st October, during operations between Les Brebis and Loos, when he was constantly employed in carrying despatches and Operations Orders over roads with heavy shell fire, and never failed to deliver his messages". The London Gazette* of 24 February 1916 (Page 2072) announced, *"The President of the French Republic has bestowed the decoration 'Médaille Militaire' on 29640 Corporal Brian Edward Glover, 47th Div. Signal Company, Royal Engineers, in recognition of distinguished service during the campaign"*. Successful in an application to join the RFC, he was, in late 1915, first gazetted Second Lieutenant to the General List and then sent for training as an observer. The gallant Brian Glover is buried alongside his pilot in Vis-en-Artois British Cemetery, Haucourt, France (Fr. 421). He was twenty-one years of age.

VICTORY NO 12

29 March 1916 FE2b (No. 6352) 23 Squadron 11.00 hours

23 Squadron FEs were assigned to fly a tactical reconnaissance sortie and Immelmann and two others were ordered off as soon as the intruding machines were reported to Douai airfield. In fact, five machines were heading for Douai itself and having climbed high, Immelmann had no difficulty in picking them out as they approached. As he closed in, he saw that two camera machines were slightly ahead of the others, the three bringing up the rear acting as escort.

Immelmann at first chose one of the leading machines but, in the event, found it easier to cut out one of the three escorts, firing round after round into it. The pilot put his FE into a steep dive and landed at 'Bethincourt' (probably Bertincourt), east of Bapaume – an indication that the fight had drifted to the south-west. As the fight started over Quéant, unless the FEs were on the way home they had obviously not got close to Douai – Immelmann later reported that the formation had turned right (south) as he approached.

Returning to his base, Immelmann reported his 'victory' to his CO and both men took a car and drove to the site of the forced landing. Upon arrival, they found the two men had been taken prisoner, the pilot having been badly wounded in both arms, which explained the precipitous spiralling descent of the FE.

23 Squadron were based at Izel le Hameau to the west of Arras, and the downed observer, Halford, was afterwards of the opinion that they had been brought down nearer to Cambrai. He also said that they were attacked by superior numbers but, in fact, only three Fokkers had taken off to intercept the five FEs.

Immelmann reported engaging another FE after he had seen his first go down but as he had already expended so much ammunition in despatching the former, he was obliged to break off his attack after firing his last burst. However, it seems he did hit and damage the 'Pusher' (No.6364) – the crew, Lieutenants S H B Harris and L C Powell later reporting a combat with a Fokker which had just shot down one of their number over Quéant. Fortunately, they returned safely.

Immelmann's twelfth 'victory' was later displayed at a Delka exhibition in Berlin, the FE2b appearing largely intact except for the absence of both wheel tyres and a slightly dented nose.

SECOND LIEUTENANT FRANK GEORGE PINDER, CANADIAN EXPEDITIONARY FORCE AND 23 SQUADRON, ROYAL FLYING CORPS

Born on 9 July 1886, Frank Pinder was raised and educated in Victoria, British Columbia, Canada. Working as a mining engineer for the Klondike Gold Mining Company, Dawson City, he travelled around various sites in the Yukon Territory until news of the outbreak of war brought him back to British Columbia so that he could volunteer his services for the war effort. He joined the Canadian Infantry early in the war and was amongst the first drafts in the build-up of the Canadian Expeditionary Force, arriving in England in the spring of 1915. He successfully applied for transfer to the RFC which occurred on 9 May 1915. Having learnt to fly, he was awarded the Royal Aero Club Aviators Certificate (No. 1825) on 2 October 1915, taking his tests at Brooklands. Gazetted as a Flying Officer on 27 November 1916, he next joined 23

Squadron and flew with the original squadron complement to France on 16 March 1916. His was one of five FE2bs carrying out a recce of the St Léger-Quéant-Marquion-Cantin-Fampoux area when he was 'set upon' on what was only his second patrol since arriving in France. Attacked in the classic manner from above and behind, the very nature of his wounds forced him to land his machine as quickly as he could. Following lengthy spells in hospital, he was exchanged into Switzerland on 9 December 1917 and finally allowed to return to England on 24 March 1918. Once fully recovered, Pinder served as a flying instructor in Britain and was given a permanent commission at Netheravon on 25 August 1919. Served with the RCAF after returning home to Canada.

SECOND LIEUTENANT
EDWARD ATHELSTAN HALFORD,
2/WILTSHIRE REGIMENT AND 23 SQUADRON, ROYAL FLYING CORPS

The son of the Reverend H H and Mrs Halford of 'Kimberley', Mount Pleasant, Weybridge, Surrey, Edward was first educated at Felsted (1910-11) until, following a family move to St. Catherine's, Crediton, Devon (where his father was to be the vicar) he 'migrated' to Exeter School to complete his education. Wishing to make the Army his career, he attended the Royal Military College, Sandhurst, from where he was gazetted Second Lieutenant to the 2nd Battalion of the Wiltshire Regiment. Kept back in England because of his youth, he took the opportunity of learning to fly at his own expense, being awarded the Aviators Certificate of the Royal Aero Club (No. 2166) on 9 December 1915 before, soon afterwards, becoming attached to the RFC. Halford was acting as an observer on the day he was shot down and was one of the very few lucky enough to walk away unhurt (if a little shocked) after a brush with one of the great German aces! Halford was exchanged into neutral Holland shortly before the end of the war and finally repatriated on 22 November 1918. On 22 October 1919, Halford returned for special duty with the 2nd Battalion, The Wiltshire Regiment.

VICTORY NO 13
30 March 1916 BE2c (No. 4116) 15 Squadron 11.15 hours

After his 'double' the day before, Immelmann was successful again. He had taken off from Douai at 11.00 hours and, approaching Bapaume, spotted three British aircraft. The three were flying a sortie to photograph a section of the trench line but as soon as the Fokker appeared, two of them hurriedly turned back. Immelmann went after the third which was at a higher altitude than his fellows. The German ace's very first burst of fire sent the British machine plummeting to earth. Immelmann was surprised that the BE had not returned his fire and at the apparent total success of his first attack. He could not know that his initial burst had hit and killed the pilot, leaving the observer with no choice but to try to get into the pilot's rear cockpit in an attempt to arrest the aircraft's death plunge. Although the observer did, eventually, manage to get a hand to the controls, he could not access the rudder pedals. Fortunately, at 300 feet, he obtained some lateral control which helped to lessen the impact somewhat when the machine finally crashed to the ground.

Immelmann had watched the erratic descent of the BE with professional interest, coming to the erroneous conclusion that both occupants were dead. Never one to waste an opportunity, he went after one of the other two remaining BEs and had the satisfaction of seeing it force-land inside its own territory, although he was disappointed that he could not conclusively claim it as a victory.

SECOND LIEUTENANT

GEOFFREY JOSEPH LIGHTBOURN WELSFORD,

2/MIDDLESEX REGIMENT AND 15 SQUADRON, ROYAL FLYING CORPS

Born on 29 May 1895, Geoffrey Welsford was the son of Harrow School Master and Fellow of Caius College, Cambridge, J W W Welsford and his wife, Mildred. He was educated at Orley Farm School, Harrow; at Marlborough (1909-1912); at Berlin-Lechter Selde-West and at Caius College, Cambridge. In fact, he had been at Cambridge for a year studying law with a view to becoming a barrister, when the war broke out. Volunteering immediately, he was sent for a four-month course at the Royal Military College, Sandhurst, from whence he was gazetted Second Lieutenant to the 3rd Battalion, Middlesex Regiment on 16 December 1914. Sent to join the 2nd Battalion of his regiment at the front, he was wounded during the battle of Aubers Ridge on 9 May 1915. Welsford was despatched home for treatment and convalescence and during the period of recuperation, he learnt to fly at his own expense at Hendon, being awarded the Royal Aero Club Aviators Certificate (No. 1702) on 6 September 1915. Shortly afterwards, he returned to his battalion at the front for a brief three-week period before coming home again and transferring to the RFC for pilot training. After receiving his 'Wings', he was sent out to join 15 Squadron in France on 24 February 1916. By an amazing co-incidence, Welsford's observer on 30 March was an old friend – their families were neighbours in Harrow and they had been at Marlborough together. Geoffrey's mother, by now a widow, had recently married Major E W Freeborn and no doubt took some small consolation from the fact that her son's friend had survived. Geoffrey Welsford is buried in Mareuil-Sur-Ay Communal Cemetery, France (Fr.1412). He was 20 years old.

LIEUTENANT

WAYLAND JOYCE,

8/BEDFORDSHIRE REGIMENT AND 15 SQUADRON, ROYAL FLYING CORPS

The son of the Reverend F W and Mrs Joyce of The Vicarage, Harrow on the Hill, Wayland was born on 30 April 1894. He was educated at Marlborough (1908-13) and at Keeble College, Oxford. Joyce had been at Oxford for two years when war broke out. Volunteering immediately, he enlisted into the ranks before being commissioned and gazetted Second Lieutenant to the Bedfordshire Regiment on 1 December 1914. He had developed an interest in flying some time before his life-long friend, George Welsford, who was strangely enough his pilot on that fateful day. Indeed he had learned to fly at his own expense at Hendon, being awarded the Aviators Certificate of the Royal Aero Club (No. 1177) on 12 April 1915. However, he was sent to France as an observer, joining 15 Squadron on 15 June 1915. Undoubtedly, the fact that Joyce could pilot an aeroplane saved his life as the BE fell to earth following Immelmann's attack. When, with great difficulty, he managed at last to struggle partially into the cockpit still occupied by his dead friend he was able, even in the few seconds that were left, to arrest the machine's headlong plunge. Wayland Joyce was eventually exchanged into neutral Holland on 30 April 1918 before finally being repatriated, unusually late, on 29 January 1919, leaving the service some weeks later on 1 April 1919. He returned to Oxford, gaining his Bachelor of Arts degree in late 1919. Joyce later became a Master at St Michael's College, Tenbury, living at 'Lions Farm', Tenbury Wells, Worcestershire.

Immelmann received word that he had been awarded the Commanders Cross, 2nd Class, of the Military St Henry Order by Crown Prince Georg of Saxony – an unprecedented and unique award for this period.

VICTORY NO 14

23 April 1916 VF5B (No. 5079) 11 Squadron 09.45 hours

An 11 Squadron Vickers Gunbus had taken off at 08.45 hours on this St George's Day morning, to fly a photo sortie after first linking up with an escorting machine over Arras. The escort later reported that despite being in the right place at the right time, there was no sign of the Gunbus. Whatever the truth of that report, Lieutenant Mortimer-Phelan, the Gunbus pilot, bravely pressed on regardless crossing the lines unescorted to seek out the AA Battery he had been ordered to locate and photograph. (Following his return from prison camp when the war ended, Mortimer-Phelan gave a different account of the events preceding the Immelmann engagement. In fact, Mortimer-Phelan reported that the escort had indeed rendezvoused with him, but had left him shortly afterwards. Left him, it transpired, to be found by Immelmann and von Mulzer).

Mulzer dived to make the first attack with Immelmann in close attendance. A sharp burst of 120 rounds from Immelmann's machine gun badly damaged the 'Pusher' and riddled the petrol tank – which made a forced landing inevitable. Immelmann continued to attack and pursue until the Gunbus was forced down to land at Monchy-le-Preux, just to the east of Arras. Mortimer-Phelan later recorded their landing place as Pelves, near Douai, although Scott-Brown placed it more accurately at Fampoux, near Arras. After their enforced landing, and before they were led away to captivity, the British crew were able to set fire to their machine. Their German captors proudly apprised the British pair of the identities of their victors – Immelmann and Mulzer. Pilot and observer shared the same prisoner of war camp for the rest of the war, both equally unforgiving of the conduct of their supposed 'escort', both convinced that the Fokkers would not have attacked had the escort stayed with them. Prior to falling to Immelmann, Mortimer-Phelan himself had enjoyed some success against the enemy when, on 1 April and flying with Corporal G J Morton as observer, he had forced down an LVG two-seater.

LIEUTENANT

WILLIAM CHARLES MORTIMER-PHELAN,

11 SQUADRON, ROYAL FLYING CORPS

Mortimer-Phelan had begun to learn to fly before the war started and passed his civilian tests just five days into the war, being awarded the Royal Aero Club Aviators Certificate (No. 866) on 9 August 1914. Sent first to Brooklands on 26 June 1915, he was given a Special Reserve commission in the Royal Flying Corps on 2 July 1915, before going on to Joyce Green and then the CFS, where he was appointed a Flying Officer on 2 November 1915. Following a short period of leave, he was sent to join 11 Squadron at the front on 17 December 1915. After his capture, Mortimer-Phelan remained in German hands until 30 April 1918 when he was exchanged into neutral Holland. From

Holland, he was repatriated to England, returning to his wife at their home at 'Colnbrook', 18 Thrale Road, Streatham Park, London SW 16, on 18 November 1918.

SECOND LIEUTENANT

WILLIAM A SCOTT-BROWN,

6/ARGYLL AND SUTHERLAND HIGHLANDERS (TF) AND 11 SQUADRON, ROYAL FLYING CORPS

The son of Mr and Mrs W M Brown of Rhuallan, Giffnock, Glasgow, William was gazetted as Second Lieutenant in the 6th (Renfrewshire) Battalion of the Argyll's on 26 February 1915, and accompanied his battalion to France for the first time on 12 May 1915 following. After a short period in the trenches, Scott-Brown successfully applied for transfer to the Royal Flying Corps and having completed his training, was posted to 11 Squadron on the last day of 1915. He was still a 'green' probationary with little experience when he had the misfortune to run into Immelmann. Surprisingly repatriated on the day before the war ended – 10 November 1918 – he continued to serve until 7 December 1919.

Immelmann's career almost came to an end only two days after he gained his 14th victory. On 25 April he encountered a two-machine patrol from 24 Squadron. The DH2s, flown by Captain J O Andrews (No.5958) and Lieutenant S E Cowan (No.5925) ran into the German ace south of Cambrai as they escorted a 15 Squadron BE. The mother and father of all dogfights ensued! Immelmann squirted a series of bursts into Dublin-born Sidney Cowan's 'Pusher' before the Irishman adroitly manoeuvred himself behind the Fokker, thus completely turning the tables. Immelmann was forced to side-slip into a vertical nose-dive to escape. His Fokker received damage to its undercarriage, boom struts, propeller and fuel tank and the ace was obliged to admit that he had been outfought and outmanoeuvred and was lucky to be alive.

Immelmann received the Turkish Imtiaz Medal in Silver with Clasp and Sabres, together with the Turkish War Medal. Shortly after, the Duchy of Anhalt joined in the general approbation by conferring the Friedrich Cross, 2nd Class, upon him.

VICTORY NO 15

16 May 1916 Bristol C Scout (No. 5301) 11 Squadron 18.00 hours

A Bristol Scout, out on an Offensive Patrol, came upon and immediately attacked two LVG two-seaters. On the ground, German AA gunners tried to help their aviators by firing at the pursuing Bristol. Immelmann happened to be in the air at the time, testing a new Fokker and his attention was caught by the grey-black bursts of exploding AA fire in the hazy distance. Intent on his own chase, the Canadian pilot of the Bristol Scout, Morden Mowat, failed to notice Immelmann manoeuvring up behind him. The German ace was very close and, choosing the moment, he loosed twenty rounds from each of his twin machine guns into the unsuspecting Canadian's cockpit. The well-aimed bursts fatally wounded Mowat, whose machine spun down through the haze and crashed to the ground. Mowat died as German troops arrived to free him from the wreckage.

Some dispute arose over this victory, as one of the LVG observers being attacked by Mowat claimed to have fired the fatal shots. The LVG man's assertion was weakened somewhat by his reporting that he had seen a second British Scout above and behind Mowat – this was in fact Immelmann. Furthermore, Mowat's wounds were consistent with him having been shot from above and behind, whereas the LVG observer's fire would have hit him in the front. The victory was awarded to Immelmann who noted the crash to have occurred at Izel – presumably Izel-les-Equerchin, west of Douai.

SECOND LIEUTENANT

MORDEN MAXWELL MOWAT,

11 SQUADRON, ROYAL FLYING CORPS

The eldest of four sons, Morden was born in New Westminster, British Columbia, on 6 December 1891 to Maxwell M and Lillian A Mowat, (later of Campbelltown, New Brunswick, Canada). After completing his education, he became a mining prospector in Northern Ontario and was employed in that profession at the time of the outbreak of the war. Mowat learned to fly at his own expense, passing his tests at the Curtiss School, Long Branch, Ontario, on 11 November 1915 and being awarded the Royal Aero Club Aviators Certificate (No. 2064). As a consequence of this accomplishment, he was accepted as a direct entrant to the RFC on 20 November 1915, arriving in Shoreham on 11 December 1915 before being posted to 23 Squadron on 6 January 1916. Mowat accompanied his squadron to France on 16 March 1916 but was singularly unimpressed by its competence. He wrote to anybody he considered could be influential in getting him, quote, "out of this bloody awful squadron" and transferred to a Canadian Air Force squadron as soon as humanly possible! His entreaties worked, for on 24 April 1916 he was sent to join 'B' Flight, 11 Squadron (Captain Champion de Crespigny commanding). A man of uncertain temper, Mowat notoriously operated on the shortest of fuses and had the reputation of being something of a loose cannon. As a prospector, he was used to a life of self-reliance and did not take kindly to discipline and routine. The sixteenth day of May 1916 had started badly for Mowat; flying a Bristol Scout (No. 5326) over his home field, he 'lost his engine' and smashed into the roof of the 'A' Flight hangar. Unhurt but furious, he took off again on this fateful day only to fall in with the greatest of the contemporary German aces. Barely alive when troops of the German infantry reached him, he died in captivity within minutes. Morden Mowat is buried in Cabaret-Rouge British Cemetery, Souchez, France (Fr. 924). He was in his twenty-fifth year.

VICTORY NO 16

18 June 1916 FE2b (No. 6940) 25 Squadron 17.00 hours

An FE2b was to be the first of Immelmann's two victories on this, his last day on earth. Two victories which from time to time have been called into question, mainly because he was not able to make personal representations for confirmations but which were, nevertheless, almost certainly his. The late afternoon saw eight British machines crossing the lines near Arras. Four Fokkers, including Immelmann's, took off to oppose the intruders. As the fight drifted south, Immelmann attacked one FE, badly wounding the pilot and forcing him to land near Bucquoy, north-west of Bapaume. Both crewmen were wounded and taken prisoner, the seriously wounded pilot dying later in the day.

LIEUTENANT

CLARENCE ELIAS ROGERS,

25 SQUADRON, ROYAL FLYING CORPS

The son of coal and wood merchant Elias Rogers and Mrs Rogers, Clarence was born in Toronto in 1892. One of three brothers and three sisters, he was a strong willed boy, independently minded and a little unruly. Somewhat despairingly, his parents – strong Quakers themselves – sent him to the Quaker School in Philadelphia, USA, in an effort to instill some discipline. Three months later he was brought back by the ear to Toronto by his irate father and enrolled in a local boys school, St Andrew's College. Leaving school as soon as he could, he joined the Royal North West Mounted Police for a time. Wanting so badly to fly, he spent money he could ill afford for training at the Curtiss Aviation School in his home town. Impatiently, his parents refused to fund this latest enterprise and he was obliged to haul cement with his brother to pay his way. His keenness must have impressed the RFC as they accepted him as a candidate and before long he found himself leaving St John's, New Brunswick, on the *ss Scandinavian* with twenty-nine other aspirants. All were dressed in their best civilian suits, each determined to enjoy the adventure. Rogers was acknowledged as nerveless by his peers and he sailed through his training at Thetford, Norfolk. He received his Royal Aeronautical Club Aviators Certificate (No. 2316) on 16 January 1916 and flew a variety of types including the ubiquitous Maurice Farman and a Vickers FB 5 'Gunbus' before, on 24 March 1916, graduating to the controls of a FE2b (No.5228) under the expert and steely gaze of his instructor, Captain M M ('Micky') Bell-Irving. Night-flying instruction – in response to the Zeppelin menace – was the order of the day and Rogers was obliged to do 33 minutes in the dark piloting a BE2c. When, finally, he was posted to 'A' Flight, 25 Squadron on 9 April 1916, he had completed 40 hours 44 minutes of solo flying. The former 'Mountie' had become a determined and experienced pilot by the time of the Immelmann encounter – indeed, it was his forty-eighth patrol. The wreck of the FE2b hit the ground one mile inside the German lines and immediately attracted artillery fire. Clarence Rogers is buried in Cabaret-Rouge British Cemetery, Souchez, France (Fr. 924). He was twenty-four.

SERGEANT

H TAYLOR

(NO. 3613), 25 SQUADRON, ROYAL FLYING CORPS

Taylor joined the Royal Flying Corps on 11 February 1915. After successfully completing the necessary training, he was posted to 25 Squadron as an observer, being promoted to Sergeant on 1 June 1916. After the forced landing, the badly injured Sergeant Taylor was taken into captivity even while German artillery shells were still bursting around the remains of the FE2b. Finally, he was led away into a captivity which would last until almost the end of the war. It was, in fact, 12 September 1918 when Taylor, still not yet fully recovered from his injuries, was at last exchanged into neutral Holland.

VICTORY NO 17

18 June 1916 FE2b (No. 4909) 25 Squadron 21.45 hours

Despite the comparative lateness of the hour, and despite having already gained a victory, Immelmann and his fellow Fokker fliers of FA62 were up and looking to counter a threat posed by a posse of 25 Squadron 'Pushers' – seven of which had been reported as crossing the lines. Von Mulzer, Oesterreicher and Prehn had been first to take off, followed by Immelmann and Heinemann. As the latter pair climbed, they saw that above them their comrades were already in action with FEs over Henin-Lietard. Immelmann, flat out, raced to engage two of the British machines. As soon as he was within range he fired, hitting an FE flown by Lieutenant L R B Savage and 2AM Robinson. Both crewmen were wounded and their machine fell to crash near Lens. The pilot, Savage, later died of his wounds. In the meantime, the occupants of the second FE, seeing their colleagues attacked by Immelmann, wheeled around to counter-attack the German. Second Lieutenant G R McCubbin, a South African from Cape Town, carefully positioned his machine so that his observer, Corporal J H Waller, could open fire on the monoplane. Waller's fire had an immediate effect; the Fokker began to break up before their eyes.

Second Lieutenant G R McCubbin who, with his observer, Corporal J H Waller, was credited with the shooting down of Max Immelmann.

The controversy over the circumstances of Immelmann's death has been well aired and hardly needs reiterating. Wishing to sustain the myth of his invincibility, the German authorities said that Immelmann had accidently shot off a blade of his own propeller and his Fokker had shaken itself to pieces. An unlikely scenario, in view of the interrupter gear that the machine carried and the fact that an experienced – nay, brilliant – pilot like Immelmann would, in the circumstances described, have simply switched off his engine and glided down.

McCubbin and Waller, on the other hand, entertained no doubts whatsoever! Predictably, they were triumphant, particularly when they learnt the identity of their victim. British propagandists also made the most of the victory. The 'Fokker Scourge' had severely undermined the confidence of not only its potential victims (there was ample evidence of a reluctance to challenge the feared single-winged fighter, even by an air service rightly renowned for its aggressive bravery) but also of the public at large, at home and abroad. The pendulum had swung and Immelmann's defeat closed one chapter of the war in the air and heralded another. His victors were acclaimed as heroes, McCubbin awarded the Distinguished Service Order, Waller promoted to Sergeant and awarded the Distinguished Conduct Medal.

Whatever the truth of the claims and counter-claims of the opposing sides, what was certain was that the gallant Max Immelmann was dead – his place in the Pantheon of Great Aces assured. Despite (by future standards) his relatively low score of victories, he was amongst the first of the

Jagdflieger aces and, uniquely, his name is enshrined in an aerial manoeuvre he developed and used in combat – a stall turn which enabled his machine to come down again on an opponent without having to make a complete turning circle with climb and dive – 'The Immelmann Turn'.

As already mentioned, Immelmann's last two victories – the 16th and 17th – seem not to have been officially confirmed. Patently, his death precluded personal claims but, in retrospect, and even in spite of von Mulzer's claim for Savage and Robinson (No. 17) there is little doubt that these victories were, indeed, Immelmann's.

SECOND LIEUTENANT

JOHN RAYMOND BOSCAWEN SAVAGE,

25 SQUADRON, ROYAL FLYING CORPS

John Savage was born in Bradford on 3 August 1898, the son of Lieutenant Colonel and Mrs A R B Savage of Harewood, Yorkshire and London. He was educated at Winton House, Winchester and at Oundle School (1912-14). He passed the examinations to enter the Royal Military Academy, Woolwich, but instead joined the RFC on his seventeenth birthday, presumably having lied about his age. Learning to fly, he was awarded the Royal Aero Club Aviators Certificate (No. 1913) on 18 October 1915 and, following formal training, received his 'Wings' on 3 February 1916. After enjoying a short leave at home, he was sent to France in March 1916. John was the last in the direct line of the 'fighting Savages' of Ards, County Down. His father fought with the Royal Field Artillery in the Great War; his grandfather, Colonel H J Savage, 91st Highlanders, fought in the South African War; his great grandfather, General J B Savage, fought with the Royal Engineers in the Peninsular War and his great great grandfather, General Sir John Boscawen Savage KCB, commanded the Royal Marines in the Battle of the Nile (1798). An uncle, Colonel Henry Savage (South Staffordshire Regiment) fought in the Zulu Wars and in the South African campaign. Immelmann's last victory truly brought a dynasty to an end. Buried first in the cemetery of the German Military Hospital at Sallaumines, near Lens, his body was finally laid to rest in Bully-Grenay Communal Cemetery, British Extension, France (Fr. 161). He was still only seventeen years of age.

AIR MECHANIC 2ND CLASS

T N U ROBINSON,

(NO. 10387), 25 SQUADRON, ROYAL FLYING CORPS

Robinson joined the Royal Flying Corps on 19 October 1915, training initially as an instrument repairer before eventually realising his ambition to serve as a gunner/observer with 25 Squadron. In addition to the wounds he received from Immelmann's bullets during the aerial combat, he suffered yet further injuries in the crash. Miraculously, Robinson survived and was at last able to return home at the war's end, after first being exchanged into neutral Holland on 12 September 1918, the same date as his Squadron colleague, Sergeant H Taylor (Victory No.16).

CHAPTER 2

OBERLEUTNANT HERMANN GÖRING

It is quite impossible to deal with any aspect of Hermann Göring's early adult life without bringing to the subject the inevitable preconceptions formed and coloured by a knowledge of his subsequent life and career. Equally, it is impossible not to reflect upon the fateful irony that allowed him to survive the Great War when so many good men died in that terrible conflict. Or does that do him an injustice? Was he, in those early days at least, just another brave young man flying and fighting for his country in a war which destroyed so many brilliant futures? Certainly he enjoyed signal success, gaining the approbation of his Kaiser and rising to command Imperial Germany's premier air fighting unit, Jagdesgeschwader Nr. I. And yet, and yet, and yet...........!

Those who try know full well the difficulties surrounding the retrospective research into combat claims and the identification of the men on the wrong end of the so-called 'victories'. However, even given all of the usual problems associated with the subject, we cannot help but be struck by the recurring inconsistencies attending so many of Göring's victories. The claims were undoubtedly contemporary and owed

Hermann Göring in the cockpit of his Albatros Scout, 1917.

nothing to his eventual attainment of power and influence and it is generally accepted that the Imperial German Air Service's system for the confirmation and recording of claims was thorough and, usually, impartial. Yet contrary to the usual high and exacting standards, Göring's claims frequently appear to be inadequately founded and generally unsubstantiated – significantly more so than of any of the other aces' claims. Why? Is this early evidence of an ambitious, forceful and devious personality that was able to bend and manipulate events and people to his own advantage? Or is this just a trite conclusion coloured by hindsight?
Hermann Wilhelm Göring was born in Rosenheim, in the Oberbayern district of Bavaria, on 12 January 1893. He was the fourth child and second son of Doctor Heinrich Ernst Göring and his wife, Franziska – "Fanny". At the age of 19, the young Göring joined the army, subsequently being commissioned on 22 June 1912. A student at the Main Cadet Institute, it was a further eighteen months before he joined Infantry Regiment Nr. 112.

When the war came, he was a platoon commander with his regiment (8/112) and saw his first action in the Vosges region of France. Before the first month of the war was out, he was appointed Adjutant of 11/112 and fought with that unit at Nancy-Épinal and Flirey, being awarded the Iron Cross 2nd Class on 15 September 1914. However, the exertions of warfare exposed a defect in his physical make-up and he was hospitalised following the onset of a severe bout of rheumatism. This condition helped him finally to decide on a change of career he had recently been contemplating – he would apply for a transfer to the newly formed Air Service.

The formalities completed by early October 1914, he was first posted to FEA 3 before being assigned as an observer to Feldflieger Abteilung 25 on the twenty-eighth day of the same month. His first period of operational duties, which extended until June 1915, was in the Argonne region of France. During this time, he met Bruno Loerzer, a pilot with whom he flew on many occasions and a friendship was struck between them which would last until the end of the Second World War. That Göring acquitted himself well at this time is evidenced by the award of the Iron Cross 1st Class on 22 March 1915, followed by the Bavarian Order of the Zahringer Lion on 8 July. By the time of the Bavarian award, Göring had started his pilot training at the Freiburg flying school. Having successfully completed all his tests, the young Göring was sent to Army Flying Park Nr. 5 in September before returning to his old unit, FFA 25, at the beginning of the following month. Accompanied by a number of different observers, his combat flying began over the Champagne area of France when he had a series of inconclusive combats with French aircraft of various types until the day of his first victory.

VICTORY NO 1

16 November 1916 Farman Tahure 14.30 hours

Göring's first successful air action was achieved with a Leutnant Bernert acting as his observer. The identity of the observer has been the source of some confusion as there was a successful fighter pilot of the same surname – Fritz Otto Bernert. However, this latter officer laid no claim for this victory and it is also unlikely that he ever flew with FFA 25. Göring and his observer in Albatros C 486/15 were on a photographic mission when, at 14.30 hours, they came across, and enthusiastically engaged, a French Farman over Tahure. After a brief fight, the French machine was sent spiralling down. The victim's identity remains unclear even to this day as, so far as can be established, the

French suffered no combat losses on the day – in fact not even a single Caudron appears to have been lost in the whole of the month!

On 14 December 1915, Göring sustained a knee injury following a crash in Germany. The injury proved superficial and he was back flying during the early stages of the Verdun build-up. As the German offensive increased, so too did the pressure on the Air Service. Göring found himself flying several times a day, every day, and not just the Albatros two-seaters but also the big twin-engined, three-seater AEG G.IIs. It was during this period that he gained his second victory.

A head-on view of a French 'Caudron'. (*via: Liverpool Scottish Museum*)

VICTORY NO 2

14 March 1916 Caudron SE Haumont Wood Noon

Flying with observer, Graf von Schaesberg and gunner, Boje, in a three-seater AEG G.II (Nr. G19/15) on a short-range photo-reconnaissance, Göring encountered three French machines which were later described as 'Caudron' types. The fight had been on for fifteen minutes when one of the French machines, in trying to 'shepherd' the AEG away from the lines, approached directly from the front. Von Schaesberg immediately poured fire into the Frenchman who slid away steeply and sharply, one engine in flames. Göring followed the French machine down, forcing it to land behind the German lines at the south-east edge of Bois Haumont. The AEG circled the crash site and saw the opposing crew – an officer and a sergeant – taken prisoner by ground troops.

The French report two losses on this day, both of them Caudrons. In the early days, identification of aircraft 'types' was not given the importance it would assume later in the war. Often a generalised description was sufficient; for example the term a 'Vickers type', would be employed to encompass the FE8, the FE2b, the DH2 as well as the original Vickers FB5. Equally, a 'Farman' type might represent either a Caudron or a Voisin. Of the two French losses on this day, one crew was killed, the other reported as 'missing'. It is reasonable to assume that the second of these crews, consisting of the pilot, Sergent Delpach and his observer, Sous-lieutenant Thevenin (both of 'C6') were Göring's victims.

Göring was in constant action throughout March, April, May, June and into July, and, while his unit was based at Stenay, even began flying a single-seater for the first time – a Halberstadt DIII. The 'Kek Stenay' deeply impressed Göring and, no doubt, helped him with his decision to become a scout pilot. Transfer to Jametz and a single-seater unit, FAA 203, followed and he quickly became embroiled in a series of combats culminating in his third 'kill'.

VICTORY NO 3

30 July 1916 Caudron Mamey 10.30 hours

Göring, thought to be flying a Halberstadt Scout, encountered five twin-engined Caudrons north-west of Nancy. The fight took place over La Côte with Göring claiming to have despatched quickly one of the French machines which fell west of the Moselle River. French records suggest that no Caudrons were lost on this day although one pilot, Sergent Girard-Varet, was wounded. However, a Voisin of V223 – flown by Caporal Pierrard with Sous-lieutenant Schmouker as observer – did fail to return.

In early August, Göring returned to FFA 25 to fly single-seaters. Days later, on the 14th of the month, the unit was disbanded and Göring was transferred again, this time to the Kampfstaffel at Metz. By now, the Jagdstaffeln were being formed and in late September, Göring was first sent to Jasta 7 before, three weeks later and in company with Bruno Loerzer, going on to join Jasta 5 then based at Gonnelieu, south-west of Cambrai. The Battle of the Somme was still raging and Jasta 5 was kept busy supporting the German ground forces. On 2 November, during an aerial combat, Göring was wounded in the right hip and was forced to spend some weeks in hospitals in both France and Munich. Just before Christmas 1916 and prior to a return to full active service, he was prescribed 'light duties' and posted to FEA 10.

Whilst enjoying a short period of leave in January 1917, Göring took the opportunity of visiting Jasta 26. This was no idle social visit as, shortly after being declared fit to return to full duty by the doctors, he was posted to that unit on 15 February. Göring was now flying the Albatros DIII Scout.

VICTORY NO 4

23 April 1917 FE2b (No. A823) 18 Squadron 17.20 hours

Four FE2b 'pushers' of 18 Squadron out on an evening bombing raid were attacked by elements of Jasta 26, including Göring, over Barelle. Göring, flying Albatros DIII (No.2049/16) picked out FE2b A823 and pressed home his attack. Flames were soon licking around the nacelle and engine of the 'pusher'. The pilot, Second Lieutenant E L Zink, despite being wounded, manoeuvred the stricken machine towards his own lines whilst the observer, Second Lieutenant G B Bate, kept Göring at a respectful distance with accurate bursts from his machine gun. Eventually, Zink managed to land the burning FE2b behind the British lines in an area north-east of Arras.

Second Lieutenant E L Zink, Suffolk Regiment and 18 Squadron, RFC (on right) in the exalted company of Major J T B McCudden VC DSO* MC* MM CdeG(Fr) (left) and Major G J C Maxwell MC DFC.

SECOND LIEUTENANT

EDMUND LEONARD ZINK,

SUFFOLK REGIMENT AND 18 SQUADRON, ROYAL FLYING CORPS

Born on 21 February 1899, Edmund was the son of Mr and Mrs Zink of 1 Randolph Gardens, Maida Vale, London. He must have lied about his age, as he was commissioned into the Suffolk Regiment on 7 October 1915 at the age of sixteen. After learning to fly at his own expense, he was awarded the Royal Aero Club Aviators Certificate, Number 5794, on 27 September 1916. He next successfully sought transfer to the Royal Flying Corps and, while flying FEs with 18 Squadron had achieved four 'victories' by April 1917. Following his brush with Göring, the culmination of an exacting and arduous period at the front, he was sent home for rest and recuperation. For a time, he was employed as an instructor at Turnberry before returning to France as a Flight Commander with 32 Squadron. Zink claimed one more victory in the last weeks of the war and so became an ace himself. Choosing to stay in the RAF after the war, he was awarded a short service commission on 21 November 1920.

SECOND LIEUTENANT

GEORGE BEAUMONT BATE,

9/LOYAL NORTH LANCASHIRE REGIMENT AND 18 SQUADRON, ROYAL FLYING CORPS

Beaumont Bate (he preferred 'Beaumont' to 'George'!) the son of George and Millicent Bate of 51 Colville Gardens, London and 'The Rhyddyn', Caergwrle, near Wrexham, North Wales, was born in 1895. He was educated at Downside (1909-1911) where his sporting achievements included playing in goal for the hockey XI. In April 1915, Bate joined the Public Schools Brigade as a private soldier. After spending the winters of 1915 and 1916 in the trenches, Bate was gazetted Second Lieutenant to the Loyal North Lancashire Regiment on 26 September 1916. A request for a transfer to the RFC granted, he returned to England in late 1916 to undergo training as an observer. Bate was sent to France in April 1917 and in fact the fight with Göring occured during his very first flight over German lines. Bate and his pilot claimed to have shot down one of their attackers before they, themselves, were forced down. Although Bate was unharmed, a machinegun bullet ploughed a furrow through the cloth of his tunic and the leather of his flying suit. His good fortune, however, proved to be short-lived. Six days later, his FE2b was attacked by three enemy machines. In a letter to his parents, his Commanding Officer said that of the three attacking planes, Beaumont had brought down one in flames, another he had sent down 'out of control' but the third, attacking from below, shot him through the heart, killing him instantaneously. Bate's pilot on this occasion, Second Lieutenant J H Dinsmore, despite having most of his controls shot away and being constantly harried by the enemy, still managed to reach British lines before crash landing. George Beaumont Bate was laid to rest after a service conducted by a Catholic priest and is buried in Queant Road Cemetery, Buissy, France (Fr. 646). He was twenty-one years old.

VICTORY NO 5

28 April 1917 Sopwith 1½ Strutter St Quentin 18.30 hours

Again flying Albatros DIII Number 2049/16 on the evening of a dark overcast day, Göring was patrolling between Bohain and St Quentin with several of his colleagues from Jasta 26. On a pass over St Quentin, the German patrol ran into a flight of six Sopwith two-seaters. The encounter occured at a point in the line where the British and French sectors met and, as both countries employed the Sopwith two-seaters, the nationality of Göring's claimed victory is impossible to ascertain. Göring reported his victim as having fallen inside the German lines, north-east of St Quentin. The Jasta 26 reports also stated that another machine fell south of the same town – but only one RFC Sopwith was lost on that day and that fell well north of the Lens front. Furthermore, there were no French losses on the day and despite Göring's assertion that his victim fell inside German lines (which should have helped to make identification simple) still this claim remains less than clearcut.

VICTORY NO 6

29 April 1917 Nieuport XVII (N3192) 6 Naval Squadron 19.45 hours

Again piloting Albatros DIII Number 2049/16, Göring flew three sorties on this day, gaining his sixth victory during the third of them. At 19.45 (German time) Jasta 26 engaged a number of scouts from 6 Naval Squadron, Royal Naval Air Service, on supporting detachment to the Royal Flying Corps. The RNAS reinforcement was made necessary by the huge demands imposed on the RFC by the Arras Offensive, not to mention the extraordinary losses already sustained throughout 'Bloody April'. During the mêlée, Göring's particular opponent on this occasion, Flight Sub-Lieutenant A H V Fletcher, a South African, received a painful and disabling calf wound which forced him into a hurried landing behind the German lines. He was immediately taken prisoner.

Shortly after this success and as Göring made his way back to his base at Bohain, another British scout attacked him, strangely enough while it in turn was being pursued by yet another Albatros! The British pilot's fire damaged Göring's lateral controls but despite the resultant problems, he still managed to land safely at his home aerodrome. His British aggressor, in the meantime, was hit by yet another German pilot and forced down. Regrettably, it has proved impossible to identify, with any degree of certainty, the name of the man who so nearly 'got Göring!' One possible contender is a colleague of Fletcher's in Naval 6, Flight Sub-Lieutenant R R Winter, flying a Nieuport (N3199). He was certainly in the same fight that saw Fletcher shot down and although his own machine was badly shot up, still he managed to get his

Nieuport down safely. Bruno Loerzer later laid claim to a Nieuport which he said he had shot up and thought he had forced down and this was almost certainly Winter. But interestingly, Winter also claimed his first victory in this fight – an Albatros DIII 'out of control'. Was this, in fact, Göring spinning away after being hit?

Winter, by then with Naval 9, was subsequently killed on 3 February 1918 – coincidently shot down by pilots of Jasta 26.

FLIGHT SUB-LIEUTENANT
ALBERT HARRY VICTOR FLETCHER,
6 (NAVAL) SQUADRON ROYAL NAVAL AIR SERVICE

Born on 24 May 1893, Harry Fletcher was the son of Mr and Mrs Fletcher of Musgrave Road, Durban, South Africa. His father was a Town Hall official in the Natal capital. Fletcher travelled to England and, on 11 February 1916, joined the RNAS. He learnt to fly at his own expense and, after satisfying the examiners at Chingford, was awarded the Aviators Certificate (No.2853) of the Royal Aero Club on 10 May 1916. Formal training and an appointment as a Flying Officer followed on 16 June 1916 with subsequent postings to Cranwell, Dover and finally across the Channel to Dunkirk on 1 April 1917. After his shooting down and capture, his injuries were slow to heal and his general state of health poor and, as a consequence, he was eventually exchanged home via The Hague, Holland. Arriving in London on 20 January 1918, he was immediately admitted to Queen Alexandria's Hospital for further treatment. His health continuing poor, his resignation was approved on 4 June 1918 and he was able to return to South Africa with the rank of Honorary Captain in the Royal Air Force. Fletcher was, however, fit enough to serve in the South African Air Force during the Second World War.

VICTORY NO 7

10 May 1917 DH4 ? Le Pave 15.05 hours

According to the official German listing – the 'Nachrichtenblatt' – Hermann Göring's next and seventh victory was achieved over an English 'Dreidekker' north-east of Le Pave. Jasta 26 records, on the other hand, identify the kill as a DH4 bomber (a biplane) that fell on the German side of the trenches at 15.05 hours. There were no reported British Triplane losses on this day, although one pilot with Naval 8 Squadron was wounded – but that happened at 10 in the morning and was by anti-aircraft fire. And whilst there certainly was an engagement involving DH4s (of 55 Squadron) and Jasta 26, the only one lost was claimed by Leutnant Walter Blume at 15.10 hours north-east of Gouzeaucourt.

Yet another unsatisfactory situation which defies explanation. Göring's successes at this time were comparatively modest, his position not yet sufficiently influential to suggest that Machiavellian skulduggery was afoot and yet, once again, the surviving records are irreconcilable with the circumstances of his claim.

Shortly after this, Göring moved to Jasta 27 with a promotion to Staffelführer. He was, of course, a 'regular' officer with five years service behind him, in contrast to most of his 'amateur' (war service only) contemporaries. His service, both in terms of duration and experience, eminently qualified him for this new role. Hermann Göring's new command was stationed at Ghistelles, up on the northern 4th Army front – opposite Ypres. Although Jasta 27 had been formed some three months earlier, it had still to register its first aerial victory. Göring insisted on taking his favourite Albatros (2049/16) with him over the border to Belgium. Despite being involved in a number of combats over the next few weeks, it was not until 3 June that Jasta 27 claimed its first success. Its second success would be credited to the new Staffelführer.

The 'business end' of a French Nieuport Scout. *(via: Liverpool Scottish Museum)*

VICTORY NO 8

8 June 1917 Nieuport XVII (No.B1656) 1 Squadron 07.30 hours

Göring led out four of his pilots on a morning patrol at 4,000 metres above Lens, Armentières and Ypres. North-east of Morslede, they ran across a patrol of Nieuport Scouts from Number 1 Squadron, Royal Flying Corps, who announced their presence by diving onto the German scouts, their machine guns blazing. The Nieuports had taken off at 05.25 on an Offensive Patrol covering Poelcapelle-Passchendaele-Wervicq. Göring evaded the clumsy attack of one of the Nieuports and executing a brilliant manoeuvre, positioned himself behind his opponent. His persistent, unrelenting attack sent his adversary down to a crash-landing near Morslede where he witnessed it turn over and burst into flames. Luckily the pilot, who had arrived at the front only four days earlier, was able to scramble out of the flaming wreck without suffering serious injury although he was immediately taken prisoner by German infantrymen.

Another of the Nieuports was also brought down in this fight, the pilot, Second Lieutenant E G Nuding (B1641), crash-landing his machine on the British side of the line after being shot-up over Becelaere. To complete a disastrous day for 1 Squadron, a third Nieuport was lost to Jasta 8 – its pilot, Second Lieutenant R S L Boote, being taken prisoner.

SECOND LIEUTENANT
FRANK DOLLOWAY SLEE,
1 SQUADRON, ROYAL FLYING CORPS

Before the war, Frank Slee lived at 690 Beauford Street, Perth, Western Australia. He volunteered for service and on 20 June 1915 was inducted into the Australian Imperial Force. After training, he was sent to Egypt on 13 October 1915 and was subsequently wounded in action against the Turks. Ordered to England for treatment and recuperation, he successfully applied for transfer to the RFC. Slee was commissioned into the Special Reserve of the Royal Flying Corps on 17 February 1917. After completing his pilot training, he was sent to join 1 Squadron in Flanders on 4 June 1917. Four days later, on his first operational flight above enemy territory, he was shot down. Frank Slee was repatriated to England on 5 December 1918 before, shortly afterwards, returning home to his native Australia. Died Bunbury, W. Australia in 1967.

VICTORY NO 9
16 July 1917 SE5 (No.A8931) 56 Squadron 20.10 hours

Over the next weeks, Jasta 27 continued to be heavily employed with only a brief lull occuring on 19 June when they moved base to Iseghem, near Ypres. Despite the intense activity, Göring did not score another victory until 16 July – and that one almost cost him his life. The Staffelführer, in his favourite Albatros (2049/16) took off at 19.30 for the second patrol of the day, accompanied by ten others of his command. Forty minutes later, at a point north-east of Ypres, he and his companions attacked a flight of SE5s from 56 Squadron. The RFC machines were themselves on an Offensive Patrol between Moorslede and Polygon Wood, covering and protecting a formation of 'Flying Elephants' – Martinsydes from 27 Squadron. After a brief and inconclusive skirmish with four Albatros scouts, the four SEs were heading back to their base only to run into the eleven-strong Jasta 27 who, at that precise and inauspicious moment, were also joined by seven more machines from Jasta 6! Nothing daunted, Captain G H Bowman immediately shot down one of the Jasta 6 machines. In the chaotic dogfight that ensued, Göring's initial attack on Second Lieutenant R G Jardine caused the latter to spin down and away, a tactic which bought him enough time to clear a gun-stoppage. The fault corrected, Jardine flew at Göring's Albatros head-on, the two exchanging fire at a range of fifty yards before breaking off. Both pilots now found themselves in trouble, Göring's engine almost shot out whilst Jardine's oil tank was smashed. Jardine watched as the Albatros spun down but then levelled out. He attacked again and later reported that he saw the German fly straight into the ground. This was something of an exaggeration as Göring actually deliberately spun down rapidly to lose height, his engine switched off. Levelling out behind the third-line trenches, he touched down – hard – his Albatros somersaulting to a shuddering halt. In the meantime, Jardine's engine seized, the lubricant drained away. He, too, was forced to land – inside Allied lines at Dranoutre –

and he, too, turned his machine over, the fuselage breaking in half behind the cockpit. Both machines were wrecked and would never fly again – the end of Göring's beloved 2049/16. Both pilots were shaken but unhurt and both sides could claim, with equal veracity, a confirmed victory – in soccer parlance, a score draw!

SECOND LIEUTENANT

ROBERT GORDON JARDINE,

56 SQUADRON, ROYAL FLYING CORPS

Gordon Jardine was born on 20 July 1887 the only boy amongst the five children of Alexander and Agnes Litster Jardine of 'Braemore', Wychwood Park, Toronto, Canada. His father, Alexander Jardine, a tea and coffee importer, enjoyed a reputation as a patron of the arts and as something of a raconteur. Mrs Jardine, who was considerably younger than her husband, died tragically and unexpectedly when Gordon was only four years old. The shock proved too much for Alexander and he, too, died shortly afterwards leaving five orphans. Thanks largely to the efforts of the eldest daughter, Jean, the children were kept together and received good educations, Gordon being sent to Ridley College in St Catherine's, Ontario. After St Catherine's, Gordon successfully completed a course at Ontario Agricultural College. Next, with the help of a hefty mortgage, he inadvisedly bought a badly drained and low-lying piece of land near to Medina in New York State. Struggling to keep up with the repayments, he was also forced to take a job as a used car saleman with the Strong Motor Car Company of Rochester, NY. With his love of speed and things mechanical, it was not surprising that he was one of those who, in August 1916, responded to Captain Lord A R Innes-Ker's call for Canadian recruits for the Royal Flying Corps. And so on 19 November 1916, he and eleven other young Innes-Ker recruits boarded the White Star Line ship *Northland* and set sail for Liverpool. After the usual training at Oxford, Reading and Netheravon, Jardine graduated as a Flying Officer on 25 April 1917. A course on machine guns at Turnberry in Scotland was followed in June by a transfer to 56 Squadron, the only squadron at that time equipped with direct-drive SE5s. His new home was at Estrées Blanche, the aerodrome occupying an expansive, sloping field on the outskirts of the French village. Captain G H 'Beery' Bowman, an experienced pilot, took Jardine under his wing and into 'C' Flight. Jardine developed into a brave and resourceful pilot as he demonstrated in his combat with Hermann Göring. Sadly, he was to lose his life on the anniversary of his thirtieth birthday over Passchendaele, only four days after the Göring fight, falling under the guns of another future German ace, Oberflugmeister Kurt Schönfelder of Jasta 7. His body was never recovered and so he is commemorated on the Arras Memorial to the Missing, France. He was thirty years old.

VICTORY NO 10

24 July 1917 Martinsyde G100 Passchendaele 20.45 hours

Yet another 'phantasmal' Göring claim? Not only were no Martinsyde G100s reported lost on this day, but, indeed, none were even reported damaged. Flying Albatros DV 2080/17 Göring, in the van of an eight-machine patrol, led the way towards Ypres in the late evening. Both Göring and Vfw Max Krauss each claimed successes against British opposition, although Krauss' was subsequently disallowed.

At this time, the only squadron in France and Flanders operating Martinsyde G100s was '27' (the 'Flying Elephants') and again they suffered no losses on this day. Göring not only identified his victim as a Martinsyde, but claimed that after it fell on the Allied side of the lines, north of Polygon Wood, he circled it several times before flying home. He also noted a large 'C' or 'G' on the upper wing – 27 Squadron carried numbers on the engine cowlings. Furthermore, there were no Belgian aircraft of any type lost on this day.

VICTORY NO 11

5 August 1917 Sopwith Camel (No. B3792) 70 Squadron 20.15 hours

Many of Göring's successes occured in the evening hours and this proved no exception. Ten of Jasta 27's Albatros Scouts took off at 19.45, formed up and headed for Ypres looking for trouble. They found what they were looking for almost half an hour later when they ran into a patrol of Sopwith Camels from 70 Squadron. Göring picked out an opponent and attacked. The Camel's pilot seemed anxious to keep the fight above the trenchlines and to avoid straying too far over the German side. Göring followed him closely, firing at a range of no more than 50 metres. According to Göring, flames began to come from the Sopwith and, trailing smoke, it went into a spin and was lost in a cloud. The Staffelführer was certain that he had shot the Camel down and it seemed his judgement was vindicated when, on 29 August, he was officially credited with the victory.

In fact, Göring's opponent was Lieutenant Gilbert Budden and although he was wounded in the combat and his machine badly damaged, he still managed to land the Camel near to Bailleul.

LIEUTENANT
GILBERT BUDDEN,
12TH FIELD COMPANY, ROYAL ENGINEERS
AND 70 SQUADRON, ROYAL FLYING CORPS

Born on 30 October 1890, the son of school master Edgar Budden and Mrs Budden of Grammar School House, Macclesfield, Cheshire, Gilbert was educated at Greenbank School, Liverpool (1903-04), Clifton College (1905-09) and Manchester University where he gained a BSc in Engineering in 1912. After qualifying, Budden secured a position as a mining engineer in Mexico. As soon as war was declared in 1914, Budden, along with thousands of other Britons then working in Central and South America, immediately returned home to fight for their country. Commissioned into the Royal Engineers, he first went to Flanders with the 12th Field Company on 30 July 1915 and was involved in the battles around Hooge on the 9th of the following month. During the summer of 1916, Budden successfully applied for transfer into the Royal Flying Corps and, after the appropriate training in England, was sent to France to join 70 Squadron (the first RFC unit to be equipped with the Camel F1). The severe injuries he sustained to his left arm in the fight with Göring were of a nature sufficient to have him declared as 'unfit for any service' with effect from 25 February 1918. After the war, he took up posts as a metallurgical engineer with the Marzipil Copper Company in Mexico and in the USA. Returning to England in 1939, he became, during the Second World War, the Assistant County Secretary for the Red Cross in Cambridgeshire, living at 43 Grange Road, Cambridge. Gilbert Budden died at Addenbrookes Hospital, Cambridge on 12 June 1953, at the age of sixty-two.

VICTORY NO 12

25 August 1917 Sopwith Camel (No.B3918) 70 Squadron 20.40 hours

Although in almost constant action, it was nearly three weeks before Göring added to his victories – again during the evening hours. En route for a position above the Salient at a height of 4,500 metres, Göring led his men into an engagement with a formation of FEs near Ypres. Frustrated by a gun jamming when he was in the very act of forcing down one of the 'pushers', Göring turned for home. He continued to struggle with gun jam and had just succeeded in clearing it when he spotted a lone Sopwith Camel. Closing up, he attacked from above and saw the Sopwith suddenly rear up, almost standing on its tail, before alternatively and erratically diving and climbing, trailing flames as it did so. Göring's report stated that the Camel, "disappeared crashing into the haze" eight to nine kilometres inside Allied lines. He added that because he was distracted by then having to engage a Sopwith Triplane that had appeared on the scene, he did not actually see the Camel crash. Certainly he was not unique in concluding that because he had seen a crippled machine hurtling into the ground haze, it must, perforce, have crashed! His 'victim', however, did not crash.

Second Lieutenant O C Bridgeman had taken off at 17.50, in company with colleagues from 70 Squadron, to fly an Offensive Patrol to Gheluwe, Houthulst and eastwards. Somehow he had become separated from his fellows and in his isolation, found himself suddenly pounced upon by Jasta 26's Staffelführer over Ypres. The fight had drifted south-west and although his machine was badly damaged (but not on fire apparently) and despite being wounded, Bridgeman still managed to get the Camel back to base. The state of Bridgeman's Camel bore mute testimony to the ferocity of Göring's attack, its starboard and bottom planes and centre section were shot through, as were parts of the bottom longeron and two inter-plane struts. The front engine bearing was smashed and the starboard wheel and engine induction pipes damaged. Bridgeman was taken off to hospital whilst his Camel was sent to No. 1 Air Depot for major repair.

SECOND LIEUTENANT
ORLANDO CLIVE BRIDGEMAN,
MC, 70 SQUADRON, ROYAL FLYING CORPS

The son of Colonel the Honorable F C Bridgeman and Mrs Bridgeman of Neachley, Shifnal, Shropshire, 'Bridget', as he was known, was like his father before him, educated at Rugby (1912-16). Bridgeman was gazetted Second Lieutenant to the General List on 17 March 1917 with an immediate transfer to the RFC. After recovering from the wounds he received in his brush with Hermann Göring, Bridgeman went on to become a Flight Commander with 80 Squadron, an ace with five victories and the recipient of a Military Cross – the first and only such award gained by the Squadron – London Gazette of 16 September 1918, Page 10926: *'Temporary Second Lieutenant (Temporary Captain) Orlando Clive Bridgeman, General List attached Royal Air Force. For conspicuous gallantry and devotion to duty. The patrol he was leading was attacked by twenty or thirty enemy aeroplanes of which he destroyed two himself, and by skilful manoeuvring enabled two others to be 'crashed' by officers of his patrol. His tactics and gallantry undoubtedly prevented what might have been a severe reverse to his patrol. On many occasions his work in attacking troops and other ground targets from low altitudes has been excellent, and his example and skilful leadership have been of great value to his squadron'*. The award was largely for the desperate courage he displayed on 10 May 1918 when his heavily out-numbered Flight was engaged by the Richthofen Circus. Despite Bridgeman's own best efforts, most of his men were lost in the ensuing dogfight. Bridgeman, still in his thirties and whose home at the time was 6 Pelham Close, South Kensington, London, died of blood poisoning on 21 December 1931.

VICTORY NO 13

3 September 1917 DH4 ? North of Lampernisse 09.00 hours

Yet more difficulties attend the circumstances of this 'victory'. Leading (in Albatros 4424/17) a seven-strong formation towards Ypres, Göring and his pilots engaged seven Spads and five two-seaters over the Dixmude area. Göring claimed a two-seater downed in an area south-west of Dixmude, the machine falling behind the Allied lines.

In a confusing and ambiguous report, Göring states that after seeing the five Rumpf DDs (two-seaters) coming from the direction of Imlande (?) and heading for Dixmude, he and his companions attacked four Spads! He goes on to add that he and Leutnant Fritz Berkemeyer picked out one opponent and between them forced him down. After a

Captain Johnny Leacroft MC was leading a 19 Squadron patrol on 3 September 1917 and fought Jasta 27.

diving turn the enemy machine suddenly went down steeply and crashed seven kilometres north of Lampernisse. Immediately afterwards, according to Göring, he and Berkemeyer returned to the fight going on above them and fought a further, albeit inconclusive, battle against the remaining Spads.

The Spads were undoubtedly from 19 Squadron – two four-man patrols had taken off that morning at 07.45. A little later one of the Flight leaders, Captain John Leacroft, watched as a formation of six Albatros scouts 'closed on a dark coloured Spad!' that was travelling west. Leacroft dived upon one of the attacking Albatri and fired, causing the German scout to break away to the east. Leacroft had to pull up and away himself, as the five other Albatri were still lurking menacingly above him. Suddenly the five turned east, following the lead given by the Albatros scout Leacroft had initially attacked – was that, in fact, Göring?

The confusion is further compounded by the strange description given by Leacroft in his report, 'a dark coloured Spad who was coming west'. Surely if it had been one of his own Squadron's machines, he would simply have said so. There are no known French or Belgian Spad losses this day.

The second four-man Spad patrol from 19 Squadron, led by Captain J Manley (B3528) took off with Leacroft's four but followed above and behind them. West of Menin they, too, saw the enemy scouts and closed in on the already mêléeing British and German machines. Manley fired at one of the EA but could not get close enough to do serious damage. With machines hurtling all around him, he was forced into a spin by trying to avoid a collision.

Leacroft, after the first clash, engaged other Albatros scouts south-east of Comines at 08.30 – an indication that the fight had drifted well to the south. Steadying his machine after one attacking pass, he was surprised by a green Albatros zooming over his top wing at great speed. With the overshot EA now clearly in his sights, Leacroft was able to unleash a good burst, causing the verdant machine to go down vertically.

It seems from all of this that Göring may well have engaged either Leacroft or Manley, or both of them, but whatever the circumstances of those particular possibilities, for sure neither of the British machines were shot down.

Jasta records vaguely indicate that the victory was over a Spad two-seater but subsequent comment drags a DH4 into the scenario. Indeed, a 57 Squadron DH4 was shot up during a photo-recce sortie, the pilot, Lieutenant G M Guillon, being wounded in the foot – but the machine did not crash. Was this the two-seater that Göring and Berkemeyer engaged? Certainly, it was the only DH4 'casualty' of the day.

A Bristol Fighter from 22 Squadron was also shot up and then forced to land on the Allied side of the lines near to Ypres; its pilot, Lieutenant G R Carmichael, unhurt, the observer, Second Lieutenant S Cleobury, wounded. But the Brisfit did not take off until 08.20 (09.20 German time) and is therefore airborne too late to come into consideration. In summation, even with the closest possible examination of events, it is just not possible to match a victim with this claimed Göring 'victory'!

VICTORY NO 14

21 September 1917 Bristol FE2b (No. A7224) 48 Squadron 09.05

Victory No. 14 is significant because the vanquished crew were a particularly experienced and accomplished duo. The pilot, Ralph Curtis, had achieved 15 victories whilst the observer, Desmond Fitzgerald-Uniacke, had scored at least a dozen. They had taken off at 08.00 hours on a combined OP and bombing sortie to Ostende and were last seen spinning down ten miles north-east of Roulers.

Göring, in 4424/17, led off a patrol at 08.25 (German time) to cover the Dixmude-Ypres area. He and four other of his pilots met a straggle of fourteen British aircraft that were seen approaching from the direction of Bruges. Göring attacked a Brisfit, taking care to keep below the 'blind-spot' underneath the tail so to avoid the observer's fire. The Staffelführer's bullets mortally wounded the pilot and the Bristol Fighter was forced down near Sleyhage.

LIEUTENANT

RALPH LUXMORE CURTIS,

48 SQUADRON, ROYAL FLYING CORPS

The son of farmer William Curtis and his wife Amy, of Berwick Manor, Rainham, Essex, Ralph was born in 1898. He was gazetted Second Lieutenant to the Special Reserve on 26 September 1916 and was subsequently awarded the Royal Aero Club Aviators Certificate (Number 4289) on 17 February 1917. After completing the usual formal pilot training, Curtis was awarded his 'Wings' on 21 March 1917 and sent out to join 48 Squadron in France. He very quickly became an extremely accomplished combat pilot. In fact, with a score of 15 victories between 16 June and his death on 21 September, one of the most successful Bristol Fighter pilots of 1917. Surprisingly, despite his spectacular success, he apparently did not even merit a Mention in Despatches. Ralph Luxmore Curtis is buried in Harlebeke New British Cemetery, Belgium (Bel.140). He was nineteen years old.

LIEUTENANT

DESMOND PERCIVAL FITZGERALD-UNIACKE,

5/ROYAL INNISKILLING FUSILIERS AND 48 SQUADRON, ROYAL FLYING CORPS

The second son of Richard Gordon Fitzgerald-Uniacke, FRSAI, assistant librarian at the College of Arms and his wife, Cecilia Monica, Desmond was born on 18 December 1895. He was educated mainly at Hurstpierpoint. Volunteering for service shortly after the war started, Desmond was commissioned into the Royal Inniskilling Fusiliers five days after his nineteenth birthday on 23 December 1914. He was sent to Gallipoli in September 1915 to reinforce the 5th Battalion of his regiment which had received heavy casualties since landing at Suvla Bay the month before. Within weeks of his arrival, the evacuation of the Peninsular got underway and the 5th Inniskilling Fusiliers were sent to the Salonika front. Desmond next successfully applied for transfer to the Royal Flying Corps, returning to England for training in 1916. Joining 48 Squadron as an observer, he formed an extremely successful partnership with Ralph Curtis, having a hand in no less than eleven of that pilot's victories before they met their own nemesis on 21 September 1917. Following the crash of their Bristol Fighter, Desmond saw that Curtis was beyond help. He himself had received a severe head wound, an injury which was to have a lasting effect and would adversely affect his personality. A local farmer took him into his home, dressed his wound and gave him a welcome drink. However, the farmer became nervous at the prospect of German soldiers finding the aviator in his home and asked him to leave before they arrived. Despite this, Desmond always remained grateful for the farmer's kindness. He remained a prisoner of the Germans until the end of the war in November 1918. Impatient with the undue delays in securing their repatriation, Desmond was one of those ex-POWs who walked from their former prisons to the Channel ports to hasten their return home. He married Beatrice Mary Swetenham in February 1920 and their only child, Sheila Beatrice, was born in December of the same year. The couple divorced in 1929. Desmond Percival Fitzgerald-Uniacke, who never fully recovered from the wounds he received in the Great War, died on 25 March 1933 at the age of thirty-eight, yet another, albeit delayed, casualty of that terrible conflict.

Göring awarded the Hohenzollern House Order 20 October 1917.

VICTORY NO 15

21 October 1917 SE5a (No.B547) 84 Squadron 15.45 hours

Jasta 27 was kept very busy opposing Allied incursions over German territory during this hectic period of the Third Battle of Ypres. On this day, exactly one month after his last success, the Staffelführer in Albatros DV 2159/17, and five of his pilots intercepted five Sopwith (*sic*) single-seaters who were pursuing a German LVG two-seater. The Germans later described the British machines as a new type with a 200hp Hispano-Suiza engine and four-bladed propellors, each carrying one fixed and one moveable machine gun. The description fits, exactly, the SE5a and what is surprising is that Göring and his men should consider a machine that had been around for six months, as a 'new' type!

In the mêlée that followed, two (*sic*) SE5s were shot down, one by the combined efforts of Leutnant Helmut Dilthey, Göring and Beckemeyer; the other by Göring alone. As the Germans did not 'share' victories, the first was credited to Beckemeyer – his fourth confirmed victory. Both SE5s fell inside German lines, Beckemeyer's south of Rumbeke at 15.55, Göring's at Lintelles ten minutes earlier.

The British machines belonged to 84 Squadron, out on an OP over Roulers at 14,000 feet. Their version of events was that at 14.40, Lieutenant J E Ralston in B564 followed his leader down to attack a two-seater they had spotted beneath them. Their combined fire seemed to have the desired effect as the two-seater went into a vertical nose-dive. Satisfied that his patrol leader, Captain K M StC G Leask, had accounted for the enemy machine (OOC), Ralston looked around and was surprised to find the rest of his formation being engaged by no less than 15 German scouts. As Ralston started his climb to rejoin the main body of his Squadron, he was attacked by three of the German planes. During the ensuing mêlée, Ralston saw one of the enemy scouts going down in a spin. The British reported that the Albatros machines appeared to carry two black sloping lines on the side of the fuselage and top of the wings. Jasta 27 distinctively sported a large white band around the fuselage just aft of the cockpit and had an inverted black chevron on the top wings. Göring's Albatros also carried a large Number 1 on the white band and it was probably these markings that the British mistook for the 'two black sloping lines'. Another of the RFC pilots later said that the EA were silver coloured and that some had yellow tails. Jasta 27 were certainly known to carry yellow cowlings and tails. The combat finally came to a halt at 15.20 with the surviving RFC machines rendezvousing over Ypres.

It has been said in the past that the German two-seater – coloured red and yellow – was a 'decoy', there to attract and distract any patrolling British machines whilst the German scouts lurked above, ready to pounce. There is, however, no actual evidence that the Germans deliberately employed the decoy tactic.

84 Squadron lost not two but, in fact, three SE5s in this fight. The three who failed to return – Second Lieutenants all – were F L Yeomans (B560), A E Hempel (B547) and R B Steele IARO attached RFC (B551). The German source, 'Abschusslist', gives B547 as Göring's victory. There are, however, doubts connected with the crash site and, furthermore, the 'Abschusslist' names the occupant of B547 as 'Lieut. Wyman'. Obviously a certain confusion has occured in the German records but, on the strength of the serial number identification, we have opted for Hempel who, there can be no doubt, was occupying B547 when it was shot down.

SECOND LIEUTENANT
ARTHUR ERNEST HEMPEL,
84 SQUADRON, ROYAL FLYING CORPS

Hempel, an Australian who, pre-war, lived in Union Street, Malvern, Victoria, volunteered as soon as the war started. He served in the Australian infantry for more than two years before a successful application to join the RFC was followed by a Special Reserve commission gazetted on 16 March 1917. After training, he was first posted to 71 Squadron before arriving at 84 on 14 August 1917. As though there was not already enough confusion surrounding the events on 21 October, Hempel later reported that he was shot down by a Pfalz machine belonging to the Werner Voss 'Circus'! In fact Voss, who never led a Circus, was dead by this time. After the war, Hempel returned to live in Bendigo, Victoria, where he joined and served with the Royal Australian Air Force.

VICTORY NO 16
7 November 1917 DH5 North-west of Poelcapelle 09.15 hours

Confusion again. The German 'Abschusslist' records this victory as occuring twelve hours after it actually took place. Jasta 26 took off at 08.30 to patrol a section from Ypres to the English Channel, Göring in 2153/17 leading nine of his command. They first engaged four DH 5s, one of which apparently Göring claimed he shot down, the machine falling behind the Allied lines. Shortly after this, they met five Sopwiths and following an inconclusive sparring match, both groups broke off and continued on their respective ways.

The problem with the claim is that there was only one British 'casualty' this day – a 'Big Ack' (an AWFK8 two-seater) from 10 Squadron and that occured in the early afternoon – hours after Göring's DH5 'victory'! An appraisal of all the possibilities – DH5 Squadrons et al – throws up nothing that could remotely substantiate Göring's claim.

VICTORY NO 17

21 February 1918 SE5a (No.C5325) 60 Squadron 10.00 hours

In contrast to the last 'victory', much more is known about this one – the first of the new year – although all may not be as it appears at first sight. In 1933, fifteen years after the event, Göring, by then Germany's Minister of the Interior, wrote an article for the British magazine, *Popular Flying* (edited by the creator of 'Biggles', Captain W E Johns). Göring gave himself over to a graphic and dramatic account of this aerial battle – a diving, looping, head-on 'in-your-face' confrontation – against a thoroughly impressive adversary but still one who the Staffelführer could overcome, the SE5a ultimately being sent down to destruction. Göring said that after the fight he had received a report to the effect that the pilot of the SE5a had been pulled from the wreckage with three bullets in his head and seven more through his chest. The article went on to say that papers taken from the body showed that, *'my brave adversary was no less a person than the famous Captain Craig, known all along the line for his audacity and daring and whose squadron was never complete by reason of the terrible losses that it always sustained. The two machines that attacked us – the second of which was also brought down in the same fight – turned out to be the last survivors of that famous squadron'.*

The probability is that some sycophant wrote-up this rubbish to enhance the reputation of the new Minister but the certainty is that Göring gave it his blessing.

'Captain' Craig was, in fact, Lieutenant George Barton Craig, a Canadian who most certainly put up a good fight – he was an experienced pilot – but who would not have recognised himself from Göring's description, as being, 'famous'! He had taken off with his Squadron at 07.40 and was last seen making a forced landing after a combat over Houthulst. He had been with 60 Squadron for more than five months and had flown 68 patrols. On this day, in the absence of his normal Flight Commander, Craig was 'acting up' in that capacity and to be fair to Göring may well have been carrying wing streamers that could have suggested an enhanced 'status'. Although mortally wounded (he died from his wounds the following day) Craig was certainly not dead when they took him from his machine as he surely would have been with, *'three bullets in his head and seven more through his body!'*

Göring was correct in saying that another SE5a (flown by Canadian Second Lieutenant W M Kent) was lost in the fight (credited to Leutnant Rudolf Klime – his seventh victory). However, Canadian historian Stewart Taylor, a good and respected friend of the authors and a man who knows all there is to know about Canadian airmen in the Great War, says that, based upon the evidence of the survivors of the battle, the two SE5as almost certainly accidently collided with each other and were not shot down by anybody.

LIEUTENANT
GEORGE BARTON CRAIG,
60 SQUADRON, ROYAL FLYING CORPS

Lieutenant G B Craig, 60 Squadron, RFC. (*via S K Taylor*)

Born in 1895, George was the son of William W and Linda Craig of Vancouver, British Columbia. He was educated in Okanagan and at Greenwood, BC, became a school teacher in Penticton, BC and was one of those who presented himself before Colonel Lord Innes-Ker as a volunteer for the Royal Flying Corps. He trained at Deseronto and Camp Borden before leaving for England with the rank of Second Lieutenant on 19 July 1917. After further training at the Central Flying School, he was given his 'Wings' on 3 September 1917 and posted to 45 Squadron. However, he found that he could not stand the fumes given out by the rotary engine and, as a direct consequence of this, was posted to 60 Squadron with its SE5as. His parents, by then living in Waterhole, Alberta, Canada, received the sad news of his death within days. George Barton Craig, scion of a pioneer British Columbian family, is buried in Moorseele Military Cemetery, Belgium (Bel. 158). He was twenty-three years old.

Shortly after this incident, Göring contracted tonsillitis and spent the period from 24 February to 7 March in a military hospital at Maresolm-Deinse. He was back in action in time to accompany his Jasta moving its base to Erchin on 12 March as part of the preparations for the launch of the Great Spring Offensive, scheduled to commence on 21 March 1918. Erchin was situated south-west of Douai on 17th Army front. Jasta 27 also began to be equipped with the Fokker Dr.1 Triplanes.

VICTORY NO 18

7 April 1918 RE8 (No.B876) 42 Squadron 12.50 hours

Göring's Jasta fought in many engagements during the March Offensive – the *Kaiserschlacht* (the Kaiser's Battle) – which began on 21 March 1918 but the Staffelführer did not gain another victory until seventeen days into the battle, his first against the newly constituted independent Service – the Royal Air Force. Shortly after midday, ten machines took off on a patrol between Merville and Hazebrouck. Before long, Göring was in the forefront of a chase after a solitary two-seater RE8 observation machine and later claimed to have shot it down 25 kilometres behind the British lines.

Two RE8s appear in the RFC casualty list for this day – one from 42 Squadron, the other from 52 Squadron. The 52 Squadron machine took off from Abbeville at 08.15 and so is unlikely to have still been airborne at 12.50 – (British and German times coinciding at this time). It also came down very close to the lines – so close that it was impossible to recover the wreck. On the other hand the 42 Squadron machine, operating out of Chocques west of Béthune, more closely follows the criteria of circumstance. Crewed by Second Lieutenant Collier and Lieutenant Musson, the RE8 (B876) took off at 12.30 on a photo-reconnaissance operation. They had barely started work when they were intercepted and forced to run for their lives. The observer, Musson, was wounded in the attack and although they were pursued most of the way, Collier brought the machine back to his base, landing it safely. They reported that they had been attacked by a Triplane which dived on their tail. Musson, in the back seat, returned fire with 200 rounds from his own gun, causing the German machine to veer away but not before Musson had been hit and the RE8 damaged. They went on to say that there were six Triplanes and four Albatros Scouts in the pursuing group, which agrees with the Jasta 27 numbers. They also said that as they headed for home the enemy were engaged and distracted by some Nieuports and Camels – an intervention which no doubt saved them.

SECOND LIEUTENANT

HARRY WALDO COLLIER,

MC, 42 SQUADRON, ROYAL AIR FORCE

Born on 31 October 1893, Harry Collier was the son of Mr and Mrs Henry C Collier of St John's Hill, Wanganui, New Zealand. A patriot, he travelled half-way around the world and learnt to fly at his own expense, being awarded the Aviators Certificate (No. 3863) of the Royal Aero Club on 20 November 1916. His initiative was rewarded with a commission in the Royal Flying Corps on 19 January 1917. Following formal training, he was appointed a Flying Officer on 18 August 1917 and posted to 42 Squadron on 2 September 1917. On 13 April 1918, less than a week after his brush with Göring, Collier was again involved in an aerial battle, sustaining wounds which resulted in him being sent back to the London Hospital for treatment on 20 April following. His work during the dire days of the Spring Offensive was acknowledged by the award of the Military Cross which was announced in the *London Gazette* of 26 July 1918 (Page 8787) : *Second Lieutenant Harry Waldo Collier, RAF Special Reserve: 'For conspicuous gallantry and devotion to duty. During recent operations this officer carried out a contact patrol in a thick mist at a height of only 150 feet under heavy machine-gun and rifle fire, and flew daily during the misty weather at low altitudes bringing back much useful information of the enemy and harrassing them with machine-gun fire and bombs. It was greatly due to his magnificent work that Headquarters were kept informed of the enemy's movements during a difficult phase of the battle. By his gallant and cheerful spirit at a time when the Squadron was suffering heavy casualties, he set a splendid example to the others'.*

Collier was later sent to the School of Artillery Co-operation, and promoted to Captain on 7 November 1918. He was finally posted to the Unemployed List on 29 July 1919, enabling him to return home to New Zealand.

LIEUTENANT

ERIC CAMPBELL MUSSON,

13/ESSEX REGIMENT AND 42 SQUADRON, ROYAL AIR FORCE

Born on 27 April 1894, Eric Musson was the son of Mr and Mrs J T Musson of 17 Grove

Göring the fighter pilot.

Crescent, Teignmouth, South Devon. Fluent in Spanish, Musson was engaged in ranching in the Argentine during 1913 and 1914. Like so many other Britons working in South and Central America, he returned to England as soon as he could after war had been declared. He was commissioned into the Essex Regiment and was first sent to France on 10 November 1915. Convalescing at home for a period after a bout of sickness, he returned to the trenches once again on 9 November 1916. In the meantime, however, he had applied for a transfer to the RFC, permission for which came through in the summer of 1917. After training, he was sent to 42 Squadron as a probationary observer on 2 October 1917. The wounds he received at the hands of Hermann Göring were sufficiently serious to have him returned to England on 20 April 1918 for further treatment. After recovery, he attended a number of technical courses before, on 9 December 1918 after the war ended on the Western Front, he was appointed an instructor. On 2 May 1919, Musson was posted to the Unemployed List and was free to return to ranching in the Argentine.

The changing criteria for the award to aviators of Imperial Germany's highest accolade, the Prussian Order Pour le Mérite (the 'Blue Max') in an odd way reflected the advance of aeronautics in the Great War. In the early days when air fighting began, the concept was so strange, even exotic, that any aerial victory was astonishing. Eight such victories – the number first needed to achieve the award – was breathtakingly prodigious. But, as aircraft developed, scout planes evolved, the interrupter-geared machine gun introduced and pilots of the calibre of Boelcke, Immelmann, Buddecke, Wintgens and von Mulzer emerged, so, inevitably, the threshold of victories that qualified for the award was increased. Without such increases the 'currency' of the award would be debased. The original qualifying 8 victories was doubled to 16 and, by mid-1917 had been rounded up to 20 (and rising!). And so it was perhaps a little surprising that Göring should receive the award somewhat prematurely, it seemed, with a score of just 18 – but receive it he did on 2 June 1918. A pre-requisite to the receipt of the Blue Max was the prior award of the Knight's Cross with Swords of the Royal Hohenzollern House Order, something Göring had achieved on 20 October 1917. He had also received his native State of Bavaria's highest award, the Military Karl-Friedrich Merit Order.

The day following the award of the Pour le Mérite, Hermann Göring and his Jasta 27 moved to a new base on the French front at Mont de Soissons Ferme.

VICTORY NO 19

5 June 1918 AR2? Vivières 10.00 hours

On mid-morning patrol in company with four of his command, Göring achieved his first victory on the new front. The combat occured to the north of Villers-Cotterêts Forest, his victim one of several machines seen co-ordinating French artillery fire onto German positions. As soon as the artillery spotting two-seaters spied the approach of the German scouts, they cut and ran towards the safety of their own bases. Göring chased and caught up with one – which he later reported to be an AR2 two-seater – sending it crashing down near a crossroads just east of Vivières. French ground troops poured fire up at his Triplane as he circled the wreck.

As already mentioned, there were often difficulties with 'type' identification and with the matching up of claims with corresponding losses. The Germans frequently confused AR2s with Caudrons and Bréguets. In fact, French records show two Bréguet XIVs lost on this day, but no AR2s. We assume, therefore, that one of these was Göring's nineteenth victim.

VICTORY NO 20

9 June 1918 Spad 1 Spa 94 08.45 hours

Göring led out a patrol of six on this summer's morning. Spotting a Spad single-seater flying low over the front lines, the Staffelführer dived down on the scout, the fire from his new Fokker DVII's (No. 324/18) machine guns quickly despatching the French machine down to a position behind German lines at the north-west corner of Horseshoe Forest. The Spad pilot, Pierre Chan, who was of Chinese extraction, was a member of Escadrille Spa 94.

VICTORY NO 21

17 June 1918 Spad 1 Spa 93 08.30 hours

On this occasion, five Spad single-seaters were spotted west of Soissons, their clear intention a destructive sally into the German balloon lines. Göring led seven machines to intercept and picking out one Frenchman at a height of 500 metres, fired 200 rounds into his hapless victim. The stricken Spad fell away and crashed by the side of a small wood west of the heights of Ambleny. As Göring climbed, he saw Leutnant Franz Brand shoot down another Spad just at the moment when two other of his Jasta's Fokkers collided in mid-air. The pilots of the crashed Fokkers, Oberleutnant Max von Forster and Vizefeldwebel Wilhelm Schäffer, were both killed. In the same fight, Leutnant Rudolf Klimke was credited with downing a third Spad.

The three Frenchmen who were shot down were Adjutant B E Breton (Göring's 21st victory), Maréchal-des-Logis Franceschi (Rudolf Klimke's 8th victory) and MdL Dol of Spa 162 – the first two being taken prisoner, the latter being killed.

Göring and Jasta 27 continued to operate on full combat status for the rest of June and into July but on the 11th of that month he was summoned to Headquarters and informed that he was to assume command, forthwith, of the German Air Service's premier fighting

Adjutant B E Breton, Spa 93 (centre), Göring's 21st victory. *(via F W Bailey)*

formation, Jagdesgeschwader Nr. I (Richthofen). The appointment followed the death in a flying accident of the Jagdesgeschwader's former commander, Hauptmann Wilhelm Reinhard, who had himself taken over after the death in action on 21 April 1918 of Manfred von Richthofen, 'the Red Baron'. To be given such a command was a great and, perhaps, an unexpected honour. Certainly, taken together with the early award of his Pour le Mérite, the appointment suggests that he was not without friends in high places! It was true that he had been in almost continuous combat for the whole of the war; that he was a professional regular soldier with twenty-one victories and long experience of command, but were there not others even more qualified? In this, as in most walks of life, patronage and influence are powerful allies. In stark contrast his successor in command of Jasta 27, Leutnant de Reserve Hermann Fromherz, formerly of Jasta 2, serves as an example of an officer who lacked 'connections'. Despite achieving 32 victories by the war's end, he did not get the Pour le Mérite he richly deserved.

VICTORY NO 22

18 July 1918 Spad 1 Spa ? 08.15 hours

Leading a morning patrol over the front in Fokker DVII (294/18) Göring happened upon and attacked two single-seaters. After a frenzied dogfight, one of the Spads went down, falling in a forested ravine near Bandry. This was the first of nine Spads which JGI would lay claim to on this day. French records list only the following Spad casualties: Caporal Louis Byers (an American) of Spa 38 taken prisoner; Lieutenant Daire of Spa 159, killed; Sous-lieutenant Jean Bourhis, Spa 80, missing; Caporal Georges Cumont, Spa 75, wounded; Sous-lieutenant Debarde, Spa 82, wounded. There were no casualties amongst the U S Air Service Spad units.

This was to be Göring's first and only claim whilst leading this élite and by now, world famous, air fighting unit. Had he decided that enough was enough? After the failure of the Spring Offensive and the build-up of American forces on the Western Front, the message on the wall must have been writ large to an astute and political animal like Göring. He had been amazingly lucky so far. Or was he simply ordered to take a more administrative, less active role by a High Command anxious not to lose yet another experienced commanding officer? After all, there were still plenty of young eagles able and willing to carry on the battle of the skies.

To be fair, it must be said that Hermann Göring was popular with the men under his command – there was no doubt that they regarded their leader not just with respect but with affection. Göring went on leave on 26 July, returning almost a month later on 22

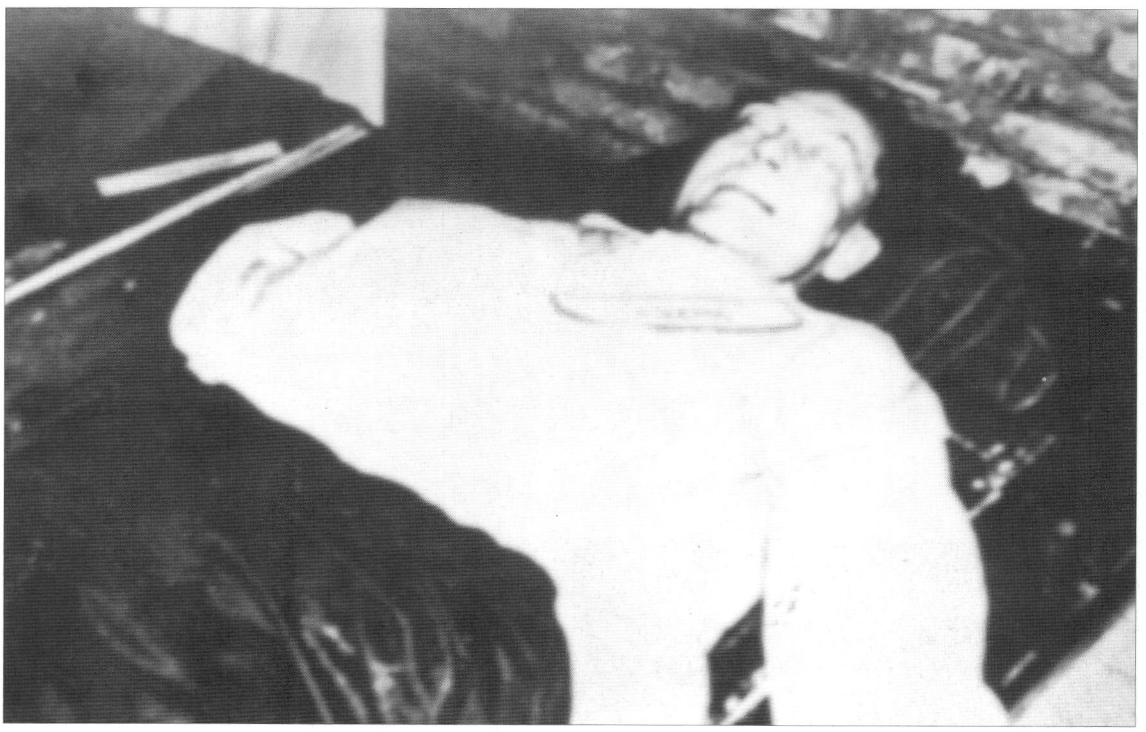

The end. Hermann Göring lies dead in his cell, the hangman cheated.

August. On 2 September he was called to attend GHQ for two days and perhaps surprisingly, he took leave yet again on 22 October. Shortages of fuel, parts and replacements curtailed flying operations and the high state of efficiency that had obtained for so long, decayed rapidly. Rumours of unrest – mutinies even – amongst the troops and sailors began to circulate as, unbeknown to the fighting men, feelers were being put out to the Allies, via the Swiss, for a negotiated armistice. The end was nigh.

Finally, on 9 November, an order was received to cease all air operations on the Western Front. On the following day, news of the Kaiser's abdication reached Jagdesgeschwader Nr. I. In direct contradiction to his orders and in a final act of defiance Göring, with the help of his Staffelführers, ensured that many of their remaining Fokkers did not fall intact into the hands of the French. The final entry of the war in the JG I day book stated: *'11 November. Armistice. Squadron flight in bad weather to Damstadt. Mist. Since its establishment, the Geschwader has shot down 644 enemy planes. Death by enemy action came to 56 officers and 6 non-commissioned pilots. 52 officers and 7 non-commissioned pilots were wounded. (Signed) Hermann Göring, Leutnant O C Geschwader'.* The end of the Flying Circus.

More than two decades afterwards, Hermann Göring's importance to Adolf Hitler's *Third Reich* was reflected by the rank and position he held. Second only to the Führer himself, Göring was Commander-in-Chief of the German Luftwaffe and Reichmarshall of Nazi Germany. He is remembered now not as one of the élite band of early military fliers but as one of the perpetrators of crimes that have rarely been parallelled in human history.

Hermann Göring's death, by his own hand, came on 15 October 1946, some 28 years after the end of his own fighting war. Found guilty of crimes against humanity by the Allies, his request to be executed by firing squad was denied. Cunning as ever, Göring used a cleverly concealed phial of cyanide to cheat the hangman. He was fifty-three years old.

CHAPTER 3

OBERLEUTNANT WERNER VOSS

The 'effectiveness' of a fighter pilot can be measured, on the face of it, by the number of his victories – his 'score'. Nothing, however, is ever that simple. So many factors enter the equation of evaluation – cool courage, flying ability and marksmanship are the constants, of course – but it is the variables that confuse the issue. The equipment available to the pilot, the strength of the opposition, the evolution of technique and so on. Immelmann is a case in point. His seventeen victories pale in a numbers-game comparison with Manfred von Richthofen (80) Ernest Udet (62) or Erich Löwenhardt (54) and yet everybody who was contemporaneously qualified to comment on 'the Eagle of Lille', acknowledged his unsurpassed ability as a brilliant and innovative fighter pilot – the best of his period. To achieve seventeen victories is a prodigious feat at any time and by any standard but, patently, it was a target much easier to attain in 1918 than ever it was in 1915/1916. Similarly, the inimitable Oswald Boelcke's 40 victories, gained by October 1916, represented a total that was equalled or overtaken by only eleven German pilots even to the war's end, but, arguably, his skill was never surpassed. The great aces – of whatever nationality – had all of the essential qualities in abundance but each had differing degrees of ability in the specialist disciplines.

Leutnant Werner Voss.

Werner Voss' main strength lay in his pure flying ability, he was an instinctive and natural pilot – the air was his element. His reading of, and positive reaction to, the shifting, changing scenario of an air battle set him apart.

Voss was born in Krefeld, in western Germany on 13 April 1897, thus he was only a couple of months past his 17th birthday

when the Great War began. He enlisted in the 11th Westphalian Hussars on 16 November 1914 and was in the ranks of that regiment when it was sent to the Eastern Front. Promotion to Gefreiter on 27 January 1915 was followed by the award of the Iron Cross Second Class and yet further elevation to the rank of Unteroffizier on 18 May. Sick of the slog and misery of the war on the ground, Voss volunteered for the Air Service in August 1915 and, following his acceptance, was sent for training at Flieger Ersatz Abteiling No. 7 at Cologne. The following month he was sent to the pilot school at Krefeld and having succeeded with his tests, returned to FEA 7 as an instructor in February 1916, a mere five months after his induction into the Air Service – mute testament in itself of his flying ability.

Promoted again on 2 March, this time to Vizefeldwebel, he was posted to Kampfgeschwader Nr. 4 and assigned to the 20th Kampf Staffel (Kasta). Whilst still training as a pilot, he frequently flew as an observer. On 28 May he was awarded his Pilot's Badge and his career took off in more ways than one! Commissioned on 9 September, another ambition – that of becoming a Jagflieger – was realised on 21 November when he was sent to join Jasta 2.

Jasta 2 had until recently been under the command of the great Oswald Boelcke but the doyen of German air fighters had been killed in an aerial collision a month earlier. Oberleutnant Stefan Kirmaier was appointed to succeed Boelcke but he, too, was killed in a fight with DH2s of 24 Squadron just days after Voss arrived. The next Staffelführer to follow Kirmaier, Oberleutnant Franz Joseph Walz, was an experienced pilot who had gained six victories while flying with Kampfstaffel 2 before his progress was checked by a foot wound received in an aerial combat. Walz, at 31, was older than most pilots and this may have had something to do with the strained relationship that would come to exist between him and his subordinates. For the moment, however, Voss was content, conscious of the singular honour done to him by his appointment to this élite Jasta. A unit which numbered amongst its members a certain Manfred von Richthofen with, at that time, 10 victories; Erwin Böhme with 6; Max Müller with 4; Hans Imelmann with 5 and Otto Höhne with 6. The Jasta, based at Lagnicourt to the west of Cambrai and east of Arras, was opposed largely by the Royal Flying Corps although there were some elements of the French Air Service in the vicinity – mainly the Groupemont de Combat de la Somme-Cachy based at Cachy aerodrome near Amiens. Voss's unit was equipped mainly with machines of the Albatros DII type, together with a few Halberstadt DII fighters.

On the day that its current commanding officer (Kirmaier) was killed – Jasta 2 achieved its 70th victory and Werner Voss his first.

VICTORY NO 1

27 November 1916 Nieuport XVII (No.A281) 60 Squadron 09.40

It was perhaps an indication of his potential that Voss claimed his first victory just five days after his arrival amongst the distinguished and accomplished group at Lagnicourt. In fact, he downed not one but two opponents on his débût day – one before noon, the other after. The morning victory was particularly impressive as it was against an experienced flyer, Captain G A Parker DSO MC, who had been at the front for some time – initially as an observer with 6 Squadron in 1915 before becoming a pilot, firstly with 8 Squadron and then on to 60 Squadron. 60 Squadron scouts had taken off at 08.00 on an Offensive Patrol over Bapaume and it was over that town that they were engaged by Jasta 2 at 09.40. Parker's Nieuport came down behind the German lines near Miraumont, west of Bapaume, the only casualty of the fight despite Offizierstellvertreter Max Müller claiming and being wrongly credited with another which he said went down into the British lines.

CAPTAIN

GEORGE ALEC PARKER

DSO, MC, MID, 2/NORTHAMPTONSHIRE REGIMENT AND 60 SQUADRON, ROYAL FLYING CORPS

The son of Lewis Jacques and Emily Parker of 26 Castle Street, Salisbury, Wiltshire, George was born on 19 December 1892, receiving part of his education at Dean Close School (1907-1909). Intent on a military career, Parker learnt to fly at his own expense, passing his test at Salisbury Plain in a Bristol and being awarded the Aviators Certificate (No.347) of the Royal Aero Club on 29 October 1912. But the possibility of joining the newly formed Royal Flying Corps was remote at that time, particularly for those without practical military training and experience. Parker was, however, gazetted Second Lieutenant from the Special Reserve on 24 March 1913 and sent to the Northamptonshire Regiment. He was in Alexandria, Egypt, with the 2nd Battalion of his regiment when war broke out and it was from there that they returned to England in the following October before finally crossing to France on 6 November 1914, thus qualifying all concerned for the award of the 1914 Star. Parker spent an unpleasant winter in the trenches and at one period was in charge of a contingent of 28 'grenadiers' (or bomb throwers) attached to the Brigade. Tragically, at the Battle of Neuve Chapelle between 10th and 12th March 1915, the 2/Northants was almost annihilated. Only three officers emerged unscathed from the battle and of those, Parker and another subaltern subsequently collapsed and were taken to hospital suffering from the effects of standing up to their waists in water for four days. After Parker recovered, he asked for a transfer to the RFC and, from May 1915, was frequently in combat when acting as an observer with 6 Squadron. Formal RFC pilot training followed and towards the end of 1915 he was sent to 13 Squadron, with which unit he was again often in combat situations. Parker, by now a Captain, was transferred to 60 Squadron and had been recommended for both the DSO and the MC just before he was killed. The announcements of his awards appeared in the same *London Gazette* of 10 January 1917 - the citation for the DSO on page 454 ; *"For conspicuous gallantry in action. He attacked hostile aeroplanes on three occasions during the same flight, killing an enemy observer. On another occasion he drove off three enemy machines, pursuing one of them down to 750 feet three miles behind the enemy lines"*. The MC citation is given on page 461: *"For conspicuous gallantry in action. He attacked a hostile scout machine and forced it to land after a long combat. He displayed great courage and skill in out-manoeuvring this machine"*. Parker's services were further acknowledged by a Mention in Despatches, the announcement of which appeared in the *London Gazette* of 13 May 1917, again long after his death. George Alec Parker's body was never recovered and so he is commemorated on the Arras Memorial to the Missing, France. He was twenty-three years old.

VICTORY NO 2

27 November 1916 FE2b (No.4915) 18 Squadron 14.15 hours

No doubt flushed with the success of his first victory in the morning, Voss was in the air again on this winter afternoon. The Jasta 2 machines encountered a number of 18 Squadron FE2bs that had taken off at 11.00 hours to patrol the V Army front. Voss attacked what he later called a 'Vickers' – the Germans often categorised aircraft by 'types', thus any 'pusher' aeroplane (those with the propeller behind the pilot) was likely to be described as a 'Vickers' after the ubiquitous Vickers FB5 'Gunbus'. Voss's attack caused the FE2b to burst into flames in the air and crash near Ginchy in an area so close to the lines that each side claimed it fell on their side! Certainly, the pilot, Lieutenant F A George, although burnt and wounded, avoided capture and was taken to a British hospital for treatment. Unfortunately the observer, AM1 O F Watts, was not so lucky, having been killed in the air by Voss's machine-gun fire.

LIEUTENANT

FREDERIC AMBROSE GEORGE,

OBE (1953) 16/NORTHUMBERLAND FUSILIERS AND 18 SQUADRON, ROYAL FLYING CORPS

Born in 1894, Frederic was the son of the Chairman of the Consett Iron Company, Sir Edward James George and his wife, Lady Eleanor George of 'Beech Grove', Consett, County Durham. He was educated at the Leys School (1909-1912) from where he entered into training with a ship-brokering firm in Newcastle-on-Tyne. Volunteering immediately upon the outbreak of war, he was initially gazetted Second Lieutenant to the Durham Light Infantry on 7 October 1914 but this appointment was quickly amended on 13 October to a gazetting to the 16th Battalion, Northumberland Fusiliers. With a wished for transfer to the RFC in mind, George learnt to fly at his own expense and was awarded the Aviators Certificate (No.3484) of the Royal Aero Club on 31 August 1916. Formal training followed and he was appointed Flying Officer and presented with his 'Wings' on 29 September 1916 before being sent, on 2 October, to join 18 Squadron in France. His career at the front was abruptly ended by his confrontation with Werner Voss as his wounds and burns were sufficiently severe so as to render him medically 'unfit for flying'. However, despite his injuries he remained in the service and was given various appointments including, at one stage, that of lecturer in propaganda. He was finally released to the Unemployed List on 7 March 1919 and was then able to return to ship-brokering in Newcastle. George was appointed Chairman of the North of England Shipowners Association in 1932 and became a traders' member of the Tyne Improvement Commission in 1944

Right: The former Lieutenant F A George, 16/Northumberland Fusiliers and 18 Squadron, RFC – photograph taken in February 1955 at the time of his appointment as the Swedish Consul in Newcastle-upon-Tyne.

before a later appointment as Vice-Chairman of the same organisation in 1957. A magistrate in the city for many years, Frederic George was awarded the OBE in the 1953 New Year Honours. He was also a director of William Dickinson and Company, Coal Exporters and in 1955 he was appointed by the Swedish government as their Consul in Newcastle-on-Tyne. He married Agnes Kathleen Blackwell by whom he had three daughters, living at 15 Graham Park Road, Gosforth, Northumberland until his death at the age of sixty-six on 23 September 1960.

AIR MECHANIC FIRST CLASS (NO. 2073)

OLIVER FRANK WATTS,

18 SQUADRON, ROYAL FLYING CORPS

The son of Thomas and Mabel Watts of Aston, Birmingham, Frank was born in 1893. Killed in the fight with Werner Voss, he was buried with full military honours in Corbie Communal Cemetery Extension, France (Fr. 23). He was twenty-three years old.

Voss received the Iron Cross 1st Class on 19 December 1916.

VICTORY NO 3

21 December 1916 BE2d No.5782 7 Squadron 11.00 hours

On 5 December Jasta 2 moved its base from Lagnicourt to Pronville, just four kilometres to the north-east. After gaining two victories on one day, Voss might have thought that it was a feat he could easily repeat but it was, in fact, almost another month before he despatched his next victim. At 08.05 British time on 21 December, Lieutenant D W Davis and Second Lieutenant W M V Cotton of 7 Squadron took off in their BE2d tasked with ranging fire from the 72nd Siege Battery, Royal Garrison Artillery, onto targets in the Miraumont area. They had started their work by calling for 'registration shots' on a silent German battery and had sent zone calls for other hostile batteries when suddenly their wireless signals came to an abrupt end. At 09.45 the RGA Battery reported an aircraft brought down at the same time as their wireless communications with their own spotting machine ceased. The artillerymen also said that the aircraft fell inside the German lines somewhere east of Beaucourt, in the vicinity of Miraumont. Voss claimed as his third victory, a BE2d over Miraumont at 11.00 hours (10.00 British time). The pilot was taken prisoner but once again, the observer was killed. This was the RFC's only loss for the day.

LIEUTENANT

DAROLD W DAVIS,

SASKATCHEWAN REGIMENT AND 7 SQUADRON, ROYAL FLYING CORPS

Born and educated in McLeod, Alberta, Canada, Darold was employed in the local branch of the Union Bank of Canada when war came. Volunteering, he served initially with the Saskatchewan Regiment, first undergoing training in Canada and England before being sent to France as part of the Canadian Expeditionary Force. After being commissioned on 23 October 1915, Davis successfully applied for transfer to the Royal Flying Corps, undergoing training as an 'artillery/observer' pilot before reporting to 7 Squadron on 19 November 1916. However, it was to be some time before he was actually sent out on his first mission, this occuring on 20 December 1916 when in fact he flew not one but two 'art/obs' jobs on the one day – accompanied on both occasions by Lieutenant W M V Cotton. So it was to be on only his second day of operational flying that he had the misfortune to run into the future ace, Werner Voss. Many years later Davis related how, badly wounded, he had lain for three days in no-man's land until he was picked up at last by advancing German soldiers who quickly sent him back behind their lines for medical treatment. Davis was well aware of the identity of the pilot who had brought him down since he was twice visited by Voss, once in hospital and, on another occasion, in Krefeld Prison Camp when he was presented with his victor's calling card! Davis was exchanged into neutral Holland on 7 May 1918 before being finally repatriated 27 November 1918. He returned to his banking job after the war but was to serve again in the Second World War as a desk-bound Squadron Leader in the Royal Canadian Air Force. In the 1980s he was living in Vancouver, BC.

SECOND LIEUTENANT
WILLIAM MARTIN VERNON COTTON,
7 SQUADRON, ROYAL FLYING CORPS

The son of Lieutenant Colonel G W V Cotton (Gordon Highlanders) and Mrs Sarah Cotton of 3 Ferndale Road, Hove, Brighton, Sussex, William was born in 1892 and educated at Brighton Grammar School. He had only just emigrated to Canada when war broke out. Cotton enlisted in November 1914 and because of his familiarity with the workings of the combustion engine, took up duties as a mechanic in the Canadian Army Service Corps. He also served as an ambulance driver, this time in France with the 4th Field Ambulance, Canadian Expeditionary Force. Cotton's father died in February 1916 and he was allowed compassionate leave to join his mother in Brighton for the funeral. Successfully applying for transfer to the RFC, Cotton was gazetted Second Lieutenant to the Special List on 4 August 1916 and was, after training, sent to join 7 Squadron as a probationary observer on 19 November 1916. His body was never found and hence he is commemorated on the Arras Memorial to the Missing, France. He was twenty-four years of age.

VICTORY NO 4
1 February 1917 DH2 (No.A2614) 29 Squadron 16.00 hours

The harsh winter weather severely curtailed operations over the front and it was some time into the new year before Voss struck again. Four DH2s of 29 Squadron set out on a patrol at 15.30 and had been in the air for thirty minutes when they met six enemy Albatros Scouts over Achiet-le-Grand. Lieutenant Peter Daly attacked one of the German machines and later said that he had just sent it down when another engaged him from behind. Fire from the Albatros shot out his engine which promptly stopped. Another bullet hit Daly in the shoulder and despite the pain and shock of his wound, he still managed to glide the DH2 down. Unfortunately, his landing place was inside the German lines near to Essarts where he was immediately taken prisoner. A communication from 5th Brigade Headquarters reported a sighting of the aerial combat and the subsequent steep headlong dive of the stricken DH2 before its descent was checked at a height of about 3,000 feet whereupon it flattened out and glided in behind the enemy lines. Days later, Werner Voss, bearing a gift of cigars, called on Peter Daly in hospital and enquired if he was being looked after properly. Before leaving, Voss gave Daly his visiting card and a signed photograph – rather an extravagant gesture for a scout pilot with only four victories.

CAPTAIN
(LATER GROUP CAPTAIN)

ALBERT PETER VINCENT DALY,

AFC (1929), MID, SWEDISH RED CROSS MEDAL (1945) 4/CONNAUGHT RANGERS AND 29 SQUADRON, ROYAL FLYING CORPS

The only son of Peter Joseph and Marie Jeanne d'Oosterwijke Daly of Daly's Grove, Ahascragh, County Galway, Ireland, Peter was born on 15 July 1891. He was educated at Stonyhurst College, the City and Guilds College and London University, becoming an Associate of the City and Guilds Institute (Civil & Mechanical Engineering). His first job was in the USA with the Pennsylvania Railway Company. After a short stay in the States, Daly secured a position with the Canadian Northern Railway Company in Toronto. Volunteering immediately upon the outbreak of war, he enlisted as a private soldier in the Canadian Grenadiers and crossed the Atlantic with the 1st Canadian Contingent. No sooner had he arrived in England than he was sent over to Ireland and gazetted Second Lieutenant to the Connaught Rangers on 16 December 1914. He went to the front in May 1915 and was wounded for the first time near Armentières when he was hit by shrapnel from a trench mortar bomb. After recovering from the effects of his wounds, he was attached to the RFC and was sent for flying training in November 1915. Awarded the Aviators Certificate (No.2626) of the Royal Aero Club on 27 March 1916, he finally received his 'Wings' on 10 May 1916 after 12 hours 56 minutes in the air (of which 3 hours 23 minutes were 'solo'). Following a brief posting to 48 Squadron, Daly joined 8 Squadron in France in June 1916. He was involved in eighteen bombing raids before being wounded for a second time after being hit twice by anti-aircraft fire. Soon after his recovery in November 1916, he was posted to 60 Squadron. On 2 December he, and another future victim of Voss, A D Whitehead (victory No.15) were part of a patrol led by Captain Eustace Grenfell MC which brought down an Albatros near Arras. Shortly afterwards, Daly was involved in yet another successful patrol but this time with an unfortunate and farcical outcome, the details of which are included in the Whitehead biographical details elsewhere in this book. Peter Daly was wounded for the third time when he was shot down by Werner Voss after being posted to 29 Squadron. At first, he was listed as missing, presumed killed, but happily the German Air Service dropped a message over the British lines which, to the relief of his mother in Galway, reported him safe albeit wounded. Daly was exchanged into Holland on 7 May 1918 and finally repatriated on 31 August 1918. Deciding to make the Royal Air Force his career, he was granted a permanent commission and continued flying – his log book shows him piloting 31 different types of aircraft between 1915 and 1922. His engineering background was, no doubt, a factor in his appointment as a delegate to the Inter-Allied Aeronautical Commission in Bulgaria in 1920. In 1922 he returned to 60 Squadron, spending two years on the North West Frontier of India during which time he was involved in seventeen bombing raids on dissident forces. Returning to Britain in 1924, he served in various Home Defence stations, his accomplishments being recognised by the award of the Air Force Cross in 1929 (*London Gazette* 3 June 1929, page 3681). He married Catherine Mary Wilson of Cossington Manor, Somerset on 9 June 1932, by whom he had one son and one daughter. The years between 1929 amd 1933 were mainly spent in the Headquarters of China Command based in Shanghai. Returning from the Far East, he was appointed to the command of RAF Marham in Norfolk with the rank of Group Captain. He went on to command other stations including Jurby, Isle of Man and St Athan, South Wales by which time the second war was underway. Sent to the Mediterranean Air Force, he was in the Operation Torch landings in Algiers in 1942, receiving a Mention in Despatches for distinguished service. Serving next in Tunisia and Italy, he was named Permanent President of Courts Martial in Naples. At the war's end he was attached to the Swedish Red Cross in Stockholm, working directly with Count Bernadotte for the repatriation of British POWs. For this work he was presented with the Swedish Red Cross Medal (silver) by Prince Carl of Sweden. Shortly afterwards, he retired to live in his home in Ireland. Group Captain Peter Daly died in Salisbury, Wiltshire, on 6 June 1985 – he was ninety-four years old.

Fédération Aéronautique Internationale
British Empire

We the undersigned, recognised by the F.A.I. as the sporting authority in the British Empire certify that	Nous soussignés pouvoir sportif reconnu par la F.A.I. pour l'Empire Britannique certifions que

Lieut. Albert Peter Vincent Daly, 4th Connaught Rangers,
Born at Ahascragh, Co. Galway, on the 15 July 1891,

having fulfilled all the conditions stipulated by the F.A.I. has been granted an	ayant rempli toutes les conditions imposées par la F.A.I. a été breveté
AVIATOR'S CERTIFICATE.	PILOTE-AVIATEUR.

THE ROYAL AERO CLUB OF THE UNITED KINGDOM.
H. C. L. Holden V. Chairman
Ass't. Secretary.
Date 27 Mar. 1916. No 2626.

166 PICCADILLY LONDON, W.
A. P. V. Daly
(Signature of Holder)

Captain A P V Daly's Royal Aero Club Certificate (Number 2626) issued on 27 March 1916.

VICTORY NO 5

4 February 1917 BE2d (No.5927) 16 Squadron 14.40 hours

Second Lieutenant H Martin-Massey and his observer, N M H Vernham, were engaged on an artillery observation sortie when they were attacked by two German fighters. Soon their BE2d was in flames and plummeting down to crash inside the British lines near Givenchy. Vernham was killed in the air but Martin-Massey, despite painful facial burns, survived the impact – even managing, during the last moments of the machine's headlong plunge, to arrest slightly the speed of the descent. Ten minutes earlier, Leutnant Erich König of Jasta 2 had shot down another of 16 Squadron machines just south of Givenchy but this later victory, timed at 14.40, was Werner Voss's.

SECOND LIEUTENANT
(LATER AIR COMMODORE)

HERBERT MARTIN-MASSEY

CBE (1950), DSO (1936), MC, CZECH WAR CROSS (1945) SHERWOOD FORESTERS AND 16 SQUADRON, ROYAL FLYING CORPS

Born in 1898, the son of Mr and Mrs E Martin-Massey of Hilton, Derbyshire, Herbert was educated at Oundle (1912-15) and at the Royal Military College, Sandhurst. From Sandhurst he was gazetted Second Lieutenant into the Notts and Derby Regiment (Sherwood Foresters) on 7 April 1916. Shortly afterwards, he was accepted into the Royal Flying Corps and after pilot training was sent to join 16 Squadron at the front. Burnt and injured in the fight with Voss, Martin-Massey was sent home for treatment and recuperation. His services to 16 Squadron were recognised by the award of a Military Cross, the announcement appearing in the King's Birthday Honours List in the *London Gazette* of 4 June 1917 (page 5481). The recipient of a permanent commission in the Royal Air Force, he remained in the service after the war. Martin-Massey, by now a Squadron Leader, was awarded the Distinguished Service Order in 1936 – the King (this was during the short-lived reign of Edward VIII) approving the award *"for gallant and distinguished services rendered in connection with the emergency operations in Palestine during the period 15 April 1936 to 14 September 1936"*. On 3 September 1936, Martin-Massey had taken part in a 6 Squadron operation to rescue a detachment of the Lincolnshire Regiment who were pinned down on the Nalbus to Tulkham road in Palestine. One Hawker Hart was lost and the crew killed. Martin-Massey was wounded but still managed to land his Hart at Tulkham. In July 1937 after receiving promotion to the rank of Wing Commander, he was appointed to command No. 5 Bomber Group. Promoted to Group Captain in 1940, he afterwards rashly insisted on accompanying a 7 Squadron bombing mission to Essen on the night of 1/2 June 1942, shortly before he was due to go to the USA. The 7 Squadron Stirling bomber was shot down in the raid; the whole crew successfully baled out but Martin-Massey suffered severe injuries to his foot in the subsequent parachute landing. Following a lengthy spell in a German hospital, he was sent as Senior British Officer to Stalag Luft III and was acting as such when the Great Escape occurred in March 1944. (The actor James Donald, assuming the name 'Ramsey', played the role of the SBO in the fanciful but highly successful 1963 Hollywood film version of 'The Great Escape'). Indeed it was Martin-Massey who first received the devastating news that fifty of the escapers had been re-captured and shot by the Gestapo on the orders of Adolf Hitler himself. Herbert Martin-Massey could be said to have been injury and accident prone – wounded and burnt in his clash with Voss, he also injured his head playing football at RAF Spittlegate in 1920; broke his right leg while roller skating in Baghdad in 1923; received wounds in Palestine in 1936 and was badly injured when escaping from the crippled Sterling bomber over Essen in 1942. Not surprisingly, he was repatriated from Germany in May 1944; the Germans making the fairly safe assumption that he would not see active service again. Martin-Massey was given the rank of Air Commodore on 21 June 1950 and retired to his home at 5 Dormers, Austen Wood, Gerrards Cross, Buckinghamshire, on the following day.

SECOND LIEUTENANT
NOEL MARK HODSON VERNHAM,
16 SQUADRON, ROYAL FLYING CORPS

Born in 1889, Noel was the son of John Edward and Julia E Vernham of 19 Woodstock Road, Poplar, London. When the war came, he was a married man living with his wife, Violet Kathleen, at 5 Warrington Crescent, Maida Vale, London. Despite his domestic responsibilities, Noel felt it was his duty to volunteer and was accepted a candidate for the Royal Flying Corps after being gazetted to the General List on 22 September 1916. Vernham is buried in Aubigny Communal Cemetery Extension, France (Fr.95). He was, at twenty-seven, older than many of his contemporaries.

VICTORY NO 6
10 February 1917 DH2 (No. A2548) 32 Squadron 11.15 hours

Captain L P Aizlewood, with Second Lieutenants M J J G Mare-Montembault MC (A5025), J H Cross (7938) and A V H Gompertz (7862) in close support, took off at 10.15 on a Line Patrol. An hour later they spotted nine enemy machines approaching from above them. The British did not have sufficient time to climb to an equitable height and so, on a signal from Aizlewood, traversed their Lewis guns and fired upwards into the enemy squadron. The Germans violently and aggressively reacted to this affront by diving down on their numerically inferior foes and soon the sky was filled with scrapping scout planes. Aizlewood focused his attention on an enemy machine which carried streamers on its struts and drove it down to 1,000 feet but was then himself attacked by three others who had gotten onto his tail. He spun his DH2 around and had been partially successful in fending off his attackers when he was wounded in the right shoulder. The pain and shock rendered him momentarily defenceless and one of his opponents took immediate advantage, pouring bullets into his engine and fuel tanks and slicing through some of the flying wires of the DH2. Collecting himself, Aizlewood broke away and dived for home, his machine holed in more than 70 places. As he moved away from the main fight, he flew immediately below two German aircraft and lifting his gun, fired his remaining ammunition at them. Both enemy machines made off, making no attempt to retaliate. By now the dogfight had exhausted itself with most of the Germans driven back, although Gompertz, too, had had his machine badly shot about.

Voss claimed Aizlewood as his sixth victory, downed into the British lines, south-west of Serre at 12.25 German time. In fact, Aizlewood made it all the way back to his base at Lealvillers although his machine was so badly damaged it was struck off charge. Aizlewood was elated to learn that a Lieutenant Ritter (a British pilot with 15 Squadron RFC despite his name!) who had been flying near to the fight, confirmed seeing the streamered machine attacked by him early in the fight and subsequently glimpsed it going down vertically 1,000 feet above the ground.

Erwin Böhme also claimed a victory within five minutes of Voss 'scoring' but again there was confusion over the 'type'. Despite the German pilot saying his adversary crashed behind British lines, it is almost certain that the 'victim' was none other than the shot-about Gompertz who actually only forced-landed at Souastre – hardly a 'victory' in the accepted sense. And despite the vaunted confirmation methods of the German Air Service, claims could still be misapplied, especially if the supposed 'victim' fell behind Allied lines!

CAPTAIN
LESLIE PEECH AIZLEWOOD,
MC, AFC, MID, 5/YORK AND LANCASTER REGIMENT AND 32 SQUADRON, ROYAL FLYING CORPS

The son of solicitor Albert Percy Aizlewood and his wife, Florence Shaw Aizlewood, of 'Blenheim House', Doncaster Road, Rotherham, Yorkshire, Leslie was born in April 1895. He was educated privately and at Uppingham School, Rutland (1909-1912). After Uppingham, Leslie studied mechanical and electrical engineering at Sheffield University and at Parkgate Iron and Steel Works. Before the war, Aizlewood had become involved with his local (Rotherham) Territorial Force unit, being commissioned into the 5th Battalion of the York and Lancaster Regiment in 1914. Mobilised in August 1914, he helped to get his battalion up to standard before accompanying them to France on 13 April 1915. Following a period at home recovering from wounds received at the front, he took flying lessons and was rewarded with the Aviators Certificate (No. 2742) of the Royal Aero Club on 18 March 1916. After the usual formal training, he was appointed a Flying Officer and sent to France in July 1916. In the following September, he single-handedly attacked five enemy machines for which action he was awarded the Military Cross, as announced in the *London Gazette* of 20 October 1916, page 10174: *'For conspicuous gallantry and skill. Seeing five hostile machines, he manoeuvred to get between them and their lines; then, diving on one of them, he reserved his fire till he was only twenty yards off. The hostile machine fell out of control, but he was so close to it that he collided with it, breaking his propellor and damaging his machine. Though it was barely controllable, he managed to get it back to our lines'.*

Shortly after this incident, Aizlewood was made a Flight Commander. Wounded in the action against Voss, he was returned to England to recuperate. His wounds healed, Aizlewood was next appointed to helping

Aizlewood (on right) with 32 Squadron colleague, Captain W G S Curphey MC* (died of wounds 15 May 1917). (*Bruce/Leslie Collection*)

with the establishment of new aerodromes in Scotland and England and, indeed, received a Mention in Despatches for this work in March 1918. On 29 September 1918, by then Major Aizlewood was killed in a flying accident over the sea off Saltburn, Yorkshire. His body was recovered and buried with full military honours near to his home aerodrome at Marske-in-Cleveland (St Germain) Yorkshire. He was twenty-three years old. The award of the Air Force Cross was announced, posthumously, in the New Year's Honours List for 1919 – *London Gazette* 1 January 1919, page 97.

VICTORY NO 7

25 February 1917 DH2 (No. A2557) 29 Squadron 14.55 hours

On this day Voss struck twice in the same combat. He had been at the front three months by now and was approaching the peak of his powers. That his 'eye was in' is evidenced by the fact that he was to take the number of his victories to 24 during the next five weeks.

DH2s from 29 Squadron had taken off on Offensive Patrol at 12.35 British Time (13.35 German time). Some minutes later, at 13.40, Jasta 2 ran into the six-machine British patrol, led by Captain H J Payn, in the air above Arras. Four of the Jasta 2 machines dropped from their superior height onto the British whilst the other two kept a watching brief on the proceedings below. The highest of the British machines, flown by Lieutenant J H R Sutherland (A2571) was attacked first and from behind. Sutherland spun round to face his attackers but his gun jammed and he had to dive away to give himself time to try to clear the stoppage. His opponent, however, continued to press home his attack and his fire smashed the DH2's rudder post. Disabled, Sutherland continued to dive, only straightening out at the last possible moment to head for his base and safety. Lieutenant R J S Lund (2557) was not so lucky; engaged by a cleverly flown Albatros, the enemy pilot's fire severely wounded him and he and his DH2 crashed into the British lines near Arras.

LIEUTENANT

REGINALD JAMES SPENCER LUND,

1/4 (TF) BATTALION, ROYAL BERKSHIRE REGIMENT AND 29 SQUADRON, ROYAL FLYING CORPS

The son of Mr and Mrs E H Lund of Coulsdon, Surrey, James (left) was born in 1894. He was educated at Sherborne School, Dorset (1910-13) and at Worcester College, Oxford. Amongst the first to volunteer upon the outbreak of war, he was gazetted as a Second Lieutenant to the 1/4th Battalion (Territorial Force) Princess Charlotte's Own (Royal Berkshire Regiment) on 2 September 1914. He accompanied his battalion to France, departing from Folkestone on the packet boat *Onward* on 30 March 1915. After a period in the trenches, his application to join the RFC was approved and he returned to England for pilot training, upon completion of which he was sent to join 29 Squadron in France. Following his recovery from the wounds received at the hands of Werner Voss, he was employed in England as an instructor. Eventually and with the rank of Captain, he again returned to the front in September 1918, this time as a Flight Commander with the crack 60 Squadron. Lund lived between the wars at 'Trelawny', Claremont Road, Redhill in Surrey and he served again in the Second World War, this time as a Squadron Leader in the Royal Air Force. He moved finally to his retirement home at 'Grange Cottage', Steeple Aston, Oxfordshire in 1960 and died on 9 April 1972 at the age of seventy-seven.

VICTORY NO 8

25 February 1917 DH2 (No. 7849) 29 Squadron 15.00 hours

The aerial battle continued after Lund's enforced departure from the scene. Lieutenants J G Aronson and S P Simpson both successfully fought off the German scouts, each firing 100 rounds at distances of 100 yards. Their opponents having fled, the British pair could now take the time to look around and spotted an Albatros pressing home an attack upon Captain Payn, who plunged into a steep dive in an attempt to shake off his tormentor. Aronson positioned himself on the Albatros's tail and opened fire, causing the German pilot to break off his pursuit of Payn and disappear into the clouds. Payn, grateful for Aronson's intervention, nursed his damaged machine away from the scene, his stuttering and spluttering engine barely functioning, to land at nearby Duisans, his descent no doubt noted by observers on the German side.

The sixth member of the 29 Squadron patrol, Lieutenant F C B Douglas, who had been seen briefly after the scrap on the British side of the lines, was soon lost from sight in cloud and mist. In point of fact, Douglas ran out of fuel and was compelled to make a forced landing.

So, in summation, 29 Squadron actually lost one DH2, had one pilot wounded and two other machines shot up. However, Jasta 2 claimed THREE DH2s down in British lines and logic tells us that the three must have been Sutherland, Lund and Payn. The German front line observers, upon whom the Jasta pilots often relied for confirmations, would have undoubtedly seen Lund come down and may well have seen Sutherland and Payn in apparently irrecoverable dives. The chronology of the claims is helpful – Leutnant Erich König's was the first, registered as being at 14.45, and as Sutherland was the first man to be attacked, he would appear to be the subject of König's claim. Voss's two are timed at 14.55 and 15.00 – suggesting that he had disposed of Lund first and, in driving down Payn, was convinced he had 'got him' too before he, himself, was forced away by Aronson and Simpson.

And so the German system of confirmation, usually very good when the victims landed on their side of the lines, was found somewhat wanting when the apparent 'victories' disappeared into Allied lines.

CAPTAIN

HAROLD JAMES PAYN

AFC (1923), ROYAL ENGINEERS (MOTOR CYCLISTS SECTION) AND 29 SQUADRON, ROYAL FLYING CORPS

Harold James Payn was born on 3 November 1887, his family living at 33 High Street, Christchurch, Hampshire. Enlisting in the Royal Engineers as a despatch rider on the outbreak of war, he was promoted to Corporal (No. 28221) and sent to France in the autumn of 1914, thus qualifying for the 1914 Star. Next, he was gazetted Second Lieutenant to the Royal Engineers (Motor

Cyclists Section) on 15 January 1915, and continued to serve in France. Eventually transferring to the RFC, he first qualified as an observer, flying behind Major Hawker VC amongst others when serving with 6 Squadron. Gaining the Aviators Certificate (No. 2528) of the Royal Aero Club on 31 January 1916, he went on successfully to complete formal pilot training before a subsequent transfer to 29 Squadron in France. Once in France, he quickly gained a reputation as an exceptional pilot, counting among his admirers the great James McCudden with whom he flew on many a patrol. After the war Payn stayed on in the Royal Air Force until 1923 when he retired from the Active List and became a Class 'A' Reservist (Flight Lieutenant) but not before his services and exceptional flying abilities were recognised by the award of the Air Force Cross in the King's Birthday Honours List (*London Gazette* 2 June 1923, page 3953). During the next five years Payn flew flying boats, living and working in Weybridge. In 1928, his outstanding ability secured him a position as a Test Pilot with Supermarine Aviation (Vickers) Ltd – later becoming Assistant Chief Designer under R J Mitchell, the man who designed the Spitfire. Given the nickname, 'Agony', Payn continued to prosper until his second marriage to a lady of foreign origins brought down on his head the disapproval of the Air Ministry. Obviously the nineteen thirties was a sensitive time and Payn's position with Vickers was – in the opinion of the Air Ministry at least – likely to be compromised by the liaison with this foreign lady! Indeed, following Mitchell's death in 1937, Payn became virtually unemployable in the aircraft industry and generally had a very bad time of it.

VICTORY NO 9

26 February 1917 BE2c (No. 2535) 16 Squadron 16.50 hours

This, and Voss's next three victories, were against the hard pressed and long suffering men flying the 'sitting duck' BE2 Corps machines. Lieutenant H E Bagot and Second Lieutenant R L M Jack had taken off at 14.15 British time on an artillery observation patrol. Observers on both sides of the lines saw them ferociously attacked by a Halberstadt Scout that unrelentingly followed their enforced descent to within a few feet of the ground before breaking off. The BE2c, as Voss carefully noted, crashed just inside Allied lines near Ecurie, a couple of kilometres due north of Arras, at 16.50 German time. Both occupants were wounded, Jack succumbing to his the following day.

LIEUTENANT

HARRY ERIC BAGOT

(LATER THE 7TH BARON BAGOT) ROYAL FIELD ARTILLERY AND 16 SQUADRON, ROYAL FLYING CORPS

Right: Lieutenant Harry Bagot (later the 7th Baron Bagot) with his dog, 'Tiggs', who often accompanied him in the cockpit! (Note the wound stripe on Harry's lower left sleeve). His half-brother, Charles (the present Lord Bagot) looks admiringly on!

Below right: The heraldic 'Device' of the Barons Bagot.

Born on 4 February 1892, Harry was the son of Charles Frederick Heneage Bagot and Florence Eleanor Bagot of Tenbury, Worcestershire. Like his father, he was educated at Marlborough (1908-1910). Harry volunteered as soon as the war broke out and was accepted for training with the Inns of Court OTC on 9 September 1914 (No. SQ1129). Following an extremely brief period of instruction, he was gazetted as a Second Lieutenant to the Royal Field Artillery on 28 September 1914. He first went to France with his battery on 29 August 1915 but shortly afterwards applied for transfer to the RFC. Several months later he was accepted into the flying service and after successfully completing pilot training, was sent to join 16 Squadron at the front. He had seen a good deal of service and had become a Flight Commander by the time of his confrontation with Werner Voss. The wounds inflicted by the German ace were sufficiently severe to curtail his active flying service and he saw out the rest of the war in less arduous situations. After the war, he went into business in London and on 5 August 1961, upon the death of the 6th Baron Bagot, he was ennobled – the titles, Baron Bagot (first conferred in 1780) and the even more ancient Baronetcy (created 1627) both passing to Harry. In 1951 he was married to Kathleen Elizabeth Saddler and following her death in 1972, married secondly, Mrs Mary Hewitt. On 20 June 1973, the Right Honourable Baron Harry Eric Bagot of Shropshire and London (the 7th Baron Bagot) died – he was seventy-nine years old.

SECOND LIEUTENANT
ROBERT LAWRENCE MUNRO JACK,
5/GORDON HIGHLANDERS ATTACHED 16 SQUADRON, ROYAL FLYING CORPS

Robert Jack was the son of Elizabeth Ann Jack who, after becoming a widow upon the death of Robert's father, married again and as Mrs Sinclair, lived with her second husband at 11 Chapel Street, Peterhead, Aberdeenshire. Robert first enlisted as a private soldier (No. 3191) in the Gordon Highlanders before eventually being picked out as officer material and gazetted Second Lieutenant to the 1/5th (Buchan and Formartin) Battalion, Gordon Highlanders, Territorial Force, on 19 December 1915. Shortly after receiving his

commission, Robert applied for a transfer to the RFC and following the almost obligatory waiting period, was sent for observer training and then on to join 16 Squadron at the front. The wounds that Jack received at the hands of Voss were very severe and he died the following day in a Casualty Clearing Station behind the British lines. He is buried in Aubigny Communal Cemetery Extension, France (Fr.95).

VICTORY NO 10

27 February 1917 BE2e (No. 2530) 8 Squadron 10.45 hours

Voss achieved the first of two victories on the morning of this day. Lurking in wait with four of his companions, he dropped on yet another unescorted BE2e – an 8 Squadron machine that had taken off at 08.25 (British time) with orders to 'range' for 148th and 149th Batteries, RFA. Obviously hyper-aware of their vulnerability, the crews of these artillery/observation machines went to great pains to protect themselves from the faster scouts. The moment they saw, or even thought they saw, an enemy scout-plane, they would dive for the comparative safety of their own lines. On this occasion the crew of the British machine, perhaps momentarily engrossed in their work of artillery directing, were surprised and after a brief chase were unable to escape the deadly attentions of the German ace. The BE2e and its crew, Second Lieutenants E A Pope and H A Johnson, were seen to fall in flames into the British lines at Blairville, south-west of the Cité de l'Arras (ref. 51C SE R.26.a.). Both men were killed and their machine totally wrecked.

SECOND LIEUTENANT EDWIN ALBERT POPE, 8 SQUADRON, ROYAL FLYING CORPS

The son of Edwin and Alice Louisa Pope of 'Buena Vista', High Level Road, Three Anchor Bay, on the slopes of Signal Bay, Capetown, South Africa, Edwin was born in 1891. He was educated at Pietermaritzberg College and at the University of Natal where he was studying when the war broke out. As soon as his studies were completed, Edwin made his way to England at his own expense and was accepted into the Inns of Court Officer Training Corps in London on 22 November 1915 (No. 6/7746). Following six months of training, he was gazetted to the General List and his preferred choice of service, the Royal Flying Corps, on 13 May 1916. Further training as an artillery/observer pilot followed, after which he was awarded his 'Wings' on 10 July 1916 and sent as a much needed replacement to 8 Squadron in France exactly one week later. He is buried alongside his observer in Warlincourt Halte British Cemetery, France (Fr.120), aged 27.

SECOND LIEUTENANT HUBERT ALFRED JOHNSON, 24/LONDON REGIMENT AND 8 SQUADRON, ROYAL FLYING CORPS

Born in 1893, Hubert was the son of Alfred de Garieb and Alice Johnson of 17 Lascotts Road, Bowes Park, London. Johnson was gazetted Second Lieutenant to the 24th (County of London) Battalion (The Queen's) on 15 December 1915. Transfer to the Royal Flying Corps was followed by observer training and a posting to 8 Squadron in France. He is buried in Warlincourt Halte British Cemetery, Saulty, France (Fr. 120), aged 23.

VICTORY NO 11

27 February 1917 BE2c (No. 7197) 12 Squadron 16.48 hours

Jasta 2's surprise tactics trapped another 'art/obs' aircraft in the afternoon. A 12 Squadron BE2c had taken off at 14.55 British time tasked with a routine artillery observation patrol. Less than an hour later, Werner Voss was amongst a pack of five Jasta 2 members that fell upon Captain J McArthur and his observer, Private J Whiteford. Voss was the first to reach the RFC machine and his fire sent it crashing to the ground inside the British lines at St Catherine on the western outskirts of Arras. Again, both of the occupants were killed. The two BEs destroyed by Werner Voss proved to be the only British aircraft losses on this day.

CAPTAIN JOHN MCARTHUR,

ROYAL BERKSHIRE REGIMENT AND 12 SQUADRON, ROYAL FLYING CORPS

The son of Mr and Mrs McArthur of Kirkmuirhill, Lesmahagow, Lanarkshire, Scotland, John was born in 1894. He was educated in Scotland and at the South Western Polytechnic where he became a member of the University of London Officer Training Corps. Probably in an attempt to offer John's parents some consolation, his Squadron Commander said in a letter to Mr and Mrs McArthur that John had been attacked by several enemy machines but that he had shot two of them down before he, himself, had been shot and thrown from his machine. Captain John McArthur is buried alongside his observer, Private J Whiteford, in Avesnes-le-Comte Communal Cemetery, France (Fr. 46), aged 22.

PRIVATE JAMES WHITEFORD,

(NO. 15814), 18 COMPANY, MACHINE GUN CORPS ATTACHED 12 SQUADRON, ROYAL FLYING CORPS

Born in 1897, James was the son of William and Mrs Whiteford of 8 Barclay Street, Paisley, Renfrewshire. He was educated locally and after leaving school, was apprenticed as an engineer with McGee and Company, Laighpark. On 25 May 1915, just as soon as he was old enough, James enlisted in the Royal Scots Fusiliers (No.19541). He proceeded to France in March 1916 and showed a particular propensity for machine guns – so much so that he was transferred to the newly formed Machine Gun Corps later in the same year. The BE Corps machine losses at this time were such that the RFC was forced to look to the ranks of the Machine Gun Corps for replacement gunners/ observers. An exceptional marksman, James was one of those selected as a probationary from the many volunteers. In a letter to his mother, his Squadron commander said that her son and his pilot had been attacked by five hostile machines and, after a short fight, had been brought down, adding that although James had only been with them for a brief time he had shown great promise. James's father, Driver William Whiteford, was also serving in France at the time, attached to a local TF unit of the Royal Engineers. Whiteford, with his pilot and fellow Scot, Captain John McArthur, were buried with full military honours in Avesnes-le-Comte Communal Cemetery, France (Fr. 46). He was nineteen years old.

VICTORY NO 12

4 March 1917 BE2d (No. 6252) 8 Squadron 11.30 hours

Yet another BE to fall victim to Voss. The pilot, Sergeant R J Moody, with Second Lieutenant E E Horn acting as observer, left their home aerodrome at 09.25 hours on a routine artillery observation patrol. Less than an hour later, spectators on the ground watched as the RFC machine was attacked by a German scout plane. The one-sided confrontation was sickenly brief, flames enveloping the BE2d as it fell on the Allied side of the lines, south of Berneville, south-west of Arras. Both crew members died, the machine smashed and burnt.

SERGEANT
REGINALD JAMES MOODY
(NO.626), 8 SQUADRON, ROYAL FLYING CORPS

The son of Charles George and Ellen Moody of Church Street, Odiham, Hampshire, Reg Moody was born in 1894. On 1 March 1913, at the age of nineteen, he enlisted in the newly formed Royal Flying Corps, then in only its second year of existence. Moody accompanied the first echelons of the flying service to France on 12 August 1914, thus qualifying for the 1914 Star. He advanced rapidly through the non-commissioned ranks, eventually qualifying as an observer. Moody gave impetus to his ambition of gaining his 'Wings' by independently taking his 'ticket', being awarded the Aviators Certificate (No. 3889) of the Royal Aero Club on 27 November 1916. Inevitably, he was, soon afterwards, selected for formal pilot training. Now sporting the cherished full 'Wings', Moody had been back at the front for the briefest of periods when he had the misfortune to run into Werner Voss. Sergeant Moody is buried in Warlincourt Halte British Cemetery, Saulty, France (Fr. 120). He was twenty-two years of age.

SECOND LIEUTENANT
EDMUND ERIC HORN,
2/MIDDLESEX REGIMENT AND 8 SQUADRON, ROYAL FLYING CORPS

Above: Voss's Albatros DIII in May 1917 – distinctive with its red heart, white border, white swastika symbol surrounded by a painted laurel wreath, white tailplane.

Right: A DH2 of 32 Squadron in flight – the type claimed by Voss as his 13th victory.

The fourth and youngest son of poultry breeder John Horn and his wife, Mary, of Loughton and North Weald, Essex, Edmund was born in June 1897. Educated at Loughton School, Essex, he volunteered on the 17th anniversary of his birthday and was accepted for service with the Royal Army Medical Corps (No. 57343). Following three months training, he was sent to France on 5 September 1915 and was continually occupied until he was gassed and sent home to recover. Next, he was gazetted as Second Lieutenant to the 2nd Battalion of the Middlesex Regiment, with which unit he saw much of the heavy fighting on the Somme in 1916. His application for transfer to the RFC was approved and effected in December 1916 but he remained in France throughout the period of his training and was still a probationary observer at the time of his death. Edmund Horn is buried in the Warlincourt Halte British Cemetery, Saulty, France (Fr.120). Despite his lengthy service at the front, he was still only nineteen years old when he lost his life.

VICTORY NO 13

6 March 1917 DH2 (No. 7941) 32 Squadron 16.35 hours

Two days after the twelfth victory, inexorably, came the thirteenth! Small consolation for the occupant of the DH2 involved but at least the recently beleaguered BEs enjoyed a temporary respite. A 32 Squadron patrol came under anti-aircraft fire as they crossed the lines into German occupied territory at 14.05 British time. Passing through unscathed, they next spotted four hostile aircraft which they lost no time in attacking. After a brief skirmish, the Germans, who had been surprised by the British attack, showed no stomach for a fight and dived away. In the immediate aftermath the pilot of one of the British machines, Captain G J King (No. 7897), who had found that his single Lewis gun was not functioning, turned for home in company with Lieutenant M L Taylor (No. A5023) whose engine was giving trouble. Taylor's erratic engine caused him to fall behind his companion – on the face of it, a sitting duck for any passing enemy. He was attacked not once, but three times, by different enemy machines. Amazingly, he escaped each time – on the third occasion by spinning down to tree top level and racing across the lines to safety.

The remaining three members of the 32 Squadron sortie, Captain H G Southon (No. 7941) Lieutenant W A G Young (No. A 2548) and Lieutenant M J J G Mare-Montembault MC continued their patrol. In the meantime, the four German scouts who had cut and run minutes earlier, now apparently regained their composure. They re-grouped and returned to attack the weakened British patrol.

Adolf von Tutscheck claimed his first of twenty-seven victories when he shot down Mare-Montembault into the German lines. A minor ace with six victories, Maximillian John Jules Gabriel Mare-Montembault had previously been fortunate enough to survive an encounter with the peerless Oswald Boelcke, crashing into his own lines but walking away unscathed. On this occasion he was slightly less fortunate although again unharmed in the crash, and was taken into captivity by German ground troops.

Werner Voss fell upon Southon's 'pusher' and despite the RFC man's attempts at evasion, quickly overcame him; the DH2 grounded at Favreuil, due north of Bapaume – its pilot wounded and taken prisoner.

CAPTAIN HERBERT GORDON SOUTHON,

4TH RESERVE BATTALION, ROYAL NAVAL DIVISION, ROYAL NAVAL VOLUNTEER RESERVE AND 32 SQUADRON, ROYAL FLYING CORPS

The son of Walter and Alice Mabel Southon of 'Haslemere', Dartford Road, Cricklewood,

London NW, Herbert was born 24 April 1891. After serving with the 4th Reserve Battalion, Royal Naval Division, Royal Naval Volunteer Reserve, Southon successfully sought transfer to the Royal Flying Corps. He was sent to Reading to commence his training on 17 August 1916. The training followed the usual pattern, finishing with a course at the School of Aerial Gunnery in the closing days of 1916. Southon received his 'Wings' and was appointed a Flying Officer on 7 January 1917 before being sent to join 32 Squadron in France. The wounds and injuries he received in the conflict with Voss were severe, so much so that he was exchanged – via the Red Cross – into Switzerland on 29 December 1917 and repatriated to England on 23 May 1918, six months before the war's end. After a period in hospital, he was able to take up light duties, instructing at the Armaments School before finally leaving the Service on 12 March 1919 and taking up residence at his home at 16 Craigwash Avenue, Norbury, London SW. Southon married Vera le Fleming in 1921 and continued to live in the London area until his death on 11 August 1937 at the age of 46.

VICTORY NO 14

11 March 1917 FE2b (No. 7685) 22 Squadron 10.00 hours

22 Squadron mounted a Line Patrol of FE2s along the 4th Army front. At 09.00 hours British time they were engaged by elements of Jasta 2. The FE2b piloted by Second Lieutenant L W Beal with 2AM F G Davin in the front cockpit, was attacked by Werner Voss, the ace's initial burst shooting away the British machine's controls and wounding Davin in the thigh. The FE spun down, engine stopped, and force landed near Combles; the impact wrecked the machine completely. On this occasion, the circumstances of the incident, as reported by both sides – German and British – coincided precisely.

SECOND LIEUTENANT
LESLIE WATTS BEAL,
MID, 22 SQUADRON, ROYAL FLYING CORPS

A Londoner, Beal lived at 37 Ferme Park Road, N4. He joined the Inns of Court Officer Training Corps (No. 6/3/6754) on 11 October 1915 and following the mandatory period of training, was gazetted Second Lieutenant to the Royal Flying Corps on 4 August 1916. Beal then went on to train as a pilot and after qualifying, was sent to France and 22 Squadron with which unit he was to lead an eventful existence. On 4 March 1917, flying with Davin, he was engaged by an enemy machine flown by the German ace, Leutnant Renatus Theiller of Jasta 5. The FE2b (No. A5441) was set on fire but the crew managed to put it out before finally wrecking the machine during a forced landing.

Although slightly wounded in the encounter with Voss on 11 March, Beal was again up on a photo reconnaissance on 26 April 1917. For a third time he was shot up but on this occasion he was quite badly wounded. Despite all, he again managed to get down behind British lines. Beal's undoubted pluck was officially recognised by a Mention in Despatches – his profligacy with FE2bs apparently forgiven by the RFC High Command!

AIR MECHANIC 2ND CLASS
F G DAVIN
(NO. 61912), 22 SQUADRON, ROYAL FLYING CORPS

Davin, an Ulsterman, joined the Special Reserve Cavalry Unit, the North Irish Horse, as a private soldier (No. 1350) on 13 November 1914, going to France for the first time on 9 February 1915, thus qualifying for the 1914/15 Star. An expert on machine guns, he was accepted into the RFC as an assistant armourer on 5 February 1917 and soon afterwards was flying as a Brisfit observer with 22 Squadron. Davin had the misfortune of meeting two German aces within seven days. Firstly on 4 March when he and his pilot, Beal, were shot down by Renatus Theiller – the German's eleventh 'victory' and secondly, on 11 March when the same crew were shot down by Werner Voss. Davin was wounded in this latter encounter.

VICTORY NO 15

11 March 1917 Nieuport XVII (No. A279) 60 Squadron 14.30 hours

Following his morning victory, Voss was in the air again in the afternoon, sent up in response to another Allied incursion into German territory. The intruders were represented by two Nieuport 17 Scouts of 60 Squadron, there to protect a 13 Squadron BE that intended crossing the lines north-east of Arras. The Scout pilots, A D Whitehead and F Bower, took up positions above and ahead of their charge and at a point above Bailleul-sur-Berthoult (not to be confused with the Bailleul some 40 kilometres to the north) Whitehead looked down and saw, 1,000 feet below him and ideally positioned for a surprise attack, about half a dozen German fighters. Somewhat rashly perhaps, Whitehead rolled his Nieuport over and dived, attacking from behind and hammering 30 rounds from his wing Lewis gun at very close range into an enemy machine that fell away, side-slipping to the left, apparently out of control. Whitehead immediately picked out and opened fire on a second German but, at the same moment, was himself attacked from behind. A bullet went through his left knee and right leg and, unsurprisingly, he lost control of the Nieuport which went into a spinning nose dive. Regaining some of his composure through the pain of his wounds, he put his machine into a controlled dive and headed for the British lines, hoping to escape the further attentions of his attacker. Within thirty seconds such hopes evaporated as a stream of bullets hit his engine and cut his elevator controls. The Nieuport again went into a spinning dive but this time Whitehead could not regain control. Probably at about a height of three or four thousand feet, he fainted – no doubt due to shock and the loss of blood – and did not regain consciousness until a week later. He awoke to find himself in Douai hospital, a prisoner of war and the owner of a fractured skull sustained in the crash after being singled out by Werner Voss for his second victory of the day.

LIEUTENANT
ARTHUR DARLEY WHITEHEAD,
ROYAL WARWICKSHIRE REGIMENT AND 60 SQUADRON, ROYAL FLYING CORPS

The son of Mr and Mrs Arthur Whitehead of 'Maison Faucon', Atalage, Biarritz, France and 11 Lesham Gardens, Belgravia, London SW, Arthur was educated at Harrow (1910-1914) and at the Royal Military College, Sandhurst. From Sandhurst, he was gazetted Second Lieutenant to the Royal Warwickshire Regiment on 12 May 1915. Anxious to emulate his elder brother, Ralph, a Flight Commander in the Royal Naval Air Service, Arthur sought transfer to the RFC and was accepted in June 1916. He was awarded his 'Wings' and following a short period of leave, was sent first to join 13 Squadron in France on 28 September 1916 before, shortly afterwards, being transferred to 60 Squadron.

On 11 December 1916, whilst still a 'green' pilot, he and five other members of the squadron (including Voss's 4th victory to be, Peter Daly) were involved in a farcical incident which, nevertheless, demonstrated the rash keenness of the young Scout pilots. A patrol, led by Captain E O Grenfell MC, with Lieutenants 'Grid' Caldwell, Weedon, 'Duke' Meintjies, Daly and Whitehead, ran across a two-seater Albatros over Dainville on the British side of the lines. All six RFC machines opened fire on the lone enemy who, unsurprisingly, immediately dived down and landed. Exuberantly, Grenfell, anxious to be first down to claim the victory, landed in a field next to that occupied by the Albatros but in so doing, not only crashed his Nieuport but also badly broke his leg in the process. If that was not bad enough, the remaining five members of the Flight had also decided to descend and examine their prize. Three of these five also crashed their machines on landing, although not sufficiently seriously so as to injure themselves. And so the scene that greeted the ground troops as they arrived was that of a German Albatros alone in a large field with, dotted around in each of the surrounding pastures, six 60 Squadron Nieuports, four of which were wrecked! To make matters even worse – if that were possible – the German observer, after pulling his wounded pilot out of the almost intact Albatros, set it alight to prevent it falling into British hands. The farce continued when the machine's petrol tank exploded, wounding not only the German observer who was standing too close to the conflagration but also several Tommies who had just arrived on the scene. It is not too difficult to imagine the reaction of the squadron commander when he learnt that not only had the ground forces failed to secure an intact Albatros but that his pilots had also unnecessarily wrecked four of their own machines!

The injuries Whitehead received at the hands of Werner Voss on 11 March 1917 were severe enough to ensure an early repatriation which occured on 20 January 1918. Whitehead wanted to make the Royal Air Force his career but despite prolonged periods in various hospitals, he was finally discharged on health grounds on 8 November 1919. He next embarked on a course of study at Trinity College, Oxford, but left without taking a degree. Still in poor health, Whitehead lived with his sister, Lillian Mary, at 'Astley House', North Berwick, East Lothian, Scotland. He finally died in a Bournemouth nursing home on 17 October 1933, yet another (albeit delayed) casualty of the Great War.

VICTORY NO 16

17 March 1917 FE2b (No. 7695) 11 Squadron 12.15 hours

Voss was really into his stride by now and scored another two victories on this day – both within a space of ten minutes! The first was a FE2b which had taken off at 08.55 hours British time on a photo-reconnaissance mission over the Hindenburg Line, part of the intelligence gathering effort necessary for the planning of the forthcoming April offensive. R W Cross, the Canadian pilot and his observer, C F Lodge, were both quite experienced airmen, indeed Cross had been an acting Flight Commander for some weeks. After they were intercepted near to Warlencourt by nine enemy scouts, they were chased northwards. Lodge's best efforts with the machine gun were in vain as Voss's fire pierced the fuel tanks and damaged the engine. Lodge was slightly wounded and Cross had no choice but to crash-land near to the village of Mory, north of Bapaume at 12.15 German time – both men being taken prisoner.

SECOND LIEUTENANT
RUSSELL WILFRED CROSS,
11 SQUADRON, ROYAL FLYING CORPS

The only son of William Henry and Clariss Lilian Cross of 275 Wellington Crescent, Winnipeg, Manitoba, Canada, Russell (right) was born in 1894. Amongst the very first to enlist in August 1914, he initially joined the Fort Garry Horse. Because of his knowledge of all things connected with the combusion engine, he was accepted as a Petty Officer

Mechanic with the Royal Naval Air Service, serving first as a motor cycle despatch rider in France and then with a motorised machine-gun unit in Gallipoli. Returning to England, he was gazetted Second Lieutenant to the RFC on 3 June 1916. Following training – mainly at Thetford – he was posted to 18 Squadron as a FE2b pilot on 24 September 1916. After serving for three months with 18 Squadron, he was transferred to 11 Squadron on 28 December 1916 and had become the acting Flight Commander of 'C' Flight by the time he was shot down on 17 March 1917.

Cross was one of those officers who lost patience awaiting the slow process of repatriation after the war was over and took it upon himself to hike to a Channel port, arriving in England and taking up residence at the Waldorf Hotel in London just in time for Christmas 1918. He returned to Canada after the war, although he did remain in the Royal Air Force. Tragically, he was killed whilst flying as a passenger in a LWF American wartime biplane at Portage La Praire, Manitoba, when it crashed in a ploughed field near to the city late in the afternoon of 24 July 1919. Another former RFC flyer, Lieutenant S P Kerr (ex-40 Squadron – WIA 17 May 1918) was acting as pilot and survived the crash. Kerr's wife, another passenger, was also killed. Russell Wilfred Cross is buried in Winnipeg (Elmwood) Cemetery. He was twenty-five years old.

LIEUTENANT CHRISTOPHER FYERS LODGE, 8/WORCESTERSHIRE REGIMENT AND 11 SQUADRON, ROYAL FLYING CORPS

A Devonian born in 1893, Lodge was the son of Mr and Mrs Lodge of 'Aish', South Brent, South Devonshire. He was admitted to the Inns of Court Officer Training Corps (No. H/1962) on 26 October 1914 and following the usual training, was gazetted Second Lieutenant to the Worcestershire Regiment on 13 March 1915. Posted to the 8th Battalion of his regiment, he landed in France with that unit on 11 July 1915. He was wounded within days, suffering the effects of gas when supervising the digging of a new communication trench from La Boisselle to a position in front of Pozières on the night of 19th/20th July 1916. After recovering in England, Lodge successfully sought transfer to the RFC. Following the completion of his training, he was sent to join 11 Squadron on 10 November 1916. Lodge was repatriated on the last day of 1918, finally leaving the service on 5 June 1919.

VICTORY NO 17

17 March 1917 DH2 (No. A2583) 32 Squadron 12.25 hours

No sooner had Voss pulled away from disposing of Cross and Lodge and their FE2b, than he and the rest of Jasta 2 were engaged by a twelve-strong DH2 patrol of 32 Squadron led by Captain W G S Curphey MC (No. A5023). A fierce dogfight ensued which resulted in three of the British machines being shot-up and forced to land. Lieutenants Frank Billinge and A C 'Snowy' Randell were claimed by other members of the Jasta but Voss fastened on to Lieutenant T A Cooch in A2583 and shot him down north-east of Warlencourt, just inside British lines. Cooch was wounded and injured in the crash and his machine was wrecked. The timing, location and circumstances of Cooch's downing coincided with the details of Voss's claim and the German ace's seventeenth victory was confirmed.

LIEUTENANT

THEODORE ALGERNON COOCH,

13/WORCESTERSHIRE REGIMENT AND 32 SQUADRON, ROYAL FLYING CORPS

The son of Mr and Mrs Cooch of 133 Christchurch Road, Boscombe, Hampshire, Theo Cooch was born on 1 February 1891. After leaving school, he became a partner in the family firm, Ewens Motors Ltd of Bournemouth and trained as a motor engineer. Cooch was gazetted Second Lieutenant to the Worcestershire Regiment on 24 June 1915. After more than a year in England, he successfully sought transfer to the RFC on 13 August 1916. Following training at the Central Flying School, he was awarded his 'Wings' and posted to 32 Squadron on 15 December 1916. A spell in hospital followed his brush with Voss, after which Cooch was posted to the Home Establishment, being employed as a delivery pilot, mainly working out of Hendon aerodrome. Unluckily, he was again injured in an aeroplane accident on 18 August 1917. Recovering from this further setback, Cooch reverted to the pilot pool before going on to serve in various of the communication squadrons, being promoted to Captain just as the war ended. Sadly and ironically, Theo Cooch was killed during his last flight on 17 September 1919, the day before his scheduled demobilisation from the RAF. With more than 2,000 flying hours to his credit, Cooch was a Flight Commander stationed at Buc, Paris, with 2nd Communications Squadron, Royal Air Force – the famous London-Paris communication squadron. He and his mechanic were testing a machine over the airfield when a wing broke away; both men were dead by the time ground-support crews reached the wreck. Cooch and his mechanic were buried in the City of Paris Cemetery, Pantin (Fr.457) with full military honours, the firing party being furnished by men from his own Squadron and from the French Air Service. The bodies were carried to the cemetery in an Air Service tender draped with the Union Jack. Amongst his effects was a strangely prophetic poem he had recently composed, entitled,

'An Airman's Aspiration'

Securely strapped within your seat,
And ear attuned to engines' beat,
Your hand around the joystick tight,
You're off! You thrill to sudden flight.

Up! Up! She goes, the azure blue
The dazzling clouds like mountain peak
Attracts and calls and beckons you
Inviting you to hide and seek.

And to your joy you give full reins,
The life-blood coursing through your veins,
As, rushing through the ether waves,
Your soul the illimitable craves.

But every joy is incomplete,
And every love is bitter sweet;

Mother Earth – ah! There's the pain –
Recalls you back to earth again.

And as you hurtle down once more,
The wind is like an angry roar;
The earth and air appear to fight,
As to whose you are by right.

Alas! Our mother is the earth,
For she claims the right by birth;
Though my Body the earth's may be,
My soul is an ethereal legacy.

So the air my spouse shall be,
And when the earth is dead in me,
Once more, I'll feel the rapturous kiss
And clinging arms of airy bliss.

All mortal fetters I shall fling
Into Earth's face, and then I'll sing
A song of unutterable delight
Upon the bosom of eternal flight.

Captain Theodore Cooch was twenty-eight years old.

VICTORY NO 18

18 March 1917 BE2e (No. 5784) 8 Squadron 18.40 hours

For the second consecutive day, Voss achieved a double victory and, astonishingly, again within minutes of each other. The first was a BE2e crewed by Second Lieutenant C R Dougall and Lieutenant S Harryman which had taken off from Sombrin on a lone reconnaissance patrol, carrying bombs in the hope of finding an appropriate target. Over just such a target at Beaurains, south-east of Arras, Dougall pulled the wired bomb release but to no effect, the bombs remaining in their cradles. Perhaps allowing themselves to be overly occupied with this problem, they 'dropped their guard' and were unexpectedly attacked by five German scouts. The observer, Harryman, was fatally wounded and Dougall was hit in the legs. The BE's elevator controls were shot away and the machine also caught fire. To his considerable credit, Dougall managed to nurse the burning, crippled machine down to the ground where the mortally wounded Harryman was dragged from the flames. Unfortunately, the observer was to die five days later in Hamblin hospital. Voss noted the time and location of the victory as 18.40 hours at Neuville-Vitasse, south-east of Beaurains, just inside the German lines.

LIEUTENANT CHARLES ROBERT DOUGALL,
7/ARGYLL AND SUTHERLAND HIGHLANDERS AND 8 SQUADRON, ROYAL FLYING CORPS

The son of Mr and Mrs C S Dougall of Dollar, Scotland, Charles was gazetted as a Second Lieutenant to the 7th Battalion, Argyll and Sutherland Highlanders on 20 September 1915. Following a successful application to transfer to the RFC in 1916, he completed his pilot training in January 1917 and was sent out to join 8 Squadron in France on 17 February 1917. Promotion to Lieutenant followed on 30 March 1917, a little more than two weeks before he was shot down and taken prisoner. He was repatriated on 2 January 1919 and transferred to the unemployed list on 4 August 1919. However, he soon rejoined the RAF and was flying again by April 1921. In the following year, he was allowed to relinquish his temporary commission in the RAF on appointment to the Territorial Force.

SECOND LIEUTENANT SYDNEY HARRYMAN,
13/GLOUCESTERSHIRE REGIMENT AND 8 SQUADRON, ROYAL FLYING CORPS

The son of Sydney and Reta Scrafton Harryman of Jubilee Cottages, High Halston, Kent, Sydney was educated at Bristol University where he became a member of the Officer Training Corps. He was gazetted Second Lieutenant to the Gloucestershire Regiment on 19 October 1915, before transferring to the Royal Flying Corps in 1916. Harryman married and he and his wife set up home at Star Elm House, Rochester, Kent. After the appropriate training, he was sent out to join 8 Squadron in France in January 1917. Initially reported as having been taken prisoner of war, his family did not learn of his death until 29 May 1917. Sydney Harryman is buried in the Cabaret-Rouge Cemetery, France (Fr. 924).

VICTORY NO 19

18 March 1917 BE2d (No. 5770) 13 Squadron 18.50 hours

Voss climbed away from his eighteenth victory, anxious to gain height as a prelude to looking for yet another victim! He had not long to wait. Captain G S Thorne and Lieutenant P E H van Baerle had taken off at 17.25 hours on a reconnaissance to establish whether camp fires were visible at Fampoux and vicinity. They were on their way back, some way south of the recce area, when Voss found them near to Boyelles. In the initial attack, Thorne was hit in the back by what van Baerle later described as an explosive bullet. Despite the shock and pain from his horrendous wound, the pilot managed to land the BE at Henin sur Cojeul before he passed out. If all of this was not enough, van Baerle bitterly recalled upon his return from captivity that they had been fired upon as they sat, defenceless, on the ground! Miraculously still unhurt, van Baerle was taken prisoner but was told by a doctor later that night that his pilot, Thorne, had died as a consequence of his terrible wounds.
(Other references to this victory as being over Captain C Holland/Second Lieutenant A C Heaven are incorrect as that crew were brought down by anti-aircraft fire during the morning of this day).

CAPTAIN

GUY STAFFORD THORNE,

13 SQUADRON, ROYAL FLYING CORPS

The younger son of solicitor Colonel E H Thorne, 3rd Volunteer Battalion, Staffordshire Regiment and Mrs Ethel Thorne of 'The Roseries', Down Road, Bexhill-on-Sea, Sussex and Wolverhampton, Staffordshire, Guy (left) was born on 15 August 1882. He was educated at Reach's Preparatory School and at Wolverhampton Grammar (1893-1899) where he represented the school at cricket, football and tennis. After leaving school he was bound by indenture to Belliss and Morcom Ltd of Birmingham. After completion of his apprenticeship he was employed as an erecting engineer until 1906 when he left Birmingham to take up a new position with the Power and Light Company of Hong Kong. Six months after his arrival in Hong Kong, he was appointed as the Engineer in Chief of the company's power station in Canton. Next he was asked by the Chinese government to take charge of the Kwang Tung Electricity Supply Company and to act as consulting engineer to the Canton-Nowloon Railway and the Government Water Works. Thorne was elected an associate member of The Institution of Mechanical Engineers in 1914. When war broke out, he had some difficulty in getting the Chinese government to accept his resignation and allow him to return home. Eventually, when he was able to return, he was given a commission (Special Reserve) in the RFC in January 1916. Learning to fly at his own expense, he was awarded the Aviators Certificate (No. 2692) of the Royal Aero Club on 1 April 1916. He then underwent further training at the Curragh in Ireland and at Northolt before gaining his 'Wings'. He proceeded to France on 25 May 1916 and was assigned to 13 Squadron, then at Savy. During the Battle of the Somme he did some valuable work including bombing raids on Bapaume and Marcoing. He was appointed Flight Commander and promoted to acting Captain in October 1916. On 6 November, he carried out a very effective bombing raid on the railway station sidings at Douai. During a brief period of home leave, he married Mary Gwendoline Charlotte Hillman in Invergordon, Scotland, on 27 November 1916. On the day of his death, he was in temporary command of his squadron and because of the importance of the reconnaissance had decided not to delegate the job to others but to go himself. His grave was lost in the subsequent fighting in the area and so he is commemorated on the Arras Memorial to the Missing, France. He was in his thirty-fifth year.

SECOND LIEUTENANT
PHILIP EDWARD HISLOP VAN BAERLE,
1/7TH WEST YORKSHIRE REGIMENT (LEEDS RIFLES) AND 13 SQUADRON, ROYAL FLYING CORPS

Philip was the son of Mr and Mrs van Baerle of 48a Clifton Gardens, London W9. Initially gazetted to the 1/7th West Yorkshires, he very soon afterwards successfully sought transfer to the Royal Flying Corps. After training, he was sent to join 13 Squadron as a probationary observer on 1 December 1916. Following a brief period of operational flying he was given two weeks leave before arriving back at the Squadron on 17 March 1917, the day before he was shot down. Van Baerle spent most of his captivity at Karlsruhe before finally being repatriated on 17 December 1918. His peace-time postings included a spell with 62 Wing at Seaton Carew followed by a brief period at RAF Killingholme.

VICTORY NO 20
19 March 1917 RE8 (No. A4165) 59 Squadron 09.30 hours

After his two victories of the previous day (numbers 18 and 19) the next, hoped for, victory – the 20th – suddenly assumed a disproportionate importance. For twenty victories was the current 'yardstick', or quantitative criteria for the award of the ultimate accolade, the Order Pour le Mérite – otherwise known as the 'Blue Max'!

59 Squadron had put up two of their RE8s on a morning patrol in the vicinity of St Leger. One of the machines (A4165) – crewed by Captain E W Bowyer-Bower and Second Lieutenant E Elgey – was delegated the reconnaissance work, whilst the other (A4168) – manned by Captain C P Bartie and Lieutenant F H Wilson – was to act as escort. More often than not at this stage of the war, direct escorts for Corps aircraft were not provided. The stategy was that scout squadrons were put up in the general areas

where the Corps machines were working so that they would be on hand and available if the enemy attempted to interrupt their work. A 'hit and miss' system that was far from effective and totally unsatisfactory from the point of view of the poor devils doing the Corps work. This was the reason why, on this occasion, 59 Squadron with their brand new RE8s, had designated one of their own to watch over the vulnerable recce machine. The problem with this tactic, however, was that a RE8 was still only a RE8, even if its crew was not distracted by onerous reconnaissance duties! The vulnerability of the 'Harry Tates' had yet to be fully brought home to 59 Squadron; which it most certainly was when, in the following month, they were to lose a whole formation of machines in a matter of moments.

Werner Voss, in company with another Jasta 2 pilot Otto Bernert, dropped on the two RE8s in the skies above St Leger and both were sent down in quick time. Bernert shot down the escort RE8 – his eighth victory – while Voss disposed of the reconnaissance machine. Three of the four RFC men concerned were killed.

CAPTAIN

ELRED WOLFERSTAN BOWYER-BOWER,

3/EAST SURREY REGIMENT AND 59 SQUADRON, ROYAL FLYING CORPS

The only son of Captain Thomas Bowyer-Bower and his wife Florence Margaret, of 30 Bramham Gardens, South Kensington, London SW, Elred was born on 8 June 1894. He was educated at Haileybury (1908-1909) and, hoping to make the Army his career, accepted a Reserve commission in 1914, being gazetted to 3rd (Reserve) Battalion of the East Surrey Regiment. On 30 April 1915, he arrived in France as part of a group of replacements sent to reinforce the badly depleted 1st Battalion of his regiment, the remnants of which were just emerging from the rigours of the capture and ensuing defence of Hill 60. Following a period in the trenches, he successfully applied for a transfer to the RFC, passing the tests for the award of the Aviators Certificate (No. 3814) of the Royal Aero Club on 14 November 1916. After formal pilot training, he was appointed a flying officer and sent to join 59 Squadron in France.

Bowyer-Bower's RE8 fell some six miles behind the German lines near to Croisilles. Some weeks later, as the Germans fell back onto the Hindenburg Line, a party of Royal

Captain E W Bowyer-Bower, East Surrey Regiment and 59 Squadron, RFC (on left) with his father, Captain T Bowyer-Bower, Royal Engineers (who later found his son's remains on the battlefield).

Engineers was in the vanguard of the British advance over the relinquished ground. By a quite amazing coincidence, the RE detachment was under the command of Captain Thomas Bowyer-Bower, Elred's father. Bowyer-Bower Senior had, of course, already learnt of his son's death and was even roughly aware of the vicinity of the crash site. One day, his men came across a grave marked by a cross made from pieces of a wrecked aeroplane. Someone had carefully marked the cross in pencil, "Two unknown captains (*sic*) of the Flying Corps". It is impossible to imagine his emotions as Thomas Bowyer-Bower cooly sought the appropriate permission to exhume the bodies. When the grave was opened, the father was able to identify the son.........

Captain Elred Wolferstan Bowyer-Bower is buried alongside his observer in Mory Abbey Military Cemetery, France (Fr.614). He was twenty-two years old.

SECOND LIEUTENANT
ERIC ELGEY,
3/WEST RIDING BRIGADE, ROYAL FIELD ARTILLERY (TF) AND 59 SQUADRON, ROYAL FLYING CORPS

The son of Alfred Hargreaves Elgey and Jessie Farrell Elgey of 'Kirland', The Grove, Shipley, Yorkshire, Eric was born on 18 December 1891. He was educated at the University of London (where he was member of the OTC) and at Oriel College, Oxford. Prevailed upon by his family to first finish his Bachelor of Arts degree at Oxford before volunteering, he was gazetted Second Lieutenant to the local 3/West Riding Brigade (Territorial Force) of the Royal Field Artillery on 2 December 1915. An application to join the RFC was sanctioned and after successfully completing his observer training, he was sent as a probationary to 59 Squadron on 29 January 1917. Eric Elgey is buried next to his pilot in Mory Abbey Military Cemetery, France (Fr. 614). He was twenty-five years old.

VICTORY NO 21
24 March 1917 FE2b (No. A5485) 23 Squadron 16.10 hours

Voss continued his deadly work with yet another 'double' in a late afternoon sortie on this day. The first to be engaged was a FE2b flown by Sergeant E P Critchley with 1AM F Russell in the observer's cockpit. The 23 Squadron machine was on a photographic reconnaissance which had begun at 13.13 hours (British time). Voss's attack killed the observer outright and wounded the pilot, Critchley. Despite his wounds, Critchley managed to force land on farmland near to Achiet-le-Grand. Voss claimed his victim came down south-east of St Leger, on the British side of the lines. (Some records indicate that his victim on this occasion was an 11 Squadron machine but the 11 Squadron losses on this day all occured in the morning. Furthermore, Achiet-le-Grand IS south-east of St Leger!).

SERGEANT
EDWARD PRESTON CRITCHLEY,
23 SQUADRON, ROYAL FLYING CORPS

Born on 23 May 1893 in the United States of America, Edward was the younger son of Mr and Mrs A W Critchley of 40 Wattville Road, Handsworth, Birmingham. He pressed his case to become a RFC pilot by learning to fly at his own expense, being awarded the Aviators Certificate (No. 3837) of the Royal Aero Club on 27 November 1916. Formal training followed and he was given his 'Wings' and promoted to Flight Sergeant on 30 December 1916, before being sent out to join 23 Squadron in France. While Critchley was recovering at home from the wounds inflicted by Werner Voss, he was able to attend his brother Godfrey's wedding in Handsworth on 24 May 1917. Godfrey Critchley had recently been discharged from the Army as a result of disabling wounds he had received in France. Recovering from the wounds inflicted by Voss, Edward Critchley returned to duty and was commissioned, being gazetted Second Lieutenant on 21 November 1917. He undertook a number of instructing roles in various of the training squadrons in the UK before going out again to join in the last advance with 55 Squadron. Critchley had the misfortune to be wounded again on 13 August 1918 and was, consequently, invalided to England where he remained until his eventual release from the service on 12 February 1919.

AIR MECHANIC FIRST CLASS
FRANK RUSSELL
(NO.12708), 23 SQUADRON, ROYAL FLYING CORPS

The son of James Thomas and Mrs Russell of Arnold Street, Rochdale, Lancashire, Frank was born in 1896. Educated locally, Frank became a tinsmith in a local factory after leaving school. He enlisted in 1915 at the age of eighteen, undergoing his preliminary training at Farnborough before going on to Hendon. Before going out to France at the beginning of March 1917, he had enjoyed a short leave at home, taking the opportunity to visit friends at the Baillie Street United Methodist Church, where he had been a regular worshipper. Killed in the air by Werner Voss, Frank Russell was buried with full military honours in Achiet-le-Grand Cemetery Extension, France (Fr.518). He was twenty years old.

VICTORY NO 22

24 March 1917 BE2d (No. 5769) 8 Squadron 16.45 hours

Just over twenty minutes had elapsed since Voss's 21st victory, when he and Bernert were in action again. Bernert claimed a BE2e – probably a 15 Squadron machine – shot down at 16.30 into the British lines to the north-east of Vaulx. In the meantime, Voss was stalking an 8 Squadron BE2d that had taken off at 14.15 hours (British time) to fly a photographic patrol over positions near to Boyelles. The British machine was actually over Boyelles and probably at work taking photographs when Voss struck. Both crew members, Lieutenant H Norton and Second Lieutenant R A W Tillett, were killed, their machine going straight down to an area south-east of Mercatel, close to Boyelles.

LIEUTENANT
HUGH NORTON,
9/KING'S OWN ROYAL LANCASTER REGIMENT AND 8 SQUADRON, ROYAL FLYING CORPS

The son of David Norton CSI and Mrs Katherine Maud Norton of 'Engedi', St Leonards Road, Eastbourne, Hugh was born in 1892. He was educated at The Grange, Eastbourne, at Wellington College (1907-10) and at King's College, London. Norton studied Chinese at King's and, after passing his examinations, secured a position with Messrs Dodwell and Company Ltd and was about to travel to the Far East offices of that company when war broke out. A marksman of some note, Norton joined the Inns of Court OTC (No. A/1173) on 14 September 1914 and after a relatively brief period of training, was gazetted Second Lieutenant to the 9th Battalion of the King's Own on 14 November 1914. Conveniently for Hugh, his battalion was quartered in the town of Eastbourne for a time and he was thus able to enjoy some home comforts before he accompanied his unit to France in September 1915. After a period serving as a signalling officer in France, he and his battalion were sent to Salonika, arriving in the Greek port on 7 November 1915. Following another brief period in the Balkans, Norton was sent to Egypt and it was there that he first became attached to the RFC. He 'clocked' up forty solo hours in the Middle East and in England before he was sent out to France just three weeks before he was killed. Two days elapsed before Norton's body was found by British troops and his parents were subsequently advised that, 'his death had been instantaneous and had taken place before his machine fell to earth'. Hugh Norton was buried with full military honours in Warlincourt Halte British Cemetery, Saulty, France (Fr. 120). He was 24.

SECOND LIEUTENANT
REGINALD ALFRED WILLIAM TILLETT,
ROYAL GLOUCESTERSHIRE HUSSARS YEOMANRY AND 8 SQUADRON, ROYAL FLYING CORPS

Born on 27 March 1894, Reginald Tillett was the son of author Arthur William Tillett and Mrs Tillett of Witton, Norfolk. After completing his education, he was appointed as a junior member of the directorate of the 'Norfolk News' Company Limited. An excellent shot and a keen and able rider, he enlisted early in the war as a private soldier in the Norfolk Yeomanry with whom he rose rapidly in non-commissioned rank. From the Norfolk Yeomanry, he joined the Inns of Court OTC (No. 6/SQ/6867) on 18 October 1915 and after three months of training was gazetted Second Lieutenant to the Royal Gloucestershire Hussars Yeomanry on 17 January 1916. Delays in obtaining a posting to his regiment in the Middle East, caused him to look elsewhere and he was eventually successful in obtaining a transfer to the RFC. Although he had trained and qualified as a pilot, the Corps was acutely short of observers in early 1917 and Tillet was sent to the front in that capacity at the end of February 1917. Only three weeks earlier, on 1 February 1917, Reginald had married Olive Mary Boston of Norwich. Reginald Tillett is buried next to his pilot, Lieutenant Norton, in Warlincourt Halte British Cemetery, Saulty, France (Fr. 120). He died just three days short of his twenty-third birthday.

NB. British and German time coincide from 25 March 1917.

Voss was awarded the Knight's Cross of the Hohenzollern House Order with Swords on 27 March 1917.

VICTORY NO 23

1 April 1917 BE2e (No. 2561) 15 Squadron 11.45 hours

At 09.30 hours on the first day of what was to become known as 'Bloody April' as a consequence of the terrible casualties inflicted on the Royal Flying Corps by the Imperial German Air Service, a 15 Squadron BE2e flown by Captain A M Wynne and Lieutenant A S Mackenzie took off on an Artillery observation patrol. Voss emerged from a low cloud and surprised the RFC machine between Ecoust and St Leger. The German's first burst wounded the pilot, Wynne, in the leg. The observer, Mackenzie, swung his machine gun and fired back in desperate retaliation. Voss came in again and this time his bullets struck the observer in the heart, killing him instantly. Despite his wounds, the pilot Wynne managed to get the falling BE across to the British side of the lines and as it hit the ground he was thrown out of the cockpit, an added mishap that subsequently proved rather fortuitous. As Wynne crawled away, an exuberant Voss came in low and, not for the first time, straffed a helpless, defeated, grounded machine. Shortly afterwards, German artillery pounded the wreck into useless junk.

CAPTAIN ARTHUR MEREDITH WYNNE, AFC, 15 SQUADRON, ROYAL FLYING CORPS

Born on 15 July 1892, Arthur was the son of Major General Sir Arthur Singleton Wynne, GCB and Lady Emily Mary Wynne of 40a Hyde Park Gate, London SW and 'Roe End', Warcop, Westmoreland. After a distinguished military career, Arthur's father, General Wynne was charged with the safekeeping of the Crown Jewels and appointed Keeper of the Jewel House in the Tower of London (1911-1917). Arthur was educated privately and at Wellington

College. He developed an early interest in aeronautics, qualifying as a (civilian) pilot on a Graham White machine at Hendon on 15 October 1912 and at the same time gaining the Aviators Certificate (No. 314) of the Royal Aero Club. Naturally enough, he volunteered immediately the war broke out, having already held a Special Reserve commission in the RFC since 4 May 1914. Wynne joined 9 Squadron in England for a brief period before being appointed Flight Commander of a Kite Balloon Section on 27 September 1915. He returned to squadron duties on 21 February 1916 when he joined 15 Squadron in France. After recovering from the wounds he received on 1 April 1917, he was given duties as an instructor with various training units. His contribution to the war effort was recognised by the award of the Air Force Cross, announced in the *London Gazette* of 1 November 1918 (Page Number 12958). Arthur Wynne, aviation pioneer and active service pilot, came through the whole of the Great War and ceased to be employed on 24 January 1919. However, he was to serve again – next time with the RAFVR during the Second World War.

LIEUTENANT
ADRIAN SOMERSET MACKENZIE,
10/HIGHLAND LIGHT INFANTRY AND 15 SQUADRON, ROYAL FLYING CORPS

Adrian was the son of Mr and Mrs Mackenzie of 34 Yald Court, West Hampstead, Middlesex. He was gazetted to the 10th Battalion of the Highland Light Infantry on 16 December 1914 and landed in France for the first time with that unit in May 1915. Following a period in the trenches, he applied for transfer to the RFC and after successfully completing his training, was sent out again to France – this time to join 15 Squadron as a probationary observer. Adrian Mackenzie is buried in Varennes Military Cemetery, France (Fr. 41).

VICTORY NO 24

6 April 1917 BE2e (No. A3157) 15 Squadron 09.30 hours

Second Lieutenants A H Vinson and E C L Gwilt were busy taking photographs over Bullecourt when they were interrupted by six Jasta 2 fighters intent on crowding them out of the sky. The observer, Gwilt, with no lack of available targets, opened fire. Almost contemptuously, five of the six enemy fighters broke away to one side allowing the sixth – Voss – to administer the *coup de grâce*. Vinson put the BE into a near vertical dive – so sudden and steep a dive in fact that it caused both Lewis guns to be lost overboard! Three bullets grazed Vinson's face and two others tore through one of Gwilt's gloves. Vinson hauled back on the controls and, pulling out of the dive, headed pell-mell for the British lines. Voss kept up the pursuit while Gwilt, *sans* machine-guns and helpless, prayed for their lives and urged his pilot onward for what seemed an eternity. Despite the petrol tank being holed, Vinson scraped in over the trenches, putting the battered machine down near to Lagnicourt. Again Voss followed his victim down and the two RFC men barely had time to evacuate the BE and dive into the nearest shell-hole before the Albatros began strafing. Counter fire from the ground persuaded the German that discretion might be the better part of valour and he peeled away. Almost immediately, German artillery opened up on the grounded BE2e. At some considerable personal risk, Vinson ran to the machine and retrieved the camera and plates before the two-seater was destroyed by the 8 inch shells raining down on it. The hard come by photographs of the Hindenburg Line and the area around Bullecourt were, one hopes, greatly appreciated by the Staff officers at Corps HQ!

SECOND LIEUTENANT

ALBERT HIGGS VINSON,

MID, 15 SQUADRON, ROYAL FLYING CORPS

The son of agricultural merchant John Albert Vinson JP and Mrs A M Vinson of Sheepcote Farm, St Mary Cray, Kent, Albert was born on 8 January 1897. He was educated at Mill Hill School, North London (1911-15) where he was a member of the OTC. As soon as he was old enough he volunteered for service with the RFC and was given a commission in the Special Reserve on 18 March 1916. Next he learnt to fly and was awarded the Aviators Certificate (No. 3001) of the Royal Aero Club on 21 May 1916, before going on to formal pilot training and the subsequent award of his 'Wings'. Vinson served with distinction in France (Mentioned in Despatches) and was lucky to escape with his life on at least one other occasion apart from the confrontation with Voss. On 16 September 1916, he was attacked by three enemy scouts and his observer, Captain A Brooke-Murray, died from the wounds he sustained in the affair. After a long stint at the front, Vinson returned to England where he took up duties as a flying instructor with the rank of Captain. In January 1918 he married Miss Williams, the couple setting up home at Parsonage Farm, Belvedere, Kent. Some weeks later, on 22 March 1918, he was accidently killed when a pupil he was teaching to fly fell across the controls of their machine, causing it to crash near to Yatesbury, Calne, Wiltshire. Albert Higgs Vinson is buried in Erith (Brook Street) Cemetery, Kent. He was twenty-one years old.

SECOND LIEUTENANT

EVERARD LESLIE CHAMPION GWILT,

NO. 4 COMPANY, FORTH BRIGADE, ROYAL GARRISON ARTILLERY (TF) AND 15 SQUADRON, ROYAL FLYING CORPS

Gwilt was gazetted Second Lieutenant to the Forth (Scotland) Brigade of the Royal Garrison Artillery (Territorial Force) on 22 November 1915. His application to transfer to the Royal Flying Corps was approved and after successfully completing observer training, he was sent out to join 15 Squadron in France. Gwilt was brought home from France and was appointed to a series of instructional posts before relinquishing his commission because of ill health on 2 April 1919. He qualified for the issue of a Silver War Badge on 5 April 1919.

The subject of the unconfirmed Werner Voss 'victory' – R M Foster (left) and pictured above as an Air Vice-Marshal in Italy in 1945 (later Air Chief Marshal Sir Robert Mordaunt Foster KCB CBE DFC MID).

Shortly after his twenty-fourth victory, Voss engaged a Sopwith Pup flown by a future ace, Second Lieutenant R M Foster of 54 Squadron. After the briefest of skirmishes, Foster was obliged to force land – like Vinson immediately before him – in the vicinity of Lagnicourt. Surprisingly, on this singularly rare occasion, Voss was unable to obtain credit for a confirmed victory.

There was, however, massive and immediate consolation in that he was at last awarded the coveted Blue Max on 8 April. This he added to the Iron Cross 1st Class and the Knight's Cross with Swords of the Royal Hohenzollern House Order that he had received on 27 March 1917. As was usual following the award of Imperial Germany's highest accolade, the recipient was allowed home leave and, in Voss's case, the timing was perfect as it allowed him to celebrate his 20th birthday with his family on 13 April 1917. His absence in Germany meant that he was to miss most of 'Bloody April' and the period of almost total dominance over the Allies enjoyed by the German Air Service. Even without him, Jasta 2 still managed to claim 21 further victories in the remainder of April. At the same time, Jasta 5 downed 32 and Jasta 11 a phenomenal 89.

In Voss's absence, the war on the ground also intensified. The long-prepared-for Arras offensive launched by the Allies in miserable weather on 9 April 1917, enjoyed an immediate success with the capture of Vimy Ridge – thanks largely to a brilliant Canadian assault. But while the land battles encompassing the fighting at Vimy, the Scarpe and Arleux went comparatively well for the Allies, the absolute opposite was the case with the war in the air above the sanguinary fields of France. The new German Jastas, with their state-of-the-art Albatros scout planes, were unleashed upon opponents still mainly using dated and technologically inferior equipment. The outcome was predictable – only the magnitude of the disaster was surprising. How many more scoring victories would Werner Voss have gained had he still been at the front during this period, rather than at home in Germany collecting his Pour le Mérite from the hands of the Kaiser? During the so-called 'Bloody April', Manfred von Richthofen scored 22; Kurt Wolff 23; Karl Schäfer 21 and Lothar von Richthofen 15. The Royal Flying Corps and the French Air Force lost an average of ten crews and machines a day during the thirty days of April 1917. When Voss did return to the front at the beginning of May, he lost no time in picking up where he left off, scoring four more victories before unexpectedly being posted to another Jasta.

VICTORY NO 25

7 May 1917 SE5 (No. A4867) 56 Squadron 19.25 hours

Although Voss returned on 5 May 1917, it was two days later before he gained his quarter century of victories. Number 25 was a SE5 from 56 Squadron, part of an OP led by Captain Albert Ball DSO MC, which had taken off into storm clouds and poor visibility at 17.30 in the late afternoon. The British crossed the lines south of the Cambrai-Bapaume road with Ball's 'A' Flight keeping just below the clouds while 'B' and 'C' Flights spread out above. Captain C M Crowe's 'B' Flight flew over Bourlon Wood and ran into even thicker cloud as they did so. One of their number, Second Lieutenant Chaworth-Musters in A4867, spotted an enemy machine in a chink in the cloud below him and, breaking away from his companions, immediately dived after the quarry. The identity of the occupant of the machine that Chaworth-Musters pursued remains unknown, but what is known is that the RFC man was shot down by Werner Voss at 19.25 hours (German time). His machine fell at Etaing, some way north-west of where he was last seen. 56 Squadron's evening patrol was also marked by the demise of the British ace Albert Ball, who died in an aerial combat with the Red Baron's brother, Lothar von Richthofen – or so it was claimed by the German Air Service.

SECOND LIEUTENANT

ROGER MICHAEL CHAWORTH-MUSTERS,

LEICESTERSHIRE REGIMENT AND 56 SQUADRON, ROYAL FLYING CORPS

The son of George and Mabel Violet Chaworth-Musters of Field Dalling, Holt, Norfolk, Roger was born on 23 March 1898. He was educated privately and at Haileybury (1912-1915). Still not yet eighteen, he was gazetted Second Lieutenant to the Leicestershire Regiment on 27 January 1916. Because of his age, he was not allowed to go to the front and becoming bored, applied for transfer to the Royal Flying Corps. After acceptance and the usual training, he was awarded his 'Wings' and, with just 39 flying hours under his belt, was sent to join 56 Squadron on 4 March 1917 – still less than three weeks short of his nineteenth birthday – and flew with them to France the following month, the first SE5 unit to go over. His remains never recovered, Roger Michael Chaworth-Musters is commemorated on the Arras Memorial to the Missing, France. He was still only nineteen years old.

VICTORY NO 26

9 May 1917 BE2e (No.7209) 52 Squadron 14.00 hours

Voss gained a hat-trick of victories in one afternoon. The first of the day was over a BE2e of 52 Squadron which had taken off at 10.55 (British time) on an Artillery Observation sortie. The BE was charged with a heavy and demanding schedule and had been in the air for more than two hours when Voss caught up with the machine and its two-man crew, sending them down north of Metz. Voss, however, stated that the British machine fell at Havrincourt, inside British lines. The location disparity is probably explained by the fact the BE was smashed into pieces in the air with wreckage falling over a wide area. Pilot and observer were, of course, both killed in the air.

LIEUTENANT

ROWLAND HUMPHREY COLES,

WEST SOMERSET YEOMANRY AND 52 SQUADRON, ROYAL FLYING CORPS

Born in Alexandria, Egypt on 15 August 1893, Humphrey Coles was the youngest of the three sons of Coles Pasha, CMG, (Charles Edward Coles) and Mrs Coles of 'Stone House', Bishop Hull, Taunton, Somerset. He was educated at Cheam, at Wellington (1907-1911) and at the Agricultural College, Cirencester, where he gained his Diploma. A good athlete, he won many long distance foot races and was a consumate and fearless rider across country. Before the war, he was appointed to be Master of the Cirencester Beagles. Coles served with the West Somerset Yeomanry in Gallipoli and in Egypt and, as the Regimental Scout Officer, had a reputation for utter fearlessness. His older brother, Second Lieutenant Crewe Coles, East Lancashire Regiment, was killed in action at Krithia in Gallipoli on 4 June 1915. Humphrey's application to join the RFC was approved in the early summer of 1916 and he returned to England from Egypt to take his ticket, being awarded the Aviators Certificate (No. 3319) of the Royal Aero Club on 18 July 1916. Formal pilot training and the award of his 'Wings' were followed by a posting to 52 Squadron in France. His Squadron Commander in writing to his parents after his death, wrote: *'He was one of the best, if not the best officer in the squadron, and I had twice recommended him for promotion to Flight Commander'*. Rowland Humphrey Coles is buried in Gouzeaucourt New British Cemetery, France (Fr.415). He was twenty-three years old.

SECOND LIEUTENANT

JOHN CHARLES SIGISMUND DAY,

3/ROYAL SUSSEX REGIMENT AND 52 SQUADRON, ROYAL FLYING CORPS

The eldest son of Edward Francis Day and Adela Mary Day of 'Inglesbatch', Henry Street, Grahamstown, South Africa, John was born in Harlesden, Middlesex, on 17 January 1890. Soon after his birth, the family moved to his mother's home in her native South Africa and he went on to be educated at St Aidan's College, Grahamstown, where he became a member of the OTC while studying for a law degree. When the war came, he enlisted in the Special Motor Car Contingent and took part in the German West African campaign. He returned to England in June 1915 and, on 29 November following, was given a commission in the 3rd (Reserve) Battalion of the Royal Sussex Regiment. Interestingly, he appears to have dropped the use of his forename, 'Sigismund' – probably because of its Germanic connotations. He was not alone in this, of course, even the House of Saxe-Coburg-Hohenzollern became the House of Windsor in 1917! Day served at the front with his regiment from January 1916 and was present at many engagements, twice suffering minor wounds. Transferring to the RFC in November 1916, he trained as an observer and was sent to France for the last time shortly before his death. John Charles Sigismund Day is buried close to his pilot in Gouzeaucourt New British Cemetery, France (Fr.415). He was 27.

VICTORY NO 27

9 May 1917 Sopwith Pup (No. A6174) 54 Squadron 16.50 hours

Following his successful encounter with the 52 Squadron art/obs BE2e, Voss returned to his home field to re-arm and re-fuel. Two hours later he was airborne again and looking for trouble. In the meantime, 22 Squadron had sent out a number of FEs on a photo patrol intended to gather intelligence for the 4th Army Staff. On this occasion, the FEs enjoyed the luxury of an escort of Sopwith Pups from 54 Squadron. Undaunted by the deterrent posed by the escorting Scouts, elements of Jasta 2 engaged the British formation with Voss picking out one of the Pups (No. A6174) flown by Lieutenant G C T Hadrill. Voss's fire hit the Sopwith, causing it to spin downwards – the German ace hanging tightly to its tail as it fell. At the last possible moment, observers in the front lines saw the Pup flatten out and land safely. After the war when Hadrill returned from captivity, he said that they had been attacked by no less than eleven enemy aircraft and, after a fight lasting five minutes, his petrol tank had been shot through and his engine hit. With his engine stopped, and wounded as he was, he had no option but to land – and as quickly as possible. Partly because of his wounds and also because of the early arrival of German troops on the scene, he was unable to burn his machine before it and he was taken into captivity.

LIEUTENANT
GEORGE COPLAND TEMPLE HADRILL,
ARMY SERVICE CORPS AND 54 SQUADRON, ROYAL FLYING CORPS

The son of Mr and Mrs Hadrill of 'Hursley', Sevenoaks, Kent, George was born in 1896. He was working with the Board of Trade in Montreal, Canada, when the war broke out and, returning to England, was commissioned into the Army Service Corps on 4 August 1915. From April 1916, he served for a brief period with the Expeditionary Force in France before successfully applying for transfer to the RFC. Following training at Netheravon and at the School of Gunnery at Hythe, Hadrill was awarded his 'Wings' and sent to join 25 Squadron on 12 September 1916. He served as part of the Home Establishment and continued with his training until finally being sent out to France and 54 Squadron on 8 April 1917, only to be taken prisoner a month and a day later. Hadrill was confined at Karlsruhe for most of the period of his captivity but finally sailed for England on 30 December 1918, arriving in Hull during the early hours of the first day of the new year of 1919. Hadrill served again as a member of the RAFVR in the Second World War.

VICTORY NO 28
9 May 1917 FE2b (No. 4991) 22 Squadron 16.45 hours

Having disposed of Hadrill and his 'Pup', Voss and six of his Jasta charged into the vulnerable FEs like wolves after sheep. The FEs were forced down to 2,000 feet and, seizing their opportunity, Voss and two others of his Jasta singled out the sub-leader who was bringing up the rear of the formation. The trailing FE, crewed by Second Lieutenants C A M Furlonger and C W Lane, was raked by the German machine guns and, like Hadrill before them, were compelled to land, again under control, in a field south-west of Hesdin. Furlonger later said that his machine had been hit by anti-aircraft fire from the ground and the resultant damage not only slowed them down but also precluded them from gaining height. When they were hit again by Voss and company the engine stopped completely and the pilot had no choice but to bring the machine down. Lane afterwards recalled that before they themselves were shot down, they had tried to protect what must have been Hadrill's Pup as it went down pursued by enemy fighters. This act of unselfishness was another reason why they had fallen behind the main body of the British formation. Another participant in the fight, Lieutenant E J Y Grevelink (A7306), had seen the enemy fighters approach from the rear and below. He dived onto a white two-seater but his gun jammed and he had to spin away. After correcting the stoppage he climbed up again and as he did so saw a Pup spinning very slowly with a white fighter on its tail and yet another Pup diving after the chasing German. Grevelink then spotted a further black and white painted scout heading for the latter Pup firing as it approached. Jasta 2 of course, did carry black and white markings on their aircraft.

Oddly, Furlonger and Lane contradicted each other in their independently prepared post-war 'de-briefing' reports. While Furlonger stated that they had not had time to burn their machine after landing, Lane insisted that they had done so. It was not unknown for returning airmen to 'bend the truth' a little in their anxiety to show that they had done their duty to the end. In one classic example a Camel pilot later reported that he

What was left of the 22 Squadron FE2d (Furlonger/Lane) shot down by Voss on 9 May 1917 at Bel Aise Farm, Le Bosquet on the Somme. It seems that Lane's memory was better than Furlonger's – the machine is completely burnt out!

had burnt his plane to a cinder, obviously forgetting that he had posed for photographs in front of his still intact machine with the German pilot who had shot him down!

SECOND LIEUTENANT CHARLES ARTHUR MACKENZIE FURLONGER

MID (1944) 22 SQUADRON, ROYAL FLYING CORPS

Born on 25 July 1897, Charles was the son of Commander Arthur Furlonger RN and Mrs Furlonger of 'Katoomba', Walton, Clevedon. He was educated at Hazelwood, Western-super-Mare, at Cheltenham College (1910-1913) and at Trinity College, Dublin, where he was a member of the OTC. Furlonger entered Trinity in June 1914 at the age of seventeen, but left to join up in July 1916 without completing his time there. Accepted into the Royal Military Academy in 1916, he soon afterwards decided upon a change of direction and applied for transfer to the RFC. Gazetted to the Special Reserve on 8 July 1916, he had completed his pilot training and been awarded his 'Wings' by the time he was sent to join 22 Squadron in France on 22 November 1916. Incarcerated in Karlsruhe from 2 June 1917, he had to wait until 3 January 1919 before he was finally repatriated. Furlonger left the Royal Air Force on 14 October 1919, eventually going on to secure a position as an accountant with the Alliance Bank of Simla, India (1920-1923). In 1923 he secured a similiar post in the Madras, India, offices of the Standard Oil Company of New York (later the Standard Vacuum Oil Company, India). In 1939 he returned to Britain to serve, once again, in the Royal Air Force attaining the rank of Squadron Leader and receiving a Mention in Despatches for distinguished service. Following his demobilisation in 1946, Charles Furlonger returned to India to take up his post with Esso.

SECOND LIEUTENANT CHARLES WILLIAM LANE,

ROYAL FUSILIERS AND 22 SQUADRON, ROYAL FLYING CORPS

Charles was the son of Mr and Mrs Lane of 17 Weybridge Road, Thornton Heath, Surrey. He was gazetted to the Royal Fusiliers on 8 January 1916, before becoming attached to the 12th Battalion of the King's Royal Rifle Corps. Next, he successfully applied for transfer to the RFC, completed his observer training and was sent to join 22 Squadron at the front on 8 May 1917 – just one day before he was shot down and made prisoner of war.

He was repatriated on 2 January 1919 and left the service exactly three months later.

In acknowledgement of his undoubted prowess, Voss was given command of Jasta 5 with effect from 20 May 1917. His new Jasta was based at Cappy-sur-Somme on the German 2 Armee front – the very base from where, in less than a year's time, Manfred von Richthofen would take off for the last time. Jasta 5, along with Jasta 46 (commanded by Oberleutnant Richard Flashar) operated as elements of Jagdgruppe 2. Voss's new command was already one of the most successful Jastas – its pilots having already amassed something like ninety victories.

VICTORY NO 29

23 May 1917 FE2b (No. A 5502) 18 Squadron 14.25 hours

Voss's first victory as a commanding officer was against yet another FE2b photo aircraft, this time an 18 Squadron machine that was working over the V Army front. Having taken off at 11.45 hours, they had the misfortune to run into Voss above Havrincourt, the German ace sending them down into the front line trenches, killing both men. Voss timed his claim at 14.25 hours (German time).

SECOND LIEUTENANT
WILFRED FERGUSON MACDONALD,
18 SQUADRON, ROYAL FLYING CORPS

Born in Ottawa, Ontario, in 1894, Wilfred was the son of Donald N and Jennie Ferguson of Mistatim, Saskatchewan, Canada. Awarded the Aviators Certificate (No.AM 437) of the Royal Aero Club on 18 March 1916, he went on to complete formal pilot training and was eventually sent out to join 18 Squadron in France. Wilfred Ferguson Macdonald is buried in Red Cross Corner Cemetery, Beugny, France (Fr. 381). He was twenty-two years old.

LIEUTENANT
FRANK CHARLES SHACKELL,
ARMY CYCLIST CORPS AND 18 SQUADRON, ROYAL FLYING CORPS

A Londoner and a keen pre-war Territorial, Shackell went through the ranks of the 2/25th (County of London) Cyclist Battalion, The London Regiment, from Private (No. 582) to Colour Sergeant to Company Quarter Master Sergeant ('F' Company). He was gazetted to the London Regiment on 14 March 1916, before transferring to the Royal Flying Corps on 15 March 1917. The final phase of his observer training at the 1/School of Gunnery was successfully completed on 11 April 1917 whereupon he was immediately sent to France and 18 Squadron, arriving the following day. Frank Charles Shackell is buried alongside his pilot in Red Cross Corner Cemetery, France (Fr. 381).

VICTORY NO 30

26 May 1917 Sopwith Pup (No. A6168) 54 Squadron 15.45 hours

Voss increased his toll to thirty by bringing down a Sopwith Pup on an afternoon patrol above the lines. A formation of FEs, escorted by Pups of 54 Squadron, took off at 13.30 hours and ran into Voss and five of his Jasta 5 pilots in Albatros Scouts. Voss got himself on the tail of a Pup flown by Second Lieutenant M B Cole, his machine-gun fire shooting away

the Sopwith's control wires, forcing the RFC machine into a headlong dive. Cole, wounded in the thigh, just about made the lines, crunching down into an inhospitable area between the support and front line trenches. The force of the crash rammed the machine gun into the petrol tank but, fortunately, there was no fire. Cole was dragged clear of the wreckage and carted away to Number 34 Casualty Clearing Station. A 54 Squadron recovery team reached the site of the crash around midnight, but such was the devastation that it was only possible to salvage a handful of the Pup's instruments.

SECOND LIEUTENANT

MORTIMER BASIL GEORGE WEBB COLE,

54 SQUADRON, ROYAL FLYING CORPS

Born on 20 July 1896, 'Monty' was the son of George F Cole and Mrs Cole of 100 Redland Road, Bristol. After completing his education at Taunton School, he took up a position as a clerk with the Corporation of Bristol Docks Committee. Gazetted Second Lieutenant to the Royal Flying Corps on 5 August 1916, he was selected for flying training, being awarded the Aviators Certificate (No. 3860) of the Royal Aero Club on 14 November 1916. Completing his training on 10 February 1917, he was appointed a Flying Officer, awarded his 'Wings' and shortly afterwards sent to France and 54 Squadron. After he recovered from the wounds he received at the hands of Werner Voss, Cole served in non-flying capacities with 115 and 118 Squadrons of the Independent Air Force throughout most of 1918. He finally left the Royal Air Force on 22 March 1919, living in Eastbourne for a number of years after the Great War. A good all-round sportsman, he was a hockey trialist for Somerset and for the South. From Eastbourne, Cole returned to the Bristol district, becoming the Licensee of the Cosmo Hotel in Portishead. In 1933, Cole moved to Minehead, Somerset, taking over the proprietorship of 'The Queen's Head Hotel' in that town. A popular and gregarious figure, he was an active member of the British Legion and the Exmoor Lodge of Freemasons, serving on various committees including the Minehead Lifeboat and the Chamber of Trade. He also often rode to hounds with the Minehead Harriers. During the Second World War, Monty Cole served in the Home Guard. A first-class marksman, he helped to win an area rifle shooting cup in 1943. Monty Cole died suddenly in the Minehead Food Office on 12 February 1947, leaving a widow and two daughters. He was fifty years old.

VICTORY NO 31

28 May 1917 FE2d (No. A6378) 25 Squadron 14.00 hours

Four 25 Squadron FEs had taken off at 11.10 hours on a routine but long-ranging reconnaissance of the Douai – St Amand – Orchies areas. Approaching Douai with some trepidation – for this was Manfred von Richthofen's Jasta 11 'patch' – their fears were realised when they were attacked by four German fighters. Not, on this occasion, by the Red Baron's men but by Werner Voss and three of his Jasta 5 command. Three of the British machines succeeded in effectively covering each other defensively and made good their escape from the marauders. The fourth FE, piloted by Captain A de Selincourt, was not so fortunate and was picked off by Voss himself. Their engine disabled by the German's fire, the RFC men were forced down, crashing between Douai and Lomain. Fortunately, neither of the Britons was wounded nor seriously injured. It is clear from remarks made by the observer, Lieutenant H Cotton, after his release from captivity, that he and his pilot were aware of the identity of the man who had shot them down – information no doubt passed on to them by their captors. Voss's claim identified the crash site as a position 'south-east of Douai'.

CAPTAIN AUBREY DE SELINCOURT, 7/NORTH STAFFORDSHIRE REGIMENT AND 25 SQUADRON, ROYAL FLYING CORPS

Born on 7 June 1894, Aubrey was the son of Martin and Mrs de Selincourt of 13 Palace Court, Bayswater, London W2. He was educated at Rugby (1908-1913) where he excelled at both games and studies, and at University College, Oxford (classical scholar). When the war came he immediately suspended his studies at Oxford and volunteered for the Army, being gazetted Second Lieutenant to the 7th Battalion of the North Staffordshire Regiment on 29 August 1914. He accompanied his battalion to Gallipoli and was involved in much heavy fighting at Sari Bair on 7 August 1915 and subsequently. After the withdrawal from the Dardanelles, de Selincourt successfully sought transfer to the RFC and returned home for pilot training. Awarded his 'Wings' in early 1917, he was sent out to join 25 Squadron on 11 April 1917. De Selincourt was released from captivity on 17 December 1918, and left the RAF on 16 February 1919, returning to Oxford to complete his studies. During the next year he was awarded a half-Blue for athletics and took his BA. He also married Irene Rutherford McLeod by whom he had two daughters. Deciding on a teaching career, he took up a position at Bembridge School (1921-1924) before doing on to Dragon School, Oxford, as senior classics master. In 1931, he was appointed headmaster of Clayesmore School. A prolific writer in several spheres of literature, he had many books published and contributed occasionally to the *Times Literary Supplement*. After retiring, he went to live at 'Nutkins Farm', Niton, Isle of Wight, but continued with his writing. One of his most successful literary efforts, *The World of*

Lieutenant Henry Cotton, 20/Canadian Reserve Battalion and 25 Squadron, RFC. Pictured during his confinement in the Karlsruhe prison camp. *(via S K Taylor)*

Herodotus, was published shortly before his death on 20 December 1962, at the age of sixty-eight.

LIEUTENANT

HENRY COTTON,

20TH CANADIAN RESERVE BATTALION AND 25 SQUADRON, ROYAL FLYING CORPS

The son of the Reverend H Cotton and Mrs Cotton, Henry was born in Plymouth, Devon, in 1890. From Devon, his father emigrated to Canada taking with him his wife, three daughters and the youngest child, his only son, Henry. Henry was educated locally in Paris, Ontario, and intending to follow in his father's footsteps, served with the Methodist Unity in various Southern Ontario townships until the war intervened. Cotton first enlisted as a private soldier in the 148th Battalion, CEF in 1916. Subsequently commissioned into the 20th Reserve Battalion, he next successfully applied for transfer to the RFC and was sent for observer training to Reading on 15 March 1917 and from there to the No. 2 School of Air Gunnery. His training completed, he was sent to join 25 Squadron at the front on 22 April 1917. Confined mainly at Karlsruhe and at Holzminden, he was finally repatriated on 14 December 1918. Returning to Canada in May 1919, he enjoyed travelling around the country with a 'Heath Robinson' contraption of a 'magic lantern', giving lectures on life in Holzminden POW Camp and generally relating his experiences in the RFC, including his shooting down by Werner Voss! Returning to the ministry, he later served as a Chaplain in the Royal Canadian Air Force during the Second World War. Henry Cotton died suddenly from a heart attack in Toronto in May 1972 at the age of 82.

VICTORY NO 32

4 June 1917 Sopwith Pup (No. B2151) 54 Squadron 07.10 hours

Having taken off at dawn, Pups from 54 Squadron were escorting FEs on an intelligence gathering sortie for the 4th Army. The formation was engaged by a countering patrol of German scouts south-south east of Douai. In the ensuing mêlée, the Pup flown by Captain R G H Pixley MC (No.B2151) was seen to be engaged by the enemy but was then lost from view. When his compatriots landed, they were heartened by the news that a British AA battery had reported seeing a Pup 'force-land' at map reference '57B.5.28'. Unfortunately, however, when German troops reached Pixley's machine they found the pilot dead, although it was nearly two years later before his family at home knew for certain of his death. Voss's claim was timed at 07.10 (German time) and he gave the location as Aubenscheul-aux-Bois, SSE of Douai.

CAPTAIN

REGINALD GEORGE HEWETT PIXLEY,

MC, 7/LONDON BRIGADE, ROYAL FIELD ARTILLERY (TF) AND 54 SQUADRON, ROYAL FLYING CORPS

Born in 1893, Reginald was the second son of Major Stewart Aitken Pixley OBE, VD, and Patricia Hindle Pixley of Maybury Knowle, Woking, Surrey. He was educated at Stratheden House, Blackheath and at Eton (1909-1912) where he was Captain of the Shooting VIII. In 1911, he was chosen to represent a combined English Schools rifle team in Canada and liked the country so much that he returned there as soon as he left school in 1912. An accident precipitated his return home to England but after recovering from the resultant injuries, he successfully passed examinations which took him into the Imperial College of Science and Technology (Royal School of Mines) which institution he was attending when war broke out. Pixley volunteered and following the example of his elder brother, was gazetted Second Lieutenant to the 7th London Brigade, Royal Field Artillery (TF) on 27 September 1914. In 1916, he successfully sought transfer to the RFC and after training and appointment as a Flying Officer, was sent to join 54 Squadron at the front. Pixley proved himself a brave and resourceful pilot and the award of a Military Cross was announced in the *London Gazette* on 26 July 1917 (Page 7637) whilst he was still posted as 'Missing' : *'For conspicuous gallantry and devotion to duty. He attacked a hostile balloon with three other pilots and, remaining after they had left, finally sent it down in flames. He has assisted in bringing down several hostile machines and has done good work throughout.'* The grave wherein the German troops had buried Pixley was discovered in 1919 by a friend who had known him since childhood and who had gone to France, at the behest of the Pixley family, with the express purpose of finally establishing his fate. The grave was in the garden of a house in Guoy and had been carefully tended by the French lady who owned the property. The Imperial War Graves Commission arranged for Pixley's remains to be re-interned at Prospect Hill Cemetery, Guoy, France (Fr.234). Reginald George Hewett Pixley – one of the many Old Etonians who died for their country in the Great War – was twenty-four years old at the time of his death.

VICTORY NO 33

5 June 1917 FE2b (No.A857) 22 Squadron 09.30 hours

The day following his 32nd victory, Voss fell upon a 22 Squadron FE2b on a 4th Army reconnaissance sortie. His attack – at 09.30 (German time) over Vaucelles – wounded both crewmen, their machine being badly shot up. The FE spiralled down and landed some 2,000 yards south-west of Lesdaines behind enemy lines. Voss repeated his dispiteous and despicable tactic of strafing helpless and wounded victims on the ground. Fortunately, neither occupant was hit again and they were eventually put into an ambulance by German troops and carted away to hospital and captivity.

CAPTAIN (LATER AIR VICE-MARSHAL)
FRANCIS PERCIVAL DON,
OBE (1934), MID (TWICE), O ST J, LÉGION D'HONNEUR (OFFICER), CROIX DE GUERRE WITH PALME (FR), 1/1ST SCOTTISH HORSE YEOMANRY AND 22 SQUADRON, ROYAL FLYING CORPS

Born on 27 February 1886, Frank was the third son of Robert Bogle Don and his wife, Lucy Flora of 'The Lodge', Broughty Ferry, Forfarshire, Scotland. He was educated at Rugby (1900-1903) and at Trinity College, Cambridge, BA (1907) MA (1912). Don had been an active member of the Scottish Horse Yeomanry since he was gazetted Second Lieutenant to that unit in 1911. A highly qualified engineer, he was in business in Dundee until war broke out in August 1914, when his unit was mobilised. His regiment spent the rest of 1914 and part of 1915 in the UK on coastal defence duties before, on 17 August 1915, departing for Gallipoli (without horses) on the SS *Transylvania*. The Scottish Horse landed at Suvla on 2 September 1915, dismounted and equipped to fight as infantrymen. Following the withdrawal from the Dardanelles, Don and the Scottish Horse were sent to join the force guarding the Suez Canal. Obviously bored with the sand and the monotony, Don volunteered for the RFC and returned home for training in 1916. He satisfied the examiners and was awarded the Aviators Certificate (No. 3717) of the Royal Aero Club on 5 October 1916, before going on for formal RFC pilot training. Sent to join 22 Squadron in France, he soon became a Flight Commander and was Mentioned in Despatches for his services. Don was severely wounded in the clash with Voss, and among his other injuries, his left arm had been particularly badly shot up. He afterwards recalled that a kindly but elderly German doctor was responsible for treating his wounds. Caring and considerate though he was, the doctor's medical and surgical techniques had apparently been developed in the nineteenth century and had not since been updated! His method of deciding on when and at what point to amputate was to first suspend the offending limb in the air, allow the wound to rot and only then to cut off the blackened and infected portion. Don lost his left arm just below the elbow in this fashion and remained convinced that he had saved his own life by frequently dipping the stump into an available bucket of an iodine solution. Because of his injuries, he was repatriated in January 1918. Recovering quickly, and despite his disability, Don decided to make the Royal Air Force his career. Between the wars, he served in Iraq and Egypt and commanded 33 Squadron, 502 Squadron and was the first C O of the Cambridge University Air Squadron at Duxford. Don was also the British Air Attaché in Berlin from 1934 to 1937. During a reception at the British Embassy in Berlin, a relative of Werner Voss asked if she could be introduced to Don as she knew of their war-time connection. Don, who remained bitter to the end of his life over the incident when Voss had shot him up on the ground, refused. He was also constantly frustrated when his frequently expressed warnings regarding the ominous build-up of German air power were ignored by his superiors. When war finally came in 1939, he was appointed Head of Mission to the French Air Forces in the field and, in 1940, AOA British Air Forces in France (Despatches). Next he was appointed AOA Flying Training Command before going on to be SASO, Ferry Command, Canada. His health was not good and he was retired from the service in 1943, going to live at Elmham House, East Dereham, Norfolk. Not content to be idle, he became the Liaison Officer for the Northern Region of Civil Defence, 1943-1945. His subsequent appointments included Hon Air Commodore, No.3620 (County of Norfolk) Fighter Control Unit; General Commissioner of Income Tax; Vice-Chairman of Norfolk Territorial Association and Deputy Lieutenant of Norfolk. His business interests included fruit farming and he was in 1959 Chairman of the Norfolk Fruit Growers Association. Air Vice-Marshal Francis Percival Don died on 18 September 1964 at the Beaufort Hotel, Tintern, Monmouthshire. He was eighty years old.

SECOND LIEUTENANT
HERBERT HARRIS,
22 SQUADRON, ROYAL FLYING CORPS

Born on 11 January 1889, Herbert was the son of Mr and Mrs O H Harris of 121 Lorita Street, St Catherine's, Ontario, Canada. Harris was a graduate of Queens University and had enjoyed a position with the engineering department of the Grand Trunk Railway in London, Ontario, before going on to become a mining engineer. He first enlisted in the ranks of the Canadian Engineers on 23 September 1914 and proceeded overseas with the first contingent of the Canadan Expeditionary Force. Harris served in France with both the 1st and 2nd Field Companies of the Divisional Engineers before becoming attached to the RFC on 29 October 1916. Gazetted Second Lieutenant on 11 April 1917, he was sent to join 22 Squadron as a probationary observer on 15 May 1917. Harris lost the index finger of his left hand in the engagement with Werner Voss and after recovering, spent most of his captivity in Karlsruhe before finally being repatriated on 17 December 1918. He went on to the Unemployed List on 28 February 1919 and returned to Canada shortly afterwards, living at 86 Wolland Avenue, back in his home town of St Catherine's, Ontario. In 1921, Harris moved to Oakland, California, USA, where he lived until 1929 when he took an appointment as Comptroller of the Jensen Radio Manufacturing Company in Oak Park, Illinois. Herbert Harris died in Oak Park, Illinois, in 1947 – he was fifty-seven years of age.

VICTORY NO 34

6 June 1917 Nieuport XVII (No. N3204) 6 (Naval) Squadron 13.10

For the third day in succession, Voss claimed a victory, although on this occasion the victim's identity was less than clear cut. Around mid-day, 6 Naval Squadron was escorting some FEs on a line west and north-west of Cambrai. The escorting Nieuports were led by Flight Commander Chris Draper (N3101) and included Flight Lieutenants F P Reeves (N3204), G Stevens (N5865) with Flight Sub-Lieutenants R F Redpath (N5861) and Norman MacGregor (N3100) (the very MacGregor who would finally account for the German ace, Kurt Wolff, on 15 September following). The British formation was above what was left of the blackened and burnt Bourlon Wood – a familiar landmark to the airmen of both sides – when they came across elements of Jasta 5, led by Werner Voss. The Germans had climbed to a position of advantage above the Nieuports before swooping to attack. Draper (who would subsequently claim one scout destroyed and another out of control in this action) later reported that the Germans put up such a large number of machines to oppose them that, by the end of the engagement, they easily out-numbered his own command. As the fight developed, Reeves found himself being chased by a German fighter. Reeves threw his Nieuport around the sky in his efforts to shake loose his tormentor but then his wings were seen to fold and peel away from his fuselage – whether shot away by the German Scout's machine-gun fire or by the stresses induced by his own violent manoeuvring remains unclear.

Voss himself had gotten on to the tail of a Nieuport which, he later reported, he sent spinning down into the British lines. But if Voss had indeed 'got' Reeves, then surely he would have reported the clearly observed break-up of the Nieuport over the German trenches, and not contented himself with the slightly vague assertion of a machine spinning down towards the British side. Certainly it does appear that Voss and Draper engaged each other, with Draper delivering telling hits on the German ace before diving away to the safety of his own lines. It seems possible that Reeves simply broke up in the air and that Voss's rather optimistic claim related to Draper and the RNAS man's hurried exit to his own side of the trenches! Werner Voss was slightly wounded by a grazing hit during the assault on his Albatros DIII by the marauding Nieuport and presumably it was Voss who Draper claimed as his 'out of control'? Of course Voss survived the subsequent crash-landing, an event which marked his last action with Jasta 5.

FLIGHT LIEUTENANT

FABIAN PEMBER REEVES,

6 (NAVAL) SQUADRON, ROYAL NAVAL AIR SERVICE

Born in Christchurch, New Zealand on 12 December 1895, Fabian was the son of the Honourable William Pember Reeves and Magdalen Stuart Reeves. His father was a particularly distinguished New Zealander, being a noted academic, a barrister and a journalist as well as a Member of the New Zealand Parliament. Reeves Senior came to England at the turn of the century, first as Agent-General for the colony and then as High Commissioner. Fabian's mother was also an author of some note. The family, which included two daughters and one son, first took up residence at 43 Cornwall Gardens, Kensington, London before moving to 31 Pembroke Square, also in Kensington. Fabian, who had been a student member of the OTC, was commissioned into the Royal Naval Air Service on 18 July 1915, training first at Eastchurch before going on to Hendon. He served with Home Defence squadrons at Yarmouth and Dover for a period, and as an instructor at Eastchurch. He had only been at the front for a short time when he met his death. Fabian Pember Reeves's remains were never recovered and he is therefore commemorated on the Arras Memorial to the Missing, France. He was twenty-one years old.

OR!

FLIGHT COMMANDER

CHRISTOPHER DRAPER

DSC, CdeG (FR), 6 (NAVAL) SQUADRON, ROYAL NAVAL AIR SERVICE

Born on 15 April 1892 at 'The Firs', Bebington on the Cheshire banks of the River Mersey, Christopher was the third of his mother's children and the seventh of his re-married father's. He was educated locally at 'Freelands', Hooton and at Rock Ferry College. Despite his family's financial difficulties, Draper managed to raise the cash necessary to take flying lessons which culminated in the award of the Aviators Certificate of the Royal Aero Club (Number 646) on 13 October 1913 – the start of a long, at times distinguished but largely eccentric career in aviation. Draper joined the Royal Naval Air Service in January 1914 and over the next two years served in various stations around the UK. In 1916, he was testing armaments when he was directed to the newly formed 3 Naval Wing, not only to become an original member of the Sopwith 1½ Strutter unit but also being appointed a Flight Commander. Following his two victory claims in the Voss fight and after a brief rest at the Eastchurch station during the summer months, Draper was given the command of the famous 8 Naval Squadron on 28 October 1917. On 1 April 1918 when the Royal Naval Air Service and the Royal Flying Corps combined to form the new arm of service, the Royal Air Force, the former 'Naval 8' was re-designated '208 Squadron'. Draper did not have to wait long to feel the full weight and isolation of command when on 9 April 1918, with his grounded Squadron lying directly in the path of the advancing German army and unable to take off because of dense fog, he took the decision to destroy all the aeroplanes under his charge. With enemy shells falling around them his men set fire to the Squadron's sixteen Sopwith Camels before beating a hurried retreat from the threatened airfield. His drastic action was obviously acceptable to the higher command as his earlier awarded Distinguished Service Cross was formally confirmed by an announcement in the *London Gazette* of 26 April 1918 (page 5059) and even more to the point, he was allowed to retain command of his squadron until December 1918. Demobbed with the rank of Major in May 1919, Draper continued to work in aviation with the British Aerial Transport Company until he was injured in a crash in March 1920. Recovering quickly, he rejoined the RAF on a short service commission with the rank of Squadron Leader. He was one of those élite few selected to fly in the Air Pageant of 1921 but he could not settle into service life and consequently resigned his commission in the following October. He returned to civil aviation but after a few years he embarked upon a new career – as a 'Thespian' treading the stage with the newly acquired name, 'George Mannering'. Never one to hide his light under a bushel Draper decided that a filmed (of course) flight under the London bridges may well bring him to the notice of the general public. On 30 September 1931 he flew a Puss Moth though Tower Bridge and under Westminster Bridge and was promptly dubbed, 'The Mad Major', by delighted newsmen. Draper's colourful career continued through the 'Thirties when he met, and was feted by, many personalities of those days including in 1932, the emerging Adolf Hitler. When the second World War came Draper joined the Fleet Air Arm as a lowly Flight Sub-Lieutenant, returning to flying duties in 1940 before being posted to the Caribbean during the following year. A Lieutenant Commander in 1942, he was next sent to Machrihanish, Scotland, to help with the training of pilots on carrier landings and take-offs. In 1943 he was posted to the Gold Coast (now Ghana) where he was later to command No.777 Squadron, FAA. The area had been known for years as 'the white man's graveyard' and it was perhaps not surprising that Draper's health suffered and that, by 1944, he had been 'grounded'. After the end of the war Draper returned to civilian life and to a number of different and diverse jobs. In 1953, at the age of 61, to demonstrate that he was not 'past it' and still perfectly employable, Draper repeated his excursion under the Thames bridges – this time in an Auster! Chris Draper – 'The Mad Major' – died on 16 January 1979, at the grand age of eighty-six.

The highly successful Werner Voss, long by now a household name in Germany, was

next sent to command Jasta 29. He succeeded Kurt Wolff (a Jasta 11 'old boy') who had been sent back to his former unit (part of Manfred von Richthofen's JGI) as its Staffelführer. Voss took up his new appointment on 28 June 1917. Almost immediately, however, Voss was ordered to take temporary charge of Jasta 14 in succession to Oberleutnant Ernst Fr. von Althaus who, in turn, had been sent to command Jasta 10 (another unit under the aegis of JGI). Von Althaus's appointment proved short-lived as Manfred von Richthofen discovered that his new Jasta commander had failing eyesight and must, perforce, be relieved. The Baron's choice as a successor to von Althaus narrowed down to the young Werner Voss and so, on 30 July 1917, he took over his third command in a matter of weeks.

These manoeuvrings had taken Voss out of active combat for some time but now, once again, he was at the head of a leading and successful Jasta and back to his deadly business. With 34 victories, Voss was second in the German Air Service only to the maestro himself, Manfred von Richthofen, who at this time had 57. If the number of victories mattered to these men (and it most certainly did) then closing such a gap between the leading ace and himself might, at one time, have seemed almost impossible to Voss. But von Richthofen was currently inactive, still recovering from the head wound he had received on 6 July, and so the discrepancy might yet be addressed by the young man from Krefeld!

That the Red Baron himself was unafraid of competition is evidenced by the fact that he, who could have chosen anybody to lead the Jastas under his command, chose Voss with 34 victories and Wolff with 33, his two closest rivals in the numbers game.

VICTORY NO 35

10 August 1917 Spad XIII Spa 31(French) 16.25 hours

Voss had settled into his new command, which was based at Marlebecke, near Courtrai, up in the northern sector of the front opposite to the Salient and now, eleven days into the Third Battle of Ypres, he was on an afternoon patrol. South of Dixmude, the German fighters engaged several French Spad XIIIs from Spa 31. Voss closed in on a machine piloted by Capitaine Henri Rousseau, a comparative newcomer who had joined the Escadrille on 13 July 1917. The German ace soon accounted for the Spad – his first victory over the French. One of his men, Unteroffizier Herman Brettel also shot down another Spad in this action, one flown by Maréchel-des-Logis Camus. Both French machines fell near to Klerken.

VICTORY NO 36

15 August 1917 FE2b (No. A5152) 20 Squadron 19.10 hours

20 Squadron sent out an evening patrol over Ypres at 16.41 hours. After more than an hour of uneventful patrolling, they ran into Jasta 10 (led by its Staffelführer, Werner Voss) in company with elements of Jasta 24. Voss concentrated on an FE2b flown by Canadian Second Lieutenant C H Cameron, the ace's machine-gun fire killing the observer, Private S E Pilbrow MM, and hitting the engine. The FE fell away from the scene of the action without, unusually, receiving the continuing attentions of Voss who, presumably, was

otherwise occupied in the ensuing dogfight. Cameron skillfully guided his crippled 'pusher' across the lines, making a 'successful' forced landing near Dickebusch Lake. The landing was successful in so far that Cameron remained unharmed, although the machine itself was wrecked beyond repair in the process. Voss timed his claim at 17.10 (German time) giving the location as between Ypres and Zillebeke. Herman Brettel, who had shot down a Frenchman the day before, was also in this fight and was wounded. One of the Jasta 24 pilots, Heinrich Kroll, also claimed an FE (A6500) north of Ypres in the action – his 8th victory.

SECOND LIEUTENANT

CHARLES HUGHIE CAMERON,

20 SQUADRON, ROYAL FLYING CORPS

Born on 14 June 1896, Charles was the son of Mr and Mrs Cameron of 308 Liscar Street, Ottawa, Canada. He was one of those chosen by Lieutenant Colonel Lord Innes-Ker DSO whose tour of Canada had the sole purpose of finding potential air crew for the Royal Flying Corps. Cameron and a number of other Innes-Ker candidates sailed for England on the SS *Olympic* in October 1916. After successfully completing his training, he was sent to join 22 Squadron on 30 May 1917. From 22 Squadron, Cameron was transferred to 20 Squadron in the July following. Cameron was badly shaken by his experience on 15 August and took a few days off before returning to patrolling over the Salient. After a week of such patrols, he was again involved in action with the enemy and wounded on 25 August 1917. Cameron was sent to England to recover and subsequently for re-training. He returned to France in May 1918, flying SE5As with 92 Squadron but his flying time was severely curtailed by bouts of sickness. Returning to Canada after the war, he joined the Royal Canadian Mounted Police in August 1920 and served with that force for twenty years before retiring. Charles Cameron died in Victoria, British Columbia, in August 1964. He was sixty-eight years old.

PRIVATE

STANLEY EDWARD PILBROW,

MM, (NO.44340) 22/MANCHESTER REGIMENT ATTACHED 20 SQUADRON, ROYAL FLYING CORPS

The son of Edward and Minnie Priscilla Pilbrow of 1 Carlyle Street, Chelsea, London, Stanley was born in 1891. He had married Elsie Mabel shortly before he was accepted from the infantry as a volunteer observer/gunner for the Royal Flying Corps. On 27 July 1917 Pilbrow, with Second Lieutenant R M Makepiece in the pilot's seat (No. A6548) had claimed three Albatros Scouts in one action – one in flames and two crashed. The following day the same two got yet another Albatros, this one 'Out of Control'! Although the citation for the award on his Military Medal (*London Gazette*, 28 September 1917) is not available, it is reasonable to assume that it was awarded for his success and gallantry in these actions. Sadly, he did not live to receive the award. Stanley Edward Pilbrow is buried in Huts Cemetery, Dickebusch, Belgium (Bel.19). He was twenty-six years old.

VICTORY NO 37

16 August 1917 Camel (No. B3756) 70 Squadron 19.45 hours

Captain Noel Webb MC & Bar led a 70 Squadron Offensive Patrol which had taken off at 18.05 to cover an area from Poelcapelle to Becelaere. Webb was a distinguished ace with 14 victories achieved since the summer of 1916 – 5 with 25 Squadron and 9 so far with 70 Squadron. The Camels crossed the lines at 12,000 feet, steadily climbing to 14,000 feet and patrolled for an hour without any sign of enemy aircraft. Webb decided to take his command down to 4,000 feet to an area above Polygon Wood. As they descended through cloud, the formation split up and Webb found himself with just one companion, Captain F H Laurence (B3872). The two continued the patrol and continued to draw a blank. Gesturing upwards, Webb led Laurence up again, this time levelling out at 15,000 feet and joining up with a group of FE2s. The crews of the FE2s soon brought the attention of the newcomers to a formation of about twenty Albatros scouts who were ominously closing in on them from above. The two Camels bravely climbed to meet the main body of the enemy but as they did so, Webb spotted two further enemy machines just below him and, using his height advantage, dived upon them. Laurence, following his leader, fired on one of the Germans who was climbing past him. Laurence broke off the engagement and cast around, searching for Webb. He was unsuccessful – Webb had vanished, almost literally, into thin air.

CAPTAIN
NOEL WILLIAM WARD WEBB,
MC & BAR, 70 SQUADRON, ROYAL FLYING CORPS

The youngest son of Professor William Trego Webb and Isabel Mary Webb of 7 Scarsdale Villas, Kensington, London, Noel was born in Margate, Kent, on 12 December 1896. He was educated at The Briary, Westgate-on-Sea and at St Paul's School, London, where he played three-quarter for the first XV. Webb was gazetted Second Lieutenant (General List) in March 1916, gained the Aviators Certificate (No.3059) of the Royal Aero Club on 29 May 1916 and his 'Wings' in June 1916. He was sent to join 25 Squadron in France on 4 July 1916, achieving five victories before he was invalided home the following October. Upon recovery, Webb was posted to a squadron in England where he acted as instructor and later as acting Squadron Commander. His first Military Cross was announced in the New Year's honours – *'for service performed under most perilous conditions'* – *London Gazette*, 1 January 1917 (Page 43). Webb returned to the front with the rank of acting Captain, joining 70 Squadron as a Flight Commander on 21 June 1917. A clever, brave and resourceful pilot, he gained another nine victories with his new squadron before he met his nemesis on 16 August 1917. The bar to his Military Cross was announced in the *London Gazette* of 9 January 1918 (Page 579) – *'For conspicuous gallantry and devotion to duty in aerial combats. He has destroyed three hostile machines and driven down four others completely out of control. By his spirit and gallantry he has set a fine example which has inspired the pilots of his flight to successfully attack formations many times more numerous than their own'*. Webb's body was never found and so he is commemorated on the Arras Memorial to the Missing, France. He was twenty years old.

VICTORY NO 38

23 August 1917 Spad VII (No. B3528) 19 Squadron 10.10 hours

This summer morning saw Voss get his second Spad but, on this occasion, one flown by a British pilot. Captain Gordon-Kidd DSO (B3528) took off alone at 07.47 on what was graphically described as an 'aerial sentry patrol' to the east of Ypres. Voss engaged the 19 Squadron machine between Noordschoote and Neuvekapelle at 10.10 (German time) and sent it spinning down towards the British side of the lines south-west of Dixmude. Although mortally wounded with a terrible injury to his thigh, the stricken pilot still managed to get his Spad down onto the 23 Squadron base at La Lovie, north of Poperinghe. He died four days later on 27 August.

CAPTAIN

ARTHUR LIONEL GORDON-KIDD,

DSO, MID, MEDAL FOR MILITARY VALOUR (MONTENEGRO), 4TH DRAGOON GUARDS AND 19 SQUADRON, ROYAL FLYING CORPS

The son of an old Indian Army family, Gordon-Kidd was privately educated near to the family home, 'Kashmir Cottage', Merre, Punjab, India. A language expert and interpreter, he first went to France as an officer of the Reserve Regiment of Cavalry, attached to Jacob's Horse, Indian Army. He next successfully applied for transfer to the RFC and gained the Aviators Certificate of the Royal Aero Club (No. 2247) on 30 December 1915, before going on to formal pilot training and the award of his 'Wings' on 15 March 1916. Gordon Kidd was sent to join 7 Squadron at the front on 20 April 1916 and he was to win a

Distinguished Service Order for gallantry on the first day of the Battle of the Somme, 1 July 1916. Specifically charged with looking for targets on the enemy's supply lines and flying without an observer to increase his machine's bomb-carrying capacity, he saw a train on the line between Aubigny-au-Bac and Cambrai. The train was approaching a cutting which had been suggested to the pilots as a likely target – a place where train wreckage would be unusually difficult to clear. Gordon-Kidd swooped down and released his bombs, scoring a direct hit on the middle of the train. The train caught fire and began to explode. An hour later another pilot dropped two more bombs on the train, causing yet further explosions and adding to the general confusion – *London Gazette* 19 August 1916 (Page 8225): *'For conspicuous gallantry and determination. On one occasion he dived his machine from 7,500 feet to 900 feet and placed a bomb on the enemy's ammunition train, which set it on fire and blocked the line. A few days afterwards he performed another very hazardous undertaking well within the enemy lines, whilst exposed the whole time to all descriptions of heavy fire'.* Later in the summer, he and his observer spotted eight enemy field guns firing from a sunken road east of Courcelette. They signalled the enemy's position to British artillery who poured shrapnel down on them. Still the enemy doggedly worked their guns. Finally Gordon-Kidd took matters into his own hands, diving down and machine-gunning the German artillerymen, killing and wounding many of them. His fire was returned and his machine suffered many hits but he still managed to keep it airborne and returned safely to base. Gordon-Kidd was Mentioned in Despatches, the announcement appearing in the *London Gazette* of 1 January 1917. He was also awarded the Silver Medal for Military Valour by the King of Montenegro – *London Gazette* 9 March 1917. After a period in England acting as an instructor, Gordon-Kidd again returned to the front, this time joining 19 Squadron as a Flight Commander on 27 July 1917. Arthur Lionel Gordon-Kidd is buried in Mendinghem Military Cemetery, Proven, Belgium (Bel. 18).

So far, all of Voss's victories had been achieved in an Albatros Scout but now, in August 1917, a new fighting scout arrived at the front – the Fokker Triplane. Voss had already flown a pre-production V4 Triplane at Schwerin earlier in the summer, during the brief period he was acting CO of Jasta 14. The first two of the new type arrived behind the lines – 102/17 was assigned to Jasta 11 for the use of Manfred von Richthofen and Kurt Wolff and 103/17 was sent to Jasta 10 for Voss to pass judgement on. Voss began flying his machine at once and had the nose cowling painted chrome yellow – Jasta 10's own colour – with white face markings about the two air cooling holes in the front plate. Confusingly, contemporary photographs of what was to become a famous Triplane appear to show the nose cowling colour as black – this was due to a faulty photo-processing technique of the time.

VICTORY NO 39

3 September 1917 Camel (No. 3917) 45 Squadron 09.52 hours

Flying the new Triplane, Voss claimed the second of his victories over Camels. Lieutenant A T Heywood had taken off at 08.15 and was last seen heading in a westerly direction at 4,000 feet over Comines. Voss claimed a Sopwith which fell inside German lines at Zandvoorde, north of Houthem at 09.52 hours. Later in the day the German Air Service dropped a message over the British lines, confirming Heywood's death.

LIEUTENANT

AUBREY TALLEY HEYWOOD,

19/MANCHESTER REGIMENT AND 45 SQUADRON, ROYAL FLYING CORPS

Born in 1896, Aubrey was the son of provision broker Alfred Heywood and his wife, Cherokee Heywood, of 43 Clyde Road, West Didsbury, Manchester. He was educated at Liverpool College (1910-1913) where, as well as a frequent speaker at the debating society, he was also a member of the OTC (Signalling Section). After leaving school, he entered his father's business at 26 Produce Exchange Buildings, 8 Victoria Street, in the commercial centre of Liverpool. Liverpool was at this time the largest fruit and produce port outside of London. Immediately upon the outbreak of war, he enlisted as a private soldier into the 19th (Pals) Battalion of the Manchester Regiment. He was selected as possible officer material and eventually gazetted Second Lieutenant to his own battalion of the Manchesters on 6 July 1915. The 19th Manchesters were sent to join the Expeditionary Force in France on 7 November 1915 – Heywood commanding the battalion's Signallers. Following a spell in the trenches, he successfully applied for transfer to the RFC and, on 7 April 1917 received the Aviators Certificate (No.4442) of the Royal Aero Club. After further training he was awarded his 'Wings' and crossed the Channel again, this time to join 45 Squadron at the front. Aubrey Heywood's actual grave site remained undiscovered after the war although German troops had buried his remains with due ceremony. Consequently, he is commemorated on the Arras Memorial to the Missing, France. He was twenty-one years old.

VICTORY NO 40

5 September 1917 Sopwith Pup (No. B1842) 46 Squadron 14.50

Voss added two victories within two hours on this September afternoon. The first encounter concerned Pups from 46 Squadron that had left their base at 13.00 hours, set for an Offensive Patrol in a southerly direction. Over St Julien they ran into Voss and Jasta 10. Voss engaged a Pup flown by Second Lieutenant C W Odell and the German ace's fire badly damaged the RFC machine. Despite the damage, Odell, skilful pilot that he was, got the Sopwith down into the British lines without injury to himself. German observers reported the Pup as severely and irreparably damaged but this was an exaggeration as the machine was able to be retrieved by RFC crash crews and sent on to No. 1 ASD for repair. Odell too lived to fight another day – in fact surviving the war as an ace with 7 victories. By the war's end he had flown two tours of duty with 46 Squadron, the second as a Flight Commander.

SECOND LIEUTENANT

CHARLES WALTER ODELL,

ROYAL INNISKILLING FUSILIERS AND 46 SQUADRON, ROYAL FLYING CORPS

Born on 25 November 1898, Charles was the son of Walter William Odell and Mrs Odell of 'Briar Bank', Newport, Isle of Wight. He was educated at Tonbridge (1912-1915) and at the Royal Military College, Sandhurst. From Sandhurst, he was, on 16 August 1916, gazetted Second Lieutenant to the Royal Inniskilling Fusiliers but, just ten days later, was attached to the Royal Flying Corps. After completing his flying training, he was awarded his 'Wings' on 21 December 1916. His first posting was to 75 Home Defence Squadron, a night flying unit based at Bedford. At the beginning of May 1917, he briefly honed his skills at 40 Training Squadron before going out to join 46 Squadron at the front on the last day of the month. Odell fought in the air in support of the great land battles of Messines (June), Passchendaele (September) and Cambrai (November), scoring two of his victories before returning to England to rest and instruct with 32 TS. On 20 August 1918, Odell crossed again to France and re-joined 46 Squadron – this time as a Flight Commander. Odell and his Squadron flew in support of the advancing British troops in the final Somme offensive and the capture of the Hindenburg Line. During this period Odell added a balloon and four more enemy aircraft to his victory 'score'. He again returned to England on 30 October 1918 and was appointed to instruct at Eastbourne. The war over at last, Odell was sent to France on 2 January 1919, firstly as a Flight Commander with 54 Squadron before being charged with the responsibility of bringing back to Britain the cadre of 108 Squadron on 21 March 1919. Odell spent the next six months at the Aircraft Acceptance Park, Lympne, which seemed to bore him as he relinquished his RAF commission and returned to Army duty on 23 September 1919. He finally retired from the Army, receiving gratuity on 12 June 1922, after six years service in war and peace. His first enterprise in civilian life was as the proprietor of Malden Garage until 1925 when he joined the Anglo-American Oil Company as circuit manager. Odell was recalled from the Reserve of Officers in 1939 and, as a Major in the Pioneer Corps, served in France until Dunkirk in 1940. He went on to command various Companies of Pioneers until his retirement with the rank of Honorary Major in 1945. After the war ended, he returned to Anglo-American Oil but was lent to the Petroleum Board as Fuel Oil Supervisor. Odell lived out his days at 3 Copse Hill, Purley, Surrey.

VICTORY NO 41

5 September 1917 Caudron 2-Seater French 16.30 hours

Voss's second claim of the afternoon was a Frenchman, this time a Caudron two-seater. Voss stated that his adversary went down into Allied lines near to Bixschoote at 16.30 (German time). There is, it has to be said, some confusion over this victory as the only reported loss of the day was a Caudron G6 of C. 53 crewed by MdL Thabaud-Deshoulières and Lt Mulard, both of whom were reported as 'Missing'. However, those

Above: A smiling Voss in the cockpit of a Fokker V4 Triplane at Schwerin, early summer 1917.

Above right: Mdl Thabald-Deshoulières, who as a sergeant in the 6th Regiment of Dragoons received a special mention for his bravery in September 1914 when, trapped behind German lines for five days, he used the opportunity to make important observations on the enemy positions which were later made good use of by the French artillery. He showed the same courage and resource as a pilot when, on 31 July 1917, he flew very low over the German lines for two hours on an important mission. He returned with his machine riddled with bullets.

two appear to have actually been the victims of a Kest 3 pilot who claimed a Caudron down near Remoncourt. The fact that Voss's claim fell into Allied lines could be significant. It might be that whilst Voss was convinced he had downed a machine, in fact it may have landed safely and intact, and hence not reported as a loss. It would certainly not be the first, or last, occasion when just such a misapprehension arose.

A letter from his Squadron Commander, Lieutenant Gobert who, before the war was a famous tennis player, stated: *'Deshouliéres died yesterday. He was shot down by German fighters. His death must have been horrible but short fortunately. He must have been taken by surprise. A lieutenant of Artillery* (Mulard) *was by his side. Deshoulières gloriously crashed on the battlefield while fighting as a brave French soldier'.*

VICTORY NO 42

6 September 1917 FE2d (No. B1895) 20 Squadron 15.35 hours

A 20 Squadron FE2d had taken off on an Offensive Patrol at 14.35 hours, meeting Voss in the air above Boesdinghe. The greatest fear airmen of any nationality had was fire in the air. The only possibility of escape from this terrible fate was by parachute and this device, even when it eventually became available, was denied to the Royal Flying Corps. On this occasion, the worst fears of the British crew were realised as the German ace's machine-gun fire ignited the wood and canvas of their machine. Both men were killed.

LIEUTENANT JOHN OSCAR PILKINGTON,

14/KING'S LIVERPOOL REGIMENT AND 20 SQUADRON, ROYAL FLYING CORPS

Born on 18 August 1892, Jack was the younger son of John Arthur and Sarah Pilkington of 'Bank House', Maghull, Liverpool and 'Mar Rowee', Port Erin, Isle of Man. He was educated at King William's

The Manx National Memorial at St John's near to Tynwald Hill in the centre of the Isle of Man. Lieutenant J O Pilkington, King's Liverpool Regiment and 20 Squadron, RFC, is commemorated here. (*Photo: Margery West*)

School, Isle of Man (1907-1909) and at Liverpool University, where he studied Electrical Engineering. He was one of those who, in September 1914, answered Lord Derby's call for volunteers by enlisting into the Liverpool 'Pals' as a private soldier. An obvious candidate for a commission, he was gazetted Second Lieutenant to the 15th (Reserve) Battalion of the King's Liverpool Regiment on 15 March 1915. Pilkington was posted to the 14th Battalion of his regiment in time to accompany it, on 5 September 1915, on its journey to Salonika via Boulogne and Marseilles. After a period in Salonika, he was transferred to Egypt in February 1916 and like so many others before him, became bored with the heat and monotony of service on the Canal and volunteered for duty with the RFC. He returned to England for training in the Spring of 1917 and had been at the front only a matter of three weeks before he was killed. His brother, Motor Mechanic Edward Geoffrey Pilkington, also served in France with the Army Service Corps. No doubt in an effort to spare the feelings of his parents, Pilkington's Commanding Officer wrote: *'He fought bravely surrounded by Huns and died heroically being shot through the head, his machine falling into our lines'*. John Oscar Pilkington is buried in Bailleul Communal Cemetery Extension, France (Fr. 285). He was twenty-five years old.

AIR MECHANIC SECOND CLASS
HERBERT FREDERICK MATTHEWS
(NO. 1712) 20 SQUADRON, ROYAL FLYING CORPS

Born in 1895, Herbert was the son of Robert and Harriet E Matthews of 'Culverdene', 14 Tower Road, Worthing, Sussex. He first joined the Royal Flying Corps in 1914 and had seen three years of active service by the time of his death. Herbert Matthews is buried along with his pilot, Lieutenant Jack Pilkington, in Bailleul Communal Cemetery Extension, France. He was twenty-two.

VICTORY NO 43
10 September 1917 Camel (No.B3927) 70 Squadron 16.50 hours

The tenth day of September brought Voss another 'hat-trick' of victories – including two in one action and the third twenty-five minutes later. 70 Squadron had taken off at 16.45 on an Offensive Patrol with a predetermined 'beat' which would take them along a line covering Houthulst Forest-Roulers-Ledeghem and Gheluvelt. The Camels spotted and dived upon a flight of four Albatros Scouts, with Second Lieutenant L F Wheeler (B3836) claiming one out of control. Wheeler next tried his luck with a Triplane but that climbed away and eluded him. Later on, after his safe return to base, Wheeler also reported seeing a German machine going down in flames. However, as

Jasta 10 suffered no losses on this day, what Wheeler actually saw was a Camel going down in flames – a common and recurring error. Another of those involved, Second Lieutenant F H Bickerton (B2342) almost collided with one of his own Camels as it went past him in flames, hotly pursued by a German Triplane and later saw another Camel gliding, powerless, to the east. Voss had firstly engaged a Camel flown by a Canadian, Second Lieutenant A J S Sisley, and after the briefest of flurried skirmishes, sent it down into the flat Flanders fields surrounding the village of Langemarck.

SECOND LIEUTENANT
ARTHUR JACKSON SMITH SISLEY,
70 SQUADRON, ROYAL FLYING CORPS

Born in 1894, Arthur was the son of Doctor and Mrs Opie Sisley of 654 Kingston Road, Toronto, Ontario, Canada. Like his two brothers (both of whom also served in the RFC), he was educated near to his home in Toronto's east end. Arthur first enlisted as a gunner in the 4th Battalion, 4th Brigade, Canadian Field Artillery on 1 January 1915. He and his unit crossed the Atlantic to England in May 1915, before going on to join the Canadian Expeditionary Force in France in the following September. Sisley was wounded at the front and, shortly after treatment in England, was allowed recuperative leave in Canada during the November and December of 1916. Whilst he was home on leave, he responded to the blandishments proffered by the ubiquitous Colonel Lord Innes-Ker who was in Canada seeking volunteers for the Royal Flying Corps. Accepted as a flight cadet, he sailed again for England on 24 January 1917. Sent first to Oxford on 15 February 1917, he was eventually gazetted Second Lieutenant to the General List on 24 May 1917 and awarded his 'Wings' on 3 July following. After all this training and preparation, when finally he did arrive at 70 Squadron for active service on 18 August 1917, he lasted only a short three weeks – unfortunately, not an uncommon occurrence. Arthur Sisley's body was never recovered and so he is commemorated on the Arras Memorial to the Missing, France. He was twenty-three.

VICTORY NO 44
10 September 1917 Camel (No. B3787) 70 Squadron 16.55

Immediately after despatching Sisley, Voss turned his attention to another Camel – this one piloted by Second Lieutenant O C Pearson. With supreme confidence bordering on arrogance, Voss accounted for Pearson in double-quick time, the Sopwith machine falling to the ground south-west of Poelcapelle close to where, on the following day, the great French ace Georges Guynemer would meet his end.

The RFC reported three machines lost on this day, two Camels and one DH5 of 24

Squadron. There were, however, four claims made by German fliers – two by Voss of course, and one each by two Jasta 28 pilots. One of the Jasta 28 men got the DH5 but the other claimed a Camel at 17.10 (German time) inside British lines north-west of Houthulst Forest. Whatever the merit of that claim, it seems not to impinge on the validity of Voss's two as the area where it reportedly fell was much further north than the crash sites of the Staffelführer's victims.

SECOND LIEUTENANT
OLIVER CHARLES PEARSON,
70 SQUADRON, ROYAL FLYING CORPS

Oliver was the son of Mr and Mrs C E Pearson of 'Hillcrest', Lowdham, Nottinghamshire. He was accepted into the Inns of Court Officer Training Corps on 23 September 1915 (No. 6/5/6405) and, following an unusually lengthy period of training, was gazetted Second Lieutenant to the Royal Flying Corps on 25 September 1916. He first reported to Oxford on 9 October 1916 and his flying training followed the usual pattern until the award of his 'Wings' on 23 May 1917. Pearson was sent to join 70 Squadron at the front on 28 July 1917 and commenced operational flying almost immediately. He was slightly wounded on 20 August and had only just recovered and re-commenced combat flying when he was killed. His remains were never found and he is therefore commemorated on the Arras Memorial to the Missing, France.

VICTORY NO 45

10 September 1917 Spad 1 Spa 37 (French) 18.15 hours

The third of Voss's victories of the day came only 25 minutes after he achieved the second! It seemed he could not miss as he cooly disposed of a French Spad flown by Adjutant Pierre Tiberghien at 18.15 hours (German time). Tiberghien had been with the Escadrille little more than three weeks, having joined the operational unit on 19 August 1917, shortly after receiving an official commendation for earlier gallantry. *'......a first class pilot who always volunteers for important and dangerous missions. (In particular) he distinguished himself for the numerous missions he did for the infantry.........often coming back with his aircraft riddled with bullets. He was injured while doing a dangerous mission........at an altitude of less than a hundred metres'.*

VICTORY NO 46

11 September 1917 Camel (No. B3775) 45 Squadron 10.30 hours
OR Bristol 2b (No. B1105) 22 Squadron

The first of Voss's two claims on this day remains, even until now, something of a mystery. He timed the claim at 10.30, placed the engagement over Langemarck and reported that his victim fell behind the German lines. In fact, two Camels were shot down in this area around the time specified – one flown by Second Lieutenant E B Denison (B3775) of 45 Squadron (POW), the other a 70 Squadron machine piloted by Second Lieutenant E H P Streather (killed). The complication arises because whilst two Camels were actually shot down, three Camels were claimed by three separate and distinctly individual German pilots! Aside from Voss, there was Vfw Max Wackwitz of

Jasta 24 claiming a Camel at 10.05 (German time) at Wallemolen, between Ypres and Roulers and, following some initial uncertainty, Vfw Menckhoff (Jasta 3) was credited with a Camel at 09.45, this one over the Ypres-Roulers Road. Self evidently, three into two will not go and despite prolonged and careful examination of the circumstances, it has not been possible to identify and eliminate the inappropriate claim.

However, Voss's first combat on this day – shortly before 10.30 – was with a 22 Squadron Bristol Fighter, crewed by Lieutenant R de L Stedman and Second Lieutenant H E Jones, which had taken off at 08.00. Voss attacked the two-seater at an altitude of 2,000 feet over Schaap Balia, between Houthulst and Poelcapelle. In the brief, fierce but apparently inconclusive engagement that followed, the Brisfit's observer was seriously wounded. The pilot, successfully disguising their distress, disengaged from the combat and headed the machine back across the lines, hurriedly coming down to a safe landing so that Jones could get the urgent medical attention he needed.

LIEUTENANT RAYMOND DE LACEY STEDMAN, 22 SQUADRON, ROYAL FLYING CORPS

Born on 24 October 1893 in Hereford, England, Stedman was one of the many who emigrated to Australia during the early years of the new century. He settled in New South Wales, in the area of Sydney where his occupation was described as 'farmer'. Amongst the first to enlist, he joined the 1st Battalion of the Australian Imperial Force on 22 August 1914. For some unknown reason he returned to Australia in 1915, just before the Gallipoli campaign got under way, a course of action which may well have saved his life. He volunteered again in July 1916 – this time joining the 6th Light Horse; his earlier service no doubt being a factor in his early promotion to corporal three months later on 18 September. Returning yet again to the Middle East, he became an Air Cadet on 2 February 1917 learning to fly at Aboukir, Egypt. Stedman was next ordered to England where he first joined 40 Reserve Squadron before going on to 36 Reserve Squadron. On 22 August 1917 he was sent out to join 22 Squadron in France to help that unit to fly their recently acquired Bristol Fighters over the front. In July 1918 after completing his tour of duty in France, Stedman was first sent to 30 TDS before transferring to 33 TDS in the following September. After the briefest of spells of instructing at Shoreham, he returned again to 33 TDS in October. By the summer of 1919 Stedman was with the Army of the Rhine as part of the 'occupation' force in post-Armistice Germany. On 15 June 1919 Stedman accompanied 48 Squadron to India where he stayed until November 1922 when he returned to England and a posting to Cranwell. In September 1925 he joined the RAF Armoured Car Company in Iraq. Promotion to Flight Lieutenant followed in early 1927 and by June 1928 he was back in England, first at Uxbridge before going on to the CFS in November. Finally, a brief posting to No. 5 STS preceded the resignation of his commission and his departure from the RAF on 9 July 1929. Stedman returned to farming and in the nineteen thirties was located in Kilfinny, county Limerick, Eire.

SECOND LIEUTENANT HARRY EDWARD JONES, 22 SQUADRON, ROYAL FLYING CORPS

Born in 1897 Harry was the son of William A and Lizzie Jones of Picton, Ontario, Canada. After his encounter with Werner Voss he received medical treatment in France before being returned to England. His wounds were severe and despite constant attention tragically he succumbed to a sudden haemorrhaging on 12 October 1917. Harry Edward Jones is buried at Brookwood (Military) Cemetery, Surrey. He was 20 years old.

VICTORY NO 47

11 September 1917 Camel (No. B6236) 45 Squadron 16.35 hours

Voss's second claim, later in the afternoon of the same day, was more conclusive. A 45 Squadron patrol lead by Captain Norman MacMillan MC (who later recounted his experiences in his book, *Into the Blue*) took off at 13.50 (British time). At 10,000 feet east of Langemarck, they met a mixed bunch of Fokker Dr.1 Triplanes and Albatroses. MacMillan (right) himself claimed two 'out of control', stating that one of the two was in the process of attacking a Camel. That attacker was almost certainly Voss engaging a Camel (B6236) flown by Lieutenant Oliver McMaking – an ace with 6 victories. Voss proceeded to send McMaking down to an area adjacent to St Julian before spinning down and away from MacMillan. In fact, MacMillan was forced to break off his attack on Voss because of a solitary RE8 that insinuated itself between him and the German ace and with which he nearly collided. MacMillan's claim to have sent Voss down 'out of control' was obviously a trifle exaggerated but few would begrudge him that.

LIEUTENANT
OSCAR LENNOX McMAKING,
3/1ST LINCOLNSHIRE YEOMANRY AND 45 SQUADRON, ROYAL FLYING CORPS

Oscar McMaking was the son of civil engineer Thomas and Mrs McMaking of 96 St Andrews Road, Southsea, Portsmouth. A keen horseman, Oscar first enlisted as a private soldier (No. 2527) into the Yorkshire Dragoons (Queen's Own) and landed in France with 'C' Squadron on 20 July 1915. Selected as a candidate for officer training, he was subsequently gazetted Second Lieutenant to the Lincolnshire Yeomanry on 2 February 1916 before successfully applying for transfer to the RFC. Sent to join 45 Squadron in France, he first enjoyed success flying 1½ Strutters – 4 victories – before going on to Camels – 2 victories. Oscar McMaking's remains were never found and he is commemorated on the Arras Memorial to the Missing, France.

Voss's famous Fokker Triplane (103/17) – the machine in which he fought his last fight.

VICTORY NO 48

23 September 1917 DH4(No. A7643) 57 Squadron 09.30 hours

Untypically, twelve days had elapsed since Voss's last victory. On the last morning of his life, Werner Voss was in the air countering an incursion into German territory by DH4 bombing planes sent out by 57 Squadron against targets in Hooglede. Closing in on the DH4s, Voss engaged A7643 crewed by Second Lieutenants S L J Bramley (an Australian) and J M DeLacey over Hetsas. The confrontation was brief, the DH4 going down south of Roulers on the German side of the lines.

SECOND LIEUTENANT
SAMUEL LESLIE JOHN BRAMLEY,
57 SQUADRON, ROYAL FLYING CORPS

Born in 1895, Sam was the son of Harry and Ely Bramley of 'Lester', 173 Ormond Road, Elwood, Melbourne, Australia. After serving as an infantryman with the Australian Imperial Force in the Middle East, Bramley came to Britain and was gazetted Second Lieutenant to the Special Reserve of the Royal Flying Corps on 17 March 1917. Following formal pilot training, he was awarded his 'Wings' and appointed a Flying Officer on 30 July 1917. A short leave and a six week sojourn with 52 Training Squadron preceded Bramley being sent out to join 57 Squadron in France on 1 September. His operational life lasted just over three weeks. Sam Bramley was buried in Harlebeke New British Cemetery, Belgium (Bel.140). He was aged 22.

SECOND LIEUTENANT

JOHN MATTHEW DELACEY,

18/WEST YORKSHIRE REGIMENT AND 57 SQUADRON, ROYAL FLYING CORPS

The son of Captain Robert Charles DeLacey (Royal Army Medical Corps) and Isabella DeLacey of 4 Jesmond Road, Newcastle-on-Tyne, Northumberland, John was born in 1896. He was educated privately and at Durham University. First gazetted to the 14th Reserve Battalion of the West Yorkshire Regiment on 1 January 1916, he was subsequently sent to join the 18th Battalion of his regiment in France. Following a spell in the trenches, DeLacey successfully applied for transfer to the Royal Flying Corps. John DeLacey is buried alongside his pilot in Harlebeke New British Cemetery, Belgium (Bel. 140). He was twenty-two years old.

Voss was due to go home on leave in the evening of this day and that fact in itself may well have had a bearing on his subsequent actions – untypical actions that contributed to his death. Yet another factor in the events of the afternoon might have been his 'score' – 48 victories. Five months earlier, on 29 April 1917, Manfred von Richthofen was also about to go home on leave and, coincidently, had achieved 48 victories. Determined to go home with the magical half-century, the Red Baron set out on that day looking for victims....... and found them. Not just the two he needed for the half century, but four – and all in one day! How much the ridiculous numbers-games that men indulge in were a factor in the demise of Werner Voss can only be guessed at, but certainly there were aspects in the day's happenings that suggest they played a part. That Voss and von Richthofen were in competition cannot be in doubt. Furthermore, Voss was rapidly closing the gap on the most famous aviator in Germany – if not the world. Since July, von Richthofen had achieved only four victories while in the same period Voss had gained fourteen.

On that very afternoon, Voss welcomed his father and two brothers to Marckebeke, who had arrived with the intention of accompanying him on his journey home.

Voss (left) with his brothers, Max and Otto, on the morning of 23 September 1917.

Above: 60 Squadron pilots, E Thornton, R L Chidlaw-Roberts, J B Crompton and H A Hamersley. Chidlaw-Roberts and Hamersley had fought with Voss shortly before 56 Squadron arrived on the scene.

Below right: Lieutenant A P F Rhys Davids, 56 Squadron: his fire finally brought down Voss.

Obviously he could have called it a day there and then, packed his bags and made his way to the nearest railway station. Instead, he took off on one last patrol – intent, perhaps, on bagging a further brace of 'birds'. The use of a sporting simile may seem tasteless when used in connection with the possible loss of young lives but, however regrettable, one cannot but feel that something like this was in the mind of Werner Voss.

In his anxiety to 'get it done', Voss took off alone although, shortly afterwards and purely by chance, he was joined by an Albatros Scout. Scanning the skies, he spotted a patrol of 60 Squadron SE5s which included in its ranks Captain H A Hamersley and R L Chidlaw-Roberts. Outnumbered though he was, Voss unhesitatingly swooped down upon the two RFC captains whose machines trailed in the rear of the larger formation. Hamersley saw his partner attacked by what he immediately recognised as one of the new Fokker Triplanes, and turned to help. Anticipating Hamersley's rescuing manoeuvre, Voss met him head on and severely shot up his SE5, forcing him down in a spinning dive. Now Chidlaw-Roberts, who the German ace had temporarily abandoned in favour of Hamersley, tried to intervene but the brilliant Voss, making full use of his equally brilliant Fokker, turned impossibly and sent a stream of bullets into the British machine. Under this deadly assault, Chidlaw-Roberts, like Hamersley before him, dived away. Elated, Voss followed them down, sure that if they were not already finished, he could quickly complete the despatch of both damaged planes – and, better still, all of this could be done within the full and confirming sight of German observers in the front lines! Suddenly, however, with the unexpected appearance of a patrol of 56 Squadron SE5s, the situation altered.

Voss must by now have felt himself almost omnipotent – after all he could shoot down opponents virtually at will, whilst he himself remained seemingly impervious to harm. Certainly, on this occasion he appeared to be undaunted by the odds of eleven to one and unhesitatingly – arrogantly even – threw his machine into the fray. There ensued a fight that must rank as one of the classics of air combat. The time was shortly before 18.30 – British and German timing having again converged on 16 September. As the fight started, a red-

SE5 (Number A4563) seen crashed as a prototype on 12 January 1917. Repaired and modified, it subsequently served with 56 Squadron and was flown by Lieutenant V P Cronyn in the Voss fight on 23 September 1917 when it was again badly damaged.

nosed Albatros suddenly entered the mêlée and, for a moment at least, cut the odds in half. However, the gallant interloper – thought to be Carl Menckhoff of Jasta 3, at that time an ace with 11 victories (later 39) – was soon hit and forced away and out of the fight. Voss in the meantime continued to perform wonders with his Triplane, twisting and turning and scoring hits on most of his adversaries and certainly inflicting significant damage on at least two of them – specifically the SEs flown by Lieutenants R A Maybery (B1) and V P Cronyn (A4563). But as good as he was, the sheer weight of numbers and the undoubted quality of the opposition, wore him down and eventually became too much. His British opponents included pilots of the calibre of James McCudden, Gerald Bowman, Reg Hoidge and Arthur Rhys Davids. At last the Fokker Triplane was fatally hit, its propeller juddering to a halt indicating either a strike to the engine or to the fuel lines. Rhys Davids was nearest and best placed to administer the *coup de grâce* and did so with despatch. His fire obviously hit the hapless Voss as his unpowered machine suddenly fell, literally out of any sort of control and crashed unchecked into the ground at Plum Farm, just north of Frezenburg and its infamous ridge. British troops buried the German ace near to where he fell but the grave was soon lost in the incessant fighting that continued to rage over the area. Werner Voss had, indeed, come very close to emulating von Richthofen's feat of four victories on the day of his triumphant departure for Germany. He had badly damaged four British aircraft – Hamersley had to force-land at 29 Squadron's base and whilst Chidlaw-Roberts did actually make it back to his home field, his machine was in need of extensive repair. Maybery and Cronyn also got home – just; but both knew that they had been in a monumental scrap and the state of their shattered machines testified to that. Indeed, Cronyn's, Maybery's and Hamersley's machines were all returned to No. 1 AD and taken off their Squadrons' strength. All who took part in Voss's last stand were unstinting in their admiration of his raw courage and the sheer brilliance of his flying.

CHAPTER 4

OBERLEUTNANT LOTHAR VON RICHTHOFEN

Almost two and a half years younger than his famous brother Manfred, Lothar Siegfried von Richthofen was born in Breslau on 27 September 1894. Unlike his elder brother who had followed his father into the Army as a cadet at the tender age of eleven, Lothar showed no particular inclination towards a military career. The Gods of War, however, had other ideas and would soon recruit not only Lothar but a whole generation into their ranks! By the time of the outbreak of war in August 1914, Lothar was serving in the Imperial German Army with the 4th Dragoon Regiment - 'Von Bredow's Own'.

Lothar von Richthofen, Jasta 11.

The brothers kept in constant touch with each other and it surprised no one in the family when Lothar followed Manfred into the Air Service in 1915. Treading in his brother's footsteps, Lothar first became an observer and saw action with Kampstaffel 23 over the Somme front and during the Verdun offensive. Next he trained as a pilot and no doubt again inspired by his brother's example, requested service with a fighter unit. Normally, the German system would, at this stage of his development, have required Lothar to be posted back to his former, or some other two-seater unit to gain further experience before going on to a Jastaschule. But by now, the rising star of the German Air Service, Manfred von Richthofen, was in command of his own Jagdstaffel (Jasta 11) and so had no difficulty in arranging for his brother to join him. Lothar arrived on 10 March 1917, with little time to get attuned to the demands of combat flying before the onset of what was to become known as 'Bloody April', the worst of the fifty-two months of the Great War for his British opponents.

As is often the case between brothers, the two von Richthofens had entirely differing

Lothar with his famous brother, Manfred.

temperaments. Manfred, in manner and in posture, was the quintessential Prussian aristocrat, reserved and rigid but with the patience and cunning of the instinctive hunter. He would attack only from a position of advantage, rarely taking unnecessary risks and if thwarted, maintained a philosophy of 'another day, another opportunity'. Lothar, on the other hand, was by nature hotly impulsive and aggressive, keen to scrap and paying little heed to the strategic or tactical aspect of a situation before charging in, 'fangs out, hair on fire'! After observing Lothar's style with its lack of verve and finesse, Manfred dubbed his brother 'Butcher' – not the most flattering of sobriquets, even for one whose sole *raison d'être* was killing the enemy. Lothar's hot-headedness was undoubtedly a contributory factor in the number of wounds and injuries he received but seemed not to detract from his effectiveness as a scout pilot – he achieved a remarkable 40 victories in just 77 days of actual combat flying. And, paradoxically, unlike his careful and methodical brother, he survived the war.

VICTORY NO 1

28 March 1917 FE2b (No. 7715) 25 Squadron 17.15 hours

Lothar learnt his trade quickly under the expert tutelage of his brother - just as Manfred himself had learnt from Oswald Boelcke. His first victory was over a pilot with even less experience than he, although Lothar did not know that when he closed in on a 25 Squadron FE2b. The RFC machine was part of a patrol that had taken off at 14.30 hours to fly a line from La Bassée to Arras, gathering intelligence as they went. The Allies were building up for the oncoming Arras offensive and the General Staff needed constant up-dates on the dispositions of the opposing German Army. The FEs were nearing the end of their patrol and on their way back to the lines when they were engaged by Jasta 11. Lothar's attack forced the RFC machine down behind the German lines east of Curency, near Lens. The pilot, Second Lieutenant N L Knight was wounded and taken prisoner, the observer, Second Lieutenant A G Severs, was killed.

SECOND LIEUTENANT

NORMAN LESLIE KNIGHT,

25 SQUADRON, ROYAL FLYING CORPS

The son of Mr and Mrs C S Knight of 'Wingfield House', Banstead, Surrey, Norman was born in 1898. He was educated at Felsted School, Essex (1911-1915) where he excelled at sports, representing the school at cricket, football, hockey and gymnastics. After leaving school, he entered the offices of an insurance broker in the City of London. However, as soon as he reached the appropriate age, he volunteered for service in the Royal Flying Corps, receiving a commission in the Special Reserve on 8 July 1916, the day his flying training began. His training completed, he was appointed a Flying Officer on 21 October 1916 but because of his comparative youth, he was posted to a series of Home Establishment squadrons in the United Kingdom. During the late summer of 1916, Knight even visited his old school, Felsted, in a Maurice Farman training aircraft, probably without official permission. His landing on the school's playing fields caused great excitement amongst the boys who 'wrapped themselves around the machine' in their dozens! So great was Knight's difficulty in manoeuvring the aircraft into a suitable position for take-off that he 'fouled the shrubbery with consequent damage to both the shrubbery and the machine!' Despite these problems and to his great relief, he was eventually able to take off, the deep roar of his engine almost drowned by the falsetto cheering of the excited pupils. At last, on 22 March 1917 - still only eighteen and a half years old - he got his wish and joined 25 Squadron at the front. A mere five days later, he met the equally 'green' and inexperienced Lothar von Richthofen but the latter's superior aircraft and fire-power was the difference between defeat and victory. Slightly wounded and badly shaken up following the forced landing, Knight was led away into captivity. He was finally repatriated on 14 December 1918, serving in the Royal Air Force for another six months before being put on the Unemployed List on 31 May 1919. Soon after this, Norman Knight returned to take up his interrupted career as an insurance broker and underwriter at 68 Fenchurch Street in the City of London.

Norman Knight makes a spectacular return to his old school, Felsted!

SECOND LIEUTENANT

ALFRED GEORGE SEVERS,

15/MIDDLESEX REGIMENT AND 25 SQUADRON, ROYAL FLYING CORPS

Born on 5 July 1893, Alfred was the son of Frederick and Frederica Severs of 11 Vincent Road, Croydon. He received his education at Whitgift School, Croydon, from where he passed the necesssary examinations to obtain a position in the Civil Service (National Insurance Department). Alfred joined the Civil Service Cadets in 1912, eventually going on to join the Inns of Court OTC on 7 June 1915 (No. 4/2/4103) from where he was gazetted Second Lieutenant to the 15th Battalion, Middlesex Regiment on 10 September 1915. Transfer to the Royal Flying Corps followed and, after training, he was sent to France as a probationary observer in December 1916. Severs' parents were advised by the Red Cross that their son had been buried by the German Air Service in Lens Cemetery but, sadly, his grave was lost in the subsequent fighting in the area and so he is commemorated on the Arras Memorial to the Missing, France. He was twenty-three years old.

VICTORY NO 2

11 April 1917 Bristol F2a (No. A3323) 48 Squadron 09.15 hours

The Battle of Arras was two days old when Lothar gained his second and third victories. The first of the day was against a new type of aeroplane – the Bristol F2a two-seater – brought out from England by 48 Squadron. The techniques initially used by the Bristol Fighter crews were faulty and inappropriate; mistakenly, it was first thought that the 'Brisfits' would be most effective if used in groups or phalanxes. In fact, lessons learnt the hard way showed that they were best used like single-seater scout planes – single seaters with a rear gunner! In the meantime, however, the lessons had still to be learnt. Six days earlier, 48 Squadron had lost four Bristol Fighters (including the senior Flight Commander, Captain William Leefe Robinson VC) to Jasta 11 and now on this day these particular newcomers, also patrolling the front in tight formation, were attacked and badly mauled by adroitly flown Albatros scouts. Three more Bristol F2as fell to the expertise of Jasta 11 – one to Lothar von Richthofen (which crashed at 09.15 north of Fresnes), a second to Kurt Wolff (his 9th victory) and the third to Emil Schäfer (his 15th victory).

SECOND LIEUTENANT

GEORGE NORMAN BROCKHURST,

48 SQUADRON, ROYAL FLYING CORPS

The son of Mr and Mrs Brockhurst of 43 Coniston Road, Muswell Hill, London N 10, George worked in the City of London prior to his acceptance into the Inns of Court OTC on 8 November 1915 (No. 6/3/7250). From the OTC, he was granted his expressed preference for service with the Royal Flying Corps, being gazetted Second Lieutenant to the General List on 8 August 1916 with an immediate transfer on that day to the Corps of his choice. Pilot training followed and he was next appointed a Flying Officer on 18 December 1916. After further training on the new Bristol Fighter, Brockhurst accompanied 48 Squadron – the first unit to fly the F2a – to Flez in France on 8 March 1917. He was wounded and taken prisoner after the fight with Lothar von Richthofen and remained in captivity until his repatriation on the last day of 1918. Shortly afterwards, Brockhurst exchanged his flying helmet for a bowler hat and returned to his position with Messrs Singleton, Benda and Company, 27 London Wall in the City of London.

SECOND LIEUTENANT

CECIL BLOCKLEY BOUGHTON,

10/WELSH REGIMENT AND 48 SQUADRON, ROYAL FLYING CORPS

The son of garage proprietor W A and Mrs Boughton of Cathedral Road, Cardiff, Cecil was born in August 1891. He was educated at Bradfield College (1906-1908) before going on to be an Exhibitioner at King's College, London in 1908. After completing his education, Boughton joined his father's garage business in Cardiff. When war came, he immediately volunteered and on 7 December 1914 was gazetted Second Lieutenant to the 10th Battalion (1st Rhondda) of the Welsh Regiment. After a period of service in England, Boughton's application to join the RFC was approved and on 15 July 1916 he was sent to train as an observer, eventually being selected for 48 Squadron with their new Bristol F2as. His formal appointment as a Flying Officer (Observer) came through on 10 April 1917, the day before he was shot down by Lothar von Richthofen and taken into captivity. Cecil Boughton was repatriated on 31 December 1918, eventually returning to civilian life and the automobile business in his native Cardiff.

VICTORY NO 3

11 April 1917 RE8 (A4190) 59 Squadron 12.35 hours

Three hours after his first victory of the day, Lothar gained a second. He recorded the 'type' as a Sopwith two-seater and as the machine fell into the British lines north-east of Fampoux at 12.35, the description remained unaltered in the German records. However, as there were no Sopwith two-seaters lost at that time of day, or, indeed, during the whole of the day, the description was obviously inappropriate. As most of the British two-seater losses on this day were 'BE2s', a type well known to the Germans and therefore readily identifiable by von Richthofen, it seems probable that his 'Sopwith' was, in fact, an 'RE8' – a type still comparatively new to the battle front. A 59 Squadron machine (No.A4190) which had taken off earlier at 12.15, was lost at about this time. Other possibilities are ruled out by timing or location.

LIEUTENANT

GEORGE TOD MORRIS,

1/1ST AYRSHIRE BATTERY, ROYAL HORSE ARTILLERY (TF) AND 59 SQUADRON, ROYAL FLYING CORPS

The youngest son of architect James Archibald Morris ARSA and Elizabeth Morris of Savoy Croft, Ayrshire, George was born on 7 March 1894. He was educated at Bilton Grange and at Haileybury (1908-1911) where he was a member of the OTC. After leaving school he obtained a position at the head

office of James Finlay & Company, Glasgow. A keen volunteer, he obtained a commission in the Ayrshire Battery of the Royal Horse Artillery (Territorial Force) on 7 March 1913, passing courses to qualify as an instructor in signalling, telephoning, map reading and despatch riding. When the war came, his Battery was mobilised and after service in the UK was eventually sent to Egypt in February 1916, becoming attached to the ANZAC Mounted Division. After a small action in which the Battery took a number of casualties, he led out a party of five volunteers some miles into the desert and, under heavy shell fire and sniping from the Turks, they buried their fallen comrades. He took part in the Battle of Romani and in the operations leading up to the advance on Palestine before transferring to the RFC on 10 August 1916. His pilot training completed, he was awarded his Wings on 16 December 1916, returning to England in the February following. After a short leave at home in Scotland, he was sent to join 59 Squadron in France on 21 March 1917. His family was told that he had been buried in a shell hole near to where he fell between Gavrelle and Ballieul. After the war, the graves of Morris and his observer, James Souter, were identified by the Imperial War Graves Commission and re-located to the Orchard Dump Cemetery, Arleux-en-Gohelle, France (Fr. 777). He was twenty-three years old at the time of his death.

LIEUTENANT
JAMES MITCHELL SOUTER,
133/CANADIAN INFANTRY AND 59 SQUADRON, ROYAL FLYING CORPS

Born on 28 March 1894, James was the son of James E and Mary E Souter of 173 East Avenue North, Hamilton, Ontario, Canada. He was educated at Hamilton Public and High Schools before attending an applied science course at the University of Toronto where he was also a member of the Canadian OTC in the 13th Militia Regiment. Posted in March 1916 to the 133rd Battalion, he proceeded overseas in October 1916. Secondment to the RFC followed on 16 February 1917 and after the completion of his training, Souter was transferred to 57 Squadron on 28 March 1917. James Souter is buried in Orchard Dump Cemetery, Arleux-en-Gohelle, France (Fr. 777). He was aged 23.

VICTORY NO 4
13 April 1917 RE8 (A3126) 59 Squadron 08.55 hours

Lothar von Richthofen was quick to repeat his double victory of two days earlier when, on this Friday the 13th, he shot down two of six 59 Squadron RE8s that fell in minutes under the onslaught of Jasta 11. Arrangements to provide fighter cover for the 59 Squadron photo-reconnaissance sortie over an area near to Douai, the home of Manfred von Richthofen's Jasta 11, had not for the first time been thwarted. These were days before wireless communication between aircraft and because of cloud, poor visibility and other factors, it was often very difficult to rendezvous with aircraft that had taken off from other airfields many miles away. Probably because they anticipated problems with the escort arrangements, 59 Squadron had sent out four RE8s to cover the two who would be doing the actual photography. After losing three of their number only a week before, it was hardly surprising that they would be cautious. However, despite these precautions, the fact remained that an RE8 was no match for an Albatros. Jasta 11, led by Manfred von Richthofen, attacked the formation of six RE8s shortly before 09.00 hours, accounting for five of them within moments – the sixth going down under the guns of a Jasta 4 pilot. Lothar first picked out A3126, which he despatched to the ground at Pelves.

CAPTAIN
GEORGE BAILEY HODGSON,
MID, ROYAL GARRISON ARTILLERY AND 59 SQUADRON, ROYAL FLYING CORPS

Born on 3 June 1895, George Hodgson was the son of hardware factor and bicycle manufacturer John Duncan and Mrs Hodgson of 'Linton Villa', Grainger Park, Newcastle-on-Tyne. Hodgson volunteered immediately upon the outbreak of war and was gazetted Second Lieutenant to the Royal Garrison Artillery on 1 October 1914. He served as a gunner on the Western Front until September 1916 although he did return briefly to 'take his ticket', being awarded the Aviators Certificate (No. 1483) of the Royal Aero Club on 29 July 1915. In September 1916 he was allowed at last to join the RFC; then going on to complete his formal pilot training. Hodgson's earlier good work with the Garrison Artillery at the front was formally acknowledged by a Mention in Despatches, the announcement of which appeared in the *London Gazette* of 1 January 1917. He was sent to join 59 Squadron in France on 10 January 1917 and lasted just three months before falling under the guns of Lothar von Richthofen. Strangely, the date of his death is variously reported as 13 April 1917, 23 April 1917 and 10 May 1917 but what is certain is that his body was never recovered and he is therefore commemorated on the Arras Memorial to the Missing, France. He was aged twenty-two.

LIEUTENANT
CHARLES HERBERT MORRIS,
13/ROYAL WELSH FUSILIERS AND 59 SQUADRON, ROYAL FLYING CORPS

One of the three sons of William and Jane Charlotte Morris of 'Severn Villa', Welshpool, Montgomeryshire, Charles was born in 1891. He was educated at Welshpool County School and, with a view to taking Holy Orders, pursued further studies at Lampeter College where he had been for two years when war broke out. Charles and his life-long friend, Ithel Davies (who would also be killed in the war) enlisted together as private soldiers in the 13th (North Wales 'Pals') Battalion of the Royal Welsh Fusiliers. After training in Rhyl, his maturity and intelligence apparent, he was picked out as officer material and gazetted Second Lieutenant to his own battalion on 14 November 1914. In November 1915, he was transferred to the

16th Battalion of his regiment, accompanying it to France during the following month. Charles saw much action at the front and took part in the capture of Mametz Wood, one of only three of the battalion's officers who emerged physically unscathed from that terrible battle. Having had his fill of trench life, Morris applied for transfer to the RFC; an ambition he achieved in December 1916. Successfully completing his observer training, Morris was sent out to join 59 Squadron as a probationary on 25 February 1917. Charles was the first of two of the three Morris boys to fall on the Western Front (brother John was killed serving with the Canadian Cavalry in August 1918). His body was never recovered and so he is commemorated on the Arras Memorial to the Missing, France. He was twenty-five years old.

VICTORY NO 5

13 April 1917 RE8 (No. A4191) 59 Squadron 08.56 hours

Lothar turned from his attack on A3126 and, after avoiding a collision with both brother Manfred and Kurt Wolff, each of whom were as busy as he amongst the straitened 59 Squadron RE8s, looked around for another victim. He fastened onto a machine crewed by an Australian and a Canadian, Lieutenants Horne and Chalk (A4191). The unequal contest was soon over with the RE8 crashing into the ground north of Biache. Still there was no sign of the overdue RFC covering escort and the triumphant Jasta 11 pilots were able to return to their base to celebrate their victories without molestation or challenge.

SECOND LIEUTENANT HERBERT GEORGE MACMILLAN HORNE, 19/LONDON REGIMENT (TF) AND 59 SQUADRON, ROYAL FLYING CORPS

Born on 24 January 1898, Horne's parents were both dead by the time of the outbreak of the Great War, his next of kin being his father's brother, Lieutenant Colonel G Horne of Queen's Parade, Clifton Hall, Melbourne, Australia and his mother's brother, Mr D MacMillan of Kingston Street, Caulfield, Melbourne. Coming to England, Horne joined the Inns of Court OTC (No.4/3/5111) on 26 July 1915 and was gazetted Second Lieutenant to the 19th Battalion of the County of London (St Pancras) Regiment (TF) on 11 November 1915. Subsequently transferring to the Royal Flying Corps, he was sent out to join 59 Squadron in France on 29 January 1917. Herbert Horne's body was never recovered and he is commemorated on the Arras Memorial to the Missing, France. He was still only nineteen years old.

LIEUTENANT WILLIAM JOSEPH CHALK, MANITOBA REGIMENT AND 59 SQUADRON, ROYAL FLYING CORPS

The son of James and Ann Chalk of 135 Saungside Street, Winnipeg, Manitoba, Canada, William was born in 1890. He received his education locally in Winnipeg and at the University of Manitoba, where he studied law. After qualifying, he practised as a barrister with a Winnipeg legal firm and, in his spare time, joined the Militia (100th Battalion, Grenadiers). In November 1915, Chalk was gazetted Second Lieutenant to the Manitoba Regiment. Some ten months later on 13 September 1916, he embarked for England, requesting a transfer to the RFC as he did so. Chalk satisfactorily completed his observer training before being sent out to 59 Squadron as a probationary on 26 March 1917. Less than three weeks later he was dead. His remains were never found and hence he is commemorated on the Arras Memorial to the Missing, France. He was aged 27.

VICTORY NO 6

14 April 1917 Nieuport XXIII (No.A6772) 60 Squadron 09.20 hours

Nieuport Scouts of 60 Squadron took off at 08.30 hours to fly an Offensive Patrol over the area above Douai – a dangerous assignment as this was Jasta 11's 'backyard'. The patrol was led by a 'devil may care' Australian, Captain Alan Binnie MC, never a man to hide from trouble! Crossing the front, the RFC men spotted a German two-seater observing railway traffic north-west of Lens. Three of the Nieuports broke away from the rest to engage the German machine. Their initial attack inflicted slight damage on the two-seater and wounded the observer but as they closed for the kill, the instantly-recognisable Jasta 11 Albatroses arrived, giving the 60 Squadron men more immediately pressing problems. Lothar von Richthofen went for the leader, his machine-gun fire shattering the Australian's left arm as he reached up to his wing-mounted Lewis gun. Blood splattered the instrument panel and to make matters worse, the machine caught fire. Binnie afterwards had a vague recollection of extinguishing the flames as he glided down and just before he finally lost consciousness – his Nieuport spinning away out of control as a consequence. Remarkably, when he came to he found himself surrounded by the wreck of his machine and by German soldiers, as surprised as he was that he was alive! Binnie was not alone in his misfortune. Manfred von Richthofen, Kurt Wolff and Sebastian Festner had each accounted for Nieuports without reply. Because of the loss of his arm, Binnie was repatriated early via the Red Cross, arriving back in England on 7 January 1918. During his debriefing, he reported what he could recall of the events of the day: *'I left the aerodrome at Filescamp in charge of an OP at about 08.00. At about 08.30, near Roclincourt, I saw three Albatros Scouts some 2,000 feet below me, my patrol being at 10,500 feet. I dived on the leader and saw him go down in a vertical nose-dive after ½ a drum. Then I broke off to reform, since as they were all new pilots I knew they would be scattered. I could only see two and they were flying into Hunland towards Lens, so I made after them to try to get them back before they were engaged with a mob of machines I had noticed previously over Lens. When I overtook the first he was in the middle of a batch of hostile aircraft and one comfortably sitting on his tail, and this one I was able to give a ½ a drum from 20 yards. He immediately went into a spinning nose-dive. I then began to change the drum, at the same time trying to keep any HA from getting on my tail. Had just finished when I got an explosive bullet through the left arm from somewhere underneath. Since I couldn't see the HA, I was now out of action and made for the lines but fainted at 3 to 4,000 feet somewhere over Lens. When I came to I was on a stretcher with my wound bound up, lying beside my machine which was a total wreck, and about 500 Huns all round me. I learned later the other two were both killed'.* Captain Binnie also recalled having nothing to eat for seven days while in the Douai hospital and that the amputation of his arm had followed the onset of gangrene.

CAPTAIN
ALAN BINNIE,
MC, 60 SQUADRON, ROYAL FLYING CORPS

Born on 22 August 1898; Alan was the son of Mr and Mrs Binnie of Quikindi, New South Wales, Australia. Binnie fought with the 29th Division in Gallipoli, before learning to fly at a school in England, being awarded the Aviators Certificate (No. 6235) of the Royal Aero Club on 27 November 1916. An extremely brave and resourceful pilot, he quickly made a name for himself with the elite 60 Squadron. He was awarded a Military Cross for his exploits before he was shot down and captured, the announcement of the award being made while he was still receiving medical treatment in a German military hospital – *London Gazette* 26 May 1917, Page 5179: *'For conspicuous gallantry and devotion to duty. He came down to 50 feet and attacked a hostile kite balloon on the ground. He has on three previous occasions shot down and destroyed three enemy machines'.* After Binnie regained consciousness in 'a little park in Lens', he was driven straight to a military hospital where, subsequently, his left arm was amputated at the shoulder. He remained in captivity until early in 1918 when he was exchanged for an equally badly injured German soldier. Upon arrival in England, he was sent to Lady Caernavon's Hospital at 48 Bayswater Road, London. Before long, however, the seemingly indestructible Alan Binnie was agitating for a return to duty. After a refresher course at the Central Flying School in November 1918 and despite the loss of his left arm, he was soon flying again. Furthermore, the indomitable Binnie served again in the Second World War, this time with the Royal Australian Air Force, first in the Western Desert as adjutant with 3 RAAF Squadron, before then going on to New Guinea, where he met his death in the crash of a 60 Squadron (RAAF) aircraft on 25 March 1945. Alan Binnie was forty-six years old.

Binnie with 3 RAAF in WWII (above) and (right) enjoying an alfresco lunch in the Western Desert during WWII. *(via R Guest)*

VICTORY NO 7

14 April 1917 Spad VII (No. A6683) 19 Squadron 18.23 hours

Another 'double' victory was achieved in the early evening of this spring day. In the fading light, Jasta 11 engaged a flight of Spads put up by 19 Squadron to patrol a line through Ballieul-Sir-Berthoult-Vitry-Sains-Bullecourt. Both Kurt Wolff and Lothar von Richthofen made claims following this fight. Wolff was successful only after a tremendous battle, his opponent almost besting him before, finally, he got behind the Briton and sent him down east of Bailleul. Lothar was luckier; quickly and without difficulty he despatched his Spad – shot-up with the pilot wounded – to crash-land at Le Hameau airfield, the machine wrecked beyond repair.

LIEUTENANT JOHN WATSON BAKER, 11/EAST SURREY REGIMENT AND 19 SQUADRON, ROYAL FLYING CORPS

Born on 17 August 1894, John was the son of Mr and Mrs J F Baker of 'Myrtlefield', Radcliffe Road, Croydon. After completing his education at Charterhouse, he secured a position as a clerk and as an apprentice produce broker in the London office of the National Bank of India. Volunteering immediately the war broke out, he was eventually gazetted Second Lieutenant to the 11th Battalion of the East Surrey Regiment on 2 November 1914. He was held back in the Regimental Training Depot in England but after learning to fly at his own expense and being awarded the Aviators Certificate (No. 4200) of the Royal Aero Club on 20 September 1916, he was accepted into the RFC. Completing his formal training, he was next sent to join 19 Squadron in France on 19 October 1916. Wounded in the fight with Lothar von Richthofen, Watson returned to England to recuperate and after recovering, served with various Home Defence units before finally leaving the service on 4 February 1919. John Watson Baker died in Marseilles, France on 2 August 1947, just 15 days short of the anniversary of his 53rd birthday.

VICTORY NO 8

16 April 1917 Nieuport Scout XVII (No. B1501) 60 Squadron 10.30

60 Squadron took off at 8.05 hours (British time was again one hour behind German time) on an Offensive Patrol in the direction of Vitry. Jasta 11 received warning of the British incursion and took off to intercept. The two sides met and in a running fight between Biache and Roeux, Lothar von Richthofen, Wolff and Festner each claimed one of the Nieuports. A fourth Nieuport was badly mauled but managed to get home, the wounded pilot dying the following day. In these circumstances, it is difficult to

attribute with absolute certainty which of the Nieuports Lothar actually shot down but the indications are that it was B1501, flown by Second Lieutenant D N Robertson, which came down south of Roeux into the front lines alongside the River Scarfe.

SECOND LIEUTENANT

DAVID NORMAN ROBERTSON,

60 SQUADRON, ROYAL FLYING CORPS

The son of David and Mary C Steel Robertson of 'Craigard', 343 Albert Drive, Pollockshields, Glasgow, David was born in 1893. He gained the Aviators Certificate (No. 2460) of the Royal Aero Club on 12 February 1916. Robertson was gazetted Second Lieutenant to the Special List, RFC on 1 August 1916 before going on to formal training and eventual appointment as a Flying Officer on 22 October 1916. Following a brief period of leave, he was sent out as a scout pilot to 60 Squadron in early 1917. David Robertson's remains were never recovered and he is commemorated on the Arras Memorial to the Missing, France. He was twenty-three.

VICTORY NO 9

21 April 1917 Nieuport Scout XVII (No. B1568) 29 Squadron 17.28

A six-strong patrol of Nieuports from 29 Squadron, led by Captain E F Elderton, crossed the lines in the late afternoon. Jasta 11 happened to be in the vicinity hunting for patrolling Corps aircraft but, indiscriminate as they were in their choice of opponent, they spotted the scout planes and pounced. Three of the six Nieuports fell, one each to Wolff, Schäfer and Lothar von Richthofen. Wolff's victim came down on the German side, the other two fell in the trench lines. As one would expect, Wolff and Schäfer claimed Nieuports in this action but, oddly, Lothar's claim does not specify a type. This has led to some confusion in the identification of his victim but after examining other possibilities, including three 16 Squadron BEs that came down on this day, the probability remains that it was, indeed, the Nieuport flown by Second Lieutenant A B Morgan that Lothar von Richthofen sent down for his ninth victory.

SECOND LIEUTENANT

ALAN BERTRAM MORGAN,

29 SQUADRON, ROYAL FLYING CORPS

Born in 1896, Alan was the son of John and Elizabeth A Morgan of 18 Station Terrace, Caerphilly, Cardiff. Joining the RFC on 16 August 1916, he went through the usual training before being appointed a Flying Officer on 20 January 1917, eventually being sent to join 29 Squadron on 4 April 1917, just seventeen days before he was shot down by Lothar von Richthofen. Alan Bertram Morgan died whilst a prisoner in German hands on 22 April 1917 and is buried in Douai Communal Cemetery, France. He was twenty years old.

VICTORY NO 10

23 April 1917 BE2g (No. A2876) 16 Squadron 12.10 hours

16 Squadron sent out two BE2s at 09.25 and 09.45 hours on this St George's Day, the first day of the second Battle of the Scarpe. The Staff urgently needed information on the current German dispositions and the two 16 Squadron machines were charged with the responsibility of taking the requisite photographs. Perhaps it was thought that if they were sent out singly, and without escort, they would slip through unseen and without detection. Predictably however, the German Air Service was up in force and the two BEs could not have been unluckier in meeting, as they did, the two von Richthofen brothers. Manfred claimed one at 12.05 hours which fell into the German lines at Mericourt. Lothar timed his claim five minutes later, the BE2g going down behind the British lines north of Vimy. The pilot, Second Lieutenant C M Crow, was wounded in the head and chest and died immediately. Happily but perhaps surprisingly, the observer Second Lieutenant E T Turner, although wounded, survived the crash.

SECOND LIEUTENANT

CHARLES MAURICE CROW,

16 SQUADRON, ROYAL FLYING CORPS

Born in 1896, Charles was the third and youngest son of Frederick Lewis Crow and Mary Crow of Shelwood Manor, Leigh, Surrey. Like his father and brothers, he was educated at Tonbridge School (1911-1914). Charles intended becoming a Chartered Surveyor and so entered his father's offices in Dorking upon leaving school. His elder brother had been crippled in a riding accident and so the second son, Percy, a brilliant scholar at Tonbridge and now a master at Epsom College, was the sole representative of the family in the Armed Services during the early days of the war. In fact, Percy Crow went on to win both the DSO and the MC with the Royal Field Artillery. Charles was gazetted Second Lieutenant to the RFC on 18 March 1916 before going on to be awarded the Aviators Certificate (No.3097) of the Royal Aero Club on 16 June 1916. Following formal training, he was awarded his 'Wings' and sent out first to 29 Squadron in August 1916. From 29 Squadron he was posted 10 Squadron before, just four days prior to his death, he was sent to join 16 Squadron. In the nine months he had been at the front, he had flown in support of the great land battles of Vimy Ridge, the Scarpe and Arras. In writing

to his mother, his commanding officer stated that had he lived, he would have been recommended for the Military Cross. His CO also said that their son had been on photographic work with another machine in attendance when they were approached by ten enemy fast scouts, five of which attacked and brought down each machine. Lieutenant Crow received two wounds in the chest and head and he was rendered unconscious at once. His observer, who had since made a good recovery, was also hit in three places but succeeded in taking control of the machine until near the ground when he fainted. Charles Crow is buried in Bruay Communal Cemetery Extension (Fr.32). He was twenty years old.

SECOND LIEUTENANT
EUSTACE THOMAS TURNER,
ROYAL ENGINEERS AND 16 SQUADRON, ROYAL FLYING CORPS

The son of Mr and Mrs Eustace Turner of 'Higher House', Mottram St Andrews, Prestbury, Cheshire, Tom Turner was born in 1895. He was educated at Manchester Grammar School (1906-1913) before taking up a position with the paper manufacturing company, J Wrigley and Sons, Bridgehall Mills, Bury, Lancashire. In March 1915, Tom enlisted as a sapper (No.36326) into the Royal Engineers (Signal Section). After training, he was promoted to Corporal and sent to France for the first time in September 1915. An obvious candidate for advancement, he was gazetted as a Second Lieutenant to the Royal Engineers on 9 April 1916. Following further service with the Engineers, Turner applied for a transfer to the Royal Flying Corps. After observer training, he was sent as a probationary to 16 Squadron on 22 April 1917 – only the day before he was shot down by Lothar von Richthofen. The wounds he received precluded further active service and he spent the rest of the war in a variety of jobs with the Department of Aircraft Production and in the Ministry of Munitions.

On the evening of 25 April 1917, Jasta 11 attacked a formation of FE2bs from 25 Squadron. As Lothar closed in on his intended victim, he saw the British observer/gunner calmly, deliberately and most effectively, returning his fire. The gunner, 2AM George Pawley, flying with Second Lieutenant Charles V Darnell in A837, hit the Albatros severing a main control wire. Lothar was unable to turn away quickly for fear of losing his top wing and, worryingly, the FE crew continued to concentrate their attention (and their machine gun) on him. Seeing his predicament Karl Schäfer leapt to the rescue, his machine guns raking Darnell's FE, sending it crashing down to flaming destruction near to Bailleul for his twenty-third victory. Lothar was now able to ease himself away from the fight and make his way, gingerly, to his home field – a lucky man!

VICTORY NO 11
26 April 1917 BE2c (No. 2826) 16 Squadron 18.30 hours

16 Squadron were again busy over the front, some of their BEs taking off in the late afternoon. Despite receiving cover from 43 Squadron Sopwith 1½ Strutters who gallantly did their best to intervene, the Corps machines were attacked by Jasta 11 with the usual deadly effect. Lothar von Richthofen and Karl Allmenröder each claimed a 16 Squadron machine with Lothar's victim, who had been engaged on Artillery Observation, going down in flames to crash south-east of Vimy Ridge on the German side of the lines. Allmenröder's BE, which had been airborne since mid-afternoon, crash-landed inside British lines, its pilot wounded. Kurt Wolff also added to Jasta 11's 'score' with another BE from 5 Squadron being shot down during the afternoon.

SECOND LIEUTENANT

WILLIAM SAMUEL SPENCE,

17/ROYAL SCOTS AND 16 SQUADRON, ROYAL FLYING CORPS

The younger son of William and Jesse Spence of 21 Bellevue Road, Edinburgh, Bill was born in Monifeith, near Dundee, on 29 July 1894. He received his education at Harris Academy, Dundee, before taking up a position in the head office of the Buttercup Dairy Company in Leith. A keen pre-war volunteer, he joined the Royal Army Medical Corps (Territorial Force) in 1912 and was mobilized with his unit immediately upon the outbreak of war in August 1914. Selected for officer training, he was gazetted as a Second Lieutenant into the 17th Battalion, The Royal Scots Regiment on 15 May 1915. The 17th Royal Scots, raised on the instigation of Lord Rosebery, was a 'Bantam' Battalion, one of the units initiated to accommodate the many men who, despite being below the minimum height of 5 foot 3 inches, still wished to serve. Spence accompanied his battalion to France on 31 January 1916, serving in the trenches just south of Armentières. An application to transfer to the RFC was approved in July 1916. Following training, he was awarded his 'Wings' and sent out to join 16 Squadron in France. In a letter to his parents, a Sergeant Pilot in his Squadron wrote, *'He had been scouting over the enemy lines and was returning when he was attacked by three enemy machines. You will be proud to know that your son put up a brave fight to the last but was finally beaten by the three of them'.* William Samuel Spence is buried in Orchard Dump Cemetery, Arleux-en-Gohelle, France (Fr.777). He was twenty-two years old.

LIEUTENANT

WILLIAM ARCHIBALD CAMPBELL,

MANITOBA REGIMENT AND 16 SQUADRON, ROYAL FLYING CORPS

Born in 1896 in Montreal, Canada, Bill received his early education in Trenton, Ontario, before going on to attend University School, Victoria, British Columbia. He was reading law when, along with many other of his fellow students, he enlisted as a private soldier into the 225th Battalion, Canadian Expeditionary Force. Very soon after being commissioned on 26 September 1916, he was seconded to the RFC for training as an observer. His training completed, he was sent to France on 12 April 1917, going on to help reinforce a depleted 16 Squadron two days later. William Archibald Campbell lasted just twelve days at the front and now lies buried alongside his pilot in Orchard Dump Cemetery, Arleux-en-Gohelle, France (Fr. 777). He was twenty years old.

VICTORY NO 12

27 April 1917 FE2b (No. 4850) 11 Squadron 20.15 hours

11 Squadron mounted a Line Patrol from their base at Izel le Hameau, taking off at 17.20 hours. Jasta 11 met them on the German side south-west of Vitry. Although the FEs later claimed one German scout down in flames and another out of control, in fact Jasta 11 suffered no pilot losses. Lothar brought down his victims, Second Lieutenant J A Cairns and AM1 F G Perry, to crash near to Fresnes. Five minutes later, Kurt Wolff forced another FE to land inside the British lines south of Gavrelle. In his debriefing after his return from captivity at the end of the war, Cairns reported that his and the two other machines in the formation had been attacked by ten machines of the Richthofen squadron. His FE had been hit in the petrol tank and, not surprisingly, burst into flames. As they neared the ground, Cairns skilfully stalled the 'Pusher' at the last possible moment, thus saving them from a severe impact. Neither man was wounded, although the FE was wrecked. Cairns said goodbye to Perry in Douai as they were led away to different camps.

SECOND LIEUTENANT JOHN ARTHUR CAIRNS, 9/ARGYLL AND SUTHERLAND HIGHLANDERS AND 11 SQUADRON, ROYAL FLYING CORPS

The son of Mr and Mrs John Cairns of 'Woodlands', 37 Cator Road, Sydenham, SE London, John junior was born in 1892. His father and uncle being Scots, it was not surprising that he should seek to be gazetted to a Scottish regiment – his hope was realised on 11 November 1915 when he was commissioned into the Argyll and Sutherland Highlanders. Soon afterwards, however, Cairns successfully sought transfer to the RFC and embarked upon a course of pilot training. After being awarded his 'Wings', he was sent to France on 18 April 1917, joining 11 Squadron five days later. His short-lived operational life came to an abrupt end after only four days at the front. Shot down and taken prisoner, Cairns remained incarcerated until 3 January 1919 when he was finally repatriated.

AM 1ST CLASS E G PERRY (NO. 8102), 11 SQUADRON, ROYAL FLYING CORPS

Perry joined the Royal Flying Corps on 31 August 1915, initially training as a motor cyclist. He went to France on 18 September 1915 and began flying in October 1916. Like his pilot, Perry was unhurt in the crash-landing after the fight with Lothar von Richthofen but remained a prisoner of the Germans until he was exchanged into neutral Holland on 16 May 1918.

VICTORY NO 13

29 April 1917 Spad VII (No. A7653) 19 Squadron 11.15 hours

A notable day in the history of air fighting. A day when one of the best known of combat fliers was himself shot down and killed. Major H D Harvey-Kelly DSO, famous for being the first British airman to land in France in the early days of the war and now the Commanding Officer of 19 Squadron was, with two others of his squadron, engaged in combat by elements of Jasta 11 led by Manfred von Richthofen. The story put out afterwards was that observers in the front line spotted the red Albatros Scouts above them and immediately summoned up Harvey-Kelly to deal with them! An unlikely story, however, as an experienced pilot as Harvey-Kelly surely was would not choose to go against the might of Jasta 11 with just two

companions – and one of those fairly inexperienced. A much more likely scenario was that it was purely a chance meeting – and an unfortunate one for the RFC men. Harvey-Kelly fell to Kurt Wolff whilst Richard Applin was falling under the guns of the Red Baron. Lothar von Richthofen, in the meantime, was having a battle-royal with the third Spad flown by Lieutenant W N Hamilton. For fully fifteen minutes the German tried everything he knew to finish Hamilton off, expending all his ammunition in the process. The Spad's petrol tank had been pierced early in the fight and, suddenly, starved of fuel the engine gave up the ghost – Hamilton gliding away to a forced landing just west of the front line trenches near Izel-lés-Equerchin, the only survivor of the combat. Upon his return from captivity after the war, Hamilton reported that they had been attacked by fourteen of von Richthofen's aircraft and, perhaps a shade extravagantly, claimed that he and Harvey-Kelly had probably shot down five of them before they themselves were shot down. So many returning pilots reported themselves as having gone down fighting against overwhelming odds. Manfred von Richthofen achieved four victories on this one day, a feat that Werner Voss was attempting to emulate on the day he was killed some months later.

SECOND LIEUTENANT WILLIAM NORMAN HAMILTON, NORTHUMBERLAND FUSILIERS AND 19 SQUADRON, ROYAL FLYING CORPS

Originally from London, Hamilton returned from his job in India to join the Inns of Court OTC (No.6/1/6126) in September 1915. After successfully completing his course, he was gazetted Second Lieutenant to the Northumberland Fusiliers on 4 February 1916, going to the front for the first time during the following month. A transfer to the RFC followed in August and, on 28 September 1916, he gained the Aviators Certificate (No. 3715) of the Royal Aero Club. After successfully completing the formal part of his training, he was awarded his 'Wings' on 23 October 1916, finally being sent out to join 19 Squadron in France on 21 February 1917. Hamilton was repatriated on the last day of 1918 and finally left the service on 1 March 1919 shortly before returning to his job in India with the Glasgow firm, Alexander Jubb and Taylor.

VICTORY NO 14

29 April 1917 BE2e (No. 7092) 12 Squadron 19.25 hours

Lothar spent the day supporting and encouraging his brother in his quest for 50 victories before his triumphal return to the Fatherland. Manfred had already claimed his 49th and 50th during the afternoon and yet even despite these successes was up once again in the evening, in company with Lothar, and looking for more. The von Richthofens ran across two artillery-ranging BE2es from 12 Squadron which were quickly despatched at 19.25 – one to each of the brothers. Lothar's victory fell north-east of Monchy-le-Preux, hard up alongside the front lines, the teenage crew both being killed.

SECOND LIEUTENANT

CYRIL JOHN PILE,

ROYAL FIELD ARTILLERY AND 12 SQUADRON, ROYAL FLYING CORPS

The youngest son of Sir Thomas Devereux Pile (1st Baronet) and Lady Caroline Pile of Kenilworth House, Willesden Lane, London and 'Sandymount', Dublin, Ireland, Cyril was born in Dublin in 1897. His father was a former Sheriff (1898) and Lord Mayor (1900) of Dublin City. Originally gazetted Second Lieutenant to the Special Reserve of the Royal Field Artillery on 29 September 1915 but wishing a transfer to the RFC, Cyril learnt to fly, being awarded the Aviators Certificate (No. 3601) of the Royal Aero Club on 22 September 1916. Subsequently accepted for formal pilot training, he was later awarded his 'Wings' and sent out to join 12 Squadron in France. The date of his death from the wounds he received at the hands of Lothar von Richthofen is variously quoted as either 29 April 1917 or 1 May 1917. He is buried in Feuchy (Chapel) British Cemetery, Wancourt, France (Fr. 531). He was still only nineteen years old.

SECOND LIEUTENANT

JOHN HOWARD WESTLAKE,

12 SQUADRON, ROYAL FLYING CORPS

The son of woollen draper Howard Westlake and Bertha Elizabeth Westlake of 66 High Street, Taunton, Somerset, John was born on 16 July 1897. He was educated locally and after leaving school, became a pupil of Mr D Edwards, a member of the Institute of Civil Engineers, being himself formally admitted as a student of that body in December 1915. The war, however, had already interrupted his apprenticeship and during the previous month he had joined the Inns of Court OTC (No 6/5/7284). Successfully completing his officer training, he was gazetted Second Lieutenant to the General List on 4 September 1916 with an immediate posting to the Royal Flying Corps. Trained as an observer, he was sent as a probationary to 12 Squadron in early 1917. John Howard Westlake is buried in Duisans British Cemetery, France (Fr. 113). Like his pilot, he was nineteen years old.

VICTORY NO 15

30 April 1917 BE2g (No. A2942) 16 Squadron 07.15 hours

As brother Manfred left for leave in Germany, he told Lothar that he was to command Jasta 11 in his absence. Although there was potential for discontent with this decision – there were others with more experience and more victories – the other pilots cheerfully accepted him as an able deputy. As though to dispel any lingering doubts, Lothar gained two victories on this, his first day as acting Staffelführer. The first of the two was yet another 16 Squadron BE. It had taken off from Bruay early in the morning to fly a Contact Patrol. After plotting the battle positions two miles to the east of Vimy Ridge, the crew turned for home but as they did so they were attacked by Lothar von Richthofen. The BE caught fire under the onslaught and crashed to earth south-east of Vimy, both crewmen being killed.

SECOND LIEUTENANT

NORMAN ALAN LAWRENCE,

ROYAL FUSILIERS AND 16 SQUADRON, ROYAL FLYING CORPS

The son of Mr and Mrs Lawrence of 7 Balfour Road, Brighton, Norman was born on 11 June 1895. He was educated at St Lawrence College, Ramsgate, Kent (1910-1912) where, as a member of the Shooting VIII, he represented his school at Bisley in 1912. By the time of the Great War Norman's mother, Edith Marie, had re-married and was living at 3 rue St George, Paris, France, with her husband, Einar Enais Abrahamsin, who had also assumed the mantle of guardian to her son. Lawrence was gazetted Second Lieutenant to the 15th (Reserve) Battalion of the Royal Fusiliers on 23 February 1915. After a period stationed at Dover he was sent, on 23 March 1916, to join the 3rd Battalion of his Regiment, then with the Mediterranean Expeditionary Force in Salonika. After successfully seeking transfer to the Royal Flying Corps, Lawrence completed pilot training and was eventually sent out to join 16 Squadron in France shortly before he was killed in action. Possibly because of his family's move to Europe, his former school apparently lost touch with the Abrahamsins and, unfortunately, his name is omitted from the St Lawrence College War Memorial – an omission which, hopefully, will now be rectified. Norman Alan Lawrence is buried in Lieven Communal Cemetery Extension, France (Fr. 557). He was twenty-one years old.

SECOND LIEUTENANT

GEORGE RONALD YORSTON STOUT

MC, 8/ARGYLL AND SUTHERLAND HIGHLANDERS (TF) AND 16 SQUADRON, ROYAL FLYING CORPS

The younger son of George and Margaret Paterson Wingate Stout of 11 Princes Gardens, Downhill, Glasgow, George junior was born in January 1897. He was educated first at Kelvinside Academy in Glasgow before going on to Fettes College, Edinburgh (1910-1913). After completing his education he entered his father's firm, Messrs Geo Stout and Company of Glasgow. Volunteering his services in 1915, George was gazetted Second Lieutenant to the 8th (The Argyllshire) Battalion of the Argyll and Sutherland Highlanders (Territorial Force) on 10 July. Transfer to the RFC followed and he joined 16 Squadron at the front on 4 January 1917. His gallantry during the attack on Vimy Ridge was formally acknowledged by the award of a Military Cross, announced after his death in the *London Gazette* of 26 May 1917, page 5184: *'For conspicuous gallantry and devotion to duty. When on infantry contact patrol he flew twice for periods of two hours at very low altitude and, on each occasion, brought a very complete and detailed report of the situation of the attack. He has at all times displayed great courage and skill'*. The original recommendation for the MC, dated

13 April 1917 and sanctioned by Brigadier G S Shephard MC, Commmanding 1st Brigade RFC, is specific in detailing the low level operations as occuring near Thelus on 9 April and near to Farbus on 10 April 1917, the latter during a particularly heavy snow storm. On both occasions his machine was damaged by rifle and machine-gun fire from the ground. The Stout family were to lose both their sons in the Great War, the oldest son, Thomas, a Lieutenant in the RNVR, dying of an illness contracted during service in the Far East. Their father, George senior, did not long survive his sons, dying himself in 1920. George Ronald Yorston Stout is buried in Lieven Communal Cemetery Extension, France (Fr. 557). He was twenty years old.

VICTORY NO 16

30 April 1917 FE2d (A 6402) 57 Squadron 07.55 hours

Forty minutes after his destruction of the 16 Squadron BE, Lothar von Richthofen and his command, together with elements of Jasta 12, spotted a formation of FEs in the morning light. The FEs, led by Captain H R Harker (A6401), were from 57 Squadron. Earlier at 06.50 the British had spotted German fighters over Lécluse but, outnumbered as they were, had decided that discretion was the better part of valour and withdrew. At 07.00 over Vitry, they were approached by yet another formation of enemy scouts, six above them and three others at their own altitude. In the initial attack, two of the FEs fell, one to Lothar, the other to the leader of Jasta 12, Adolf von Tutschek. The RFC machines came down close together in an area around Izel-lés-Equerchin, west of Douai, the crews being taken prisoner. Strangely, after these initial successes the German planes kept a cautious distance, circling the remaining FEs and only firing as targets presented themselves. Another of the FEs (A1966) was picked off by the three enemy scouts operating at the lower level; the crew, Lieutenants C S Morice and F Leathley, later reported that they had been hit in the radiator and chased east by enemy scouts. Crossing the lines at 500 feet, they met intense ground fire before Morice managed to land some 3,000 yards behind the British lines as his engine finally seized. An enemy machine was also hit, going down two miles SW of Douai. Yet another of the German planes went down under the fire of the FEs, landing near to Vitry at 07.15. The German losses were soon more than made good by the arrival of reinforcements – now there were 12 machines above the 57 Squadron FEs, with 8 others circling them at their own level. Still the Germans continued not to commit themselves to an all-out attack, a situation which allowed Harker and three other FEs to edge their way slowly back to the British lines.

It transpired that the 57 Squadron CO, Major C A Pattinson (with Lieutenant A H Mearns in A 6423) was also in the vicinty of the engagement – Pattinson later said they were up on an engine test! Seeing the fight, they went over to help. Pattinson later reported seeing an Albatros with red fuselage, green wings, a yellow stripe around the fuselage and a blue ring around a red propeller boss. Lothar von Richthofen usually flew an Albatros with yellow markings similar to his old regimental colour. Two of the other RFC crews also reported seeing an Albatros painted flame red, its upper fuselage silver, the wings green.

Lothar's 16th victory was undoubtedly one of the two shot down in the first attack – but which? Both came down at the same time and in roughly the same vicinity. On balance, the evidence suggests that, by the finest of margins, Lieutenant P T Bowers and Second Lieutenant S T Wills in A6402 were Lothar's victims; the other FE2d (A6352) crewed by Second Lieutenants E D Jennings and J R Lingard, shot down by Adolf von Tutschek. In his debriefing after the war,

Bowers reported: *'While on an OP I broke off from the formation of six machines to attack five enemy scouts and after 15 minutes fighting was forced to land being hit in both tanks and engine; the propeller was shattered. I was not wounded but crashed on landing, and whilst extricating myself from the wreckage was surrounded by German soldiers who prevented me from setting the aircraft on fire'.*

LIEUTENANT

PERCY THOMAS BOWERS,

ARMY SERVICE CORPS AND 57 SQUADRON, ROYAL FLYING CORPS

The son of Mr and Mrs Bowers of 67 Waterloo Road, Northampton, Tom was gazetted to the Army Service Corps on 9 October 1915. Promotion to Lieutenant followed on 21 April 1916 and an application for transfer to the RFC was approved in August 1916 – his formal training commencing on 3 October 1916. Having successfully passed through the various stages, he was appointed a Flying Officer on 17 January 1917 and sent to join 57 Squadron as a fighter/reconnaissance pilot exactly one week later. Bowers was repatriated on 14 December 1918 and continued to serve with the RAF until 22 October 1919, when he was released; free to return to civilian life in Northampton. Bowers served again during the Second World War, being appointed to an emergency commission as a Second Lieutenant in the Pioneer Corps with effect from 8 January 1942.

SECOND LIEUTENANT

SAMUEL TORTON WILLS,

NORTHAMPTONSHIRE REGIMENT AND 57 SQUADRON, ROYAL FLYING CORPS

Born on 23 October 1895, Sam was the son of Mr and Mrs Wills of 'Eskerhouse', Lucan near Dublin, Ireland. Originally gazetted Second Lieutenant to the Northamptonshire Regiment on 11 August 1915, he soon sought a transfer to the RFC – an ambition he eventually achieved in late 1916. After training, Wills joined 57 Squadron as a probationary observer on 13 April 1917. Repatriated on 14 December 1918, he finally left the RAF on 10 March 1919.

The end of a memorable month for both sides, but for very different reasons. The technological superiority enjoyed by the Imperial German Air Service, allied with their undoubted edge in technique and tactics, presented them with advantages they had exploited to the full and none more so than the pilots of Jasta 11. The four top 'scorers' for the bloody month of April – Wolff with 23; Manfred von Richthofen with 22; Schäfer with 21 and Lothar von Richthofen with 15 – were all members of the Richthofen 'squadron'. And, on the first day of the month of May 1917 – with sixteen victories and the acting command of an élite Jasta – Lothar von Richthofen could be said to have come a long way in his six short weeks as a scout pilot.

VICTORY NO 17

1 May 1917 FE2b (No. A782) 25 Squadron 19.00 hours

A formation of FEs took off at 16.50 in the afternoon to fly a combined bombing raid and Line Patrol. At 18.15, as the RFC machines approached Izel-lés-Equerchin, they were confronted by Jasta 11. No less than four enemy scouts came down on the FE flown by Lieutenant Berry King from Jamaica. Bullets thudded into the FE's engine and some of the machine's controls were shot through. With his observer, Sergeant H G Taylor, seriously wounded in the thigh, King was forced to put his nose down and head for the British lines as best he could. Fortunately unmolested by the German scouts who doubtless had other fish to fry, King nursed the crippled FE over the lines and attempted to land on Arras racecourse. The elevator cables severed, King was unable to control his machine's descent and they hit the ground hard. King's luck held – for the moment – and he was unhurt but his already wounded observer had his collar bone broken in the crash. Lothar's claim is timed at 19.00 hours with the victim going down on the British side of the lines west of Acheville.

LIEUTENANT
BERRY KING,
6/KING'S OWN YORKSHIRE LIGHT INFANTRY AND 25 SQUADRON, ROYAL FLYING CORPS

The son of Mr and Mrs A O'Reilly King of 85 Barry Street, Kingston, Jamaica, British West Indies, Berry was born on 26 October 1890. He was educated at the Allen School, West Newton, Massachusetts, USA where, in his last year, he captained the football, baseball and basketball teams. After finishing school, he joined the Jamaica Artillery Militia as a Second Lieutenant but later transferred to the Kingston Infantry, attached to the West India Regiment. Leaving for England in 1915, he was gazetted Second Lieutenant to the 3rd Reserve Battalion of the King's Own Yorkshire Light Infantry on 6 March. King spent the next six months training recruits in the KOYLI barracks in Hull before going out to join the 6th Battalion of his regiment in France in September 1915. He served a full twelve months in the trenches, mainly on the Somme and on the Ypres Salient, before successfully applying for a transfer to the RFC. King proved himself a natural pilot and qualified quickly, returning again to France in January 1917, this time to join 25 Squadron. During the next five months he was almost constantly involved in combat flying, claiming victories against enemy aircraft on 6 and 14 April. He also received a letter of appreciation from Major Cheny, the Officer Commanding 16 Squadron – '*......thanks and admiration for the gallant way in which you protected 16th Squadron machines....against superior numbers.....*' Berry King's luck finally ran out just two days after his encounter with Lothar von Richthofen. In these days of trauma and stress counselling for almost any unpleasant happening or experience, it is quite astonishing to learn that just forty-eight hours after having his machine shot from under him, his observer wounded and injured and being himself involved in a crash, King was up again on a combined bombing and Line Patrol. Returning after dropping their bombs, King was observed to fire a flare, an indication that he was experiencing engine or other trouble. Later in the day, news came that his machine (A842) was seen to catch fire and nose dive to the ground near Fiefs, about 10 miles west of the aerodrome. King and his observer, Trumpeter James Gibson Lawrence, 1/1 Westmorland and Cumberland Yeomanry, were killed. Both are buried in Lapugnoy Military Cemetery, France (Fr. 88). Berry King was twenty-six years old.

SERGEANT
H G TAYLOR
(NO. 65386), 25 SQUADRON, ROYAL FLYING CORPS

Taylor was something of an 'old sweat' by the time of the engagement with Lothar von Richthofen, having first joined the Army on 22 September 1914. Strangely enough, this 'May Day' in 1917 was Taylor's first in the rank of Sergeant. Seriously wounded in the thigh and with his collar bone broken in the crash, Sergeant Taylor was put into an ambulance and taken to hospital, the start of his long journey home to Britain. Out of the war at last.

VICTORY NO 18

6 May 1917 RE8 (No. A4596) 16 Squadron 10.50 hours

According to the Jasta 11 records, Lothar von Richthofen claimed an RE8 at 10.50, south-east of Givenchy, the machine going down into the British lines. Neither of the two possibilities precisely fits the circumstances of location and time but, of the two, the most likely was the RE8 crewed by Second Lieutenant A C Sanderson and Lieutenant H K Lytton. They were part of a 16 Squadron sortie led by Captain A L Neale (A4256) who later reported that they were approached at 09.55 (British time) by five red (Halberstadt-type) Scouts north-east of Mericourt – one of the Scouts having a black band around its fuselage. Three of the Scouts broke away from the rest and attacked. The leading German machine was met by a hail of fire and passed below the RE8s without returning the British fusillade. The second machine did fire into the RE8s but then pulled away and dived towards its own lines. Sanderson was hit in the hand and the shock caused him to dive his RE8 steeply and sharply before he regained control and headed for his own lines. They made a forced landing at Farbus at 10.00 (11.00 German time) the crew hurriedly evacuating the machine as it came under shell fire. On 19 May, Sanderson wrote to his Squadron Commander from his bed in the Acheson Hospital in Albert Road, Regent's Park, London. Happily, he was able to tell his CO that despite his hand being badly damaged, the doctors were optimistic about him being able to regain full use. The quality of the handwriting – obviously executed with the undamaged hand – indicated that this was usually the least favoured of the two!

The possibility has been mooted that this victory of Lothar's relates to the shooting down of a 2 Squadron AWFK8. However, that machine was shot down at about 15.15 in the afternoon after taking off at 12.15 on an artillery 'shoot'. Furthermore, Hans Klein of Jasta 4 claimed an AW at 16.30 (German time) between Lens and Lieven.

Captain (later Air Marshal) A C Sanderson DFC (on left) with Major G Allen, 46 Squadron, RAF, four days after the war's end. *(via F Cheesman)*

SECOND LIEUTENANT (LATER AIR MARSHAL SIR CLIFFORD)

ALFRED CLIFFORD SANDERSON,

KBE (1953), CBE (1941), CB (1948), DFC, 16 SQUADRON, ROYAL FLYING CORPS

The son of Mr and Mrs Alfred Sanderson of 'Sunnycroft', 57 Kingshall Road, Hayes, Kent, Clifford was born on 19 February 1898. He was educated at Dulwich College (1910-1916) from where he entered directly into the RFC, being gazetted Second Lieutenant on 5 August 1916. Having completed his training, he was awarded his 'Wings' on 15 March 1917 and almost immediately sent out to join 16 Squadron. Wounded in the action with Lothar von Richthofen, he spent some months recovering in England before again returning to France in 1918, this time as a pilot with 46 Squadron. He was awarded the Distinguished Flying Cross during the final advance to victory, the announcement being made in the *London Gazette* of 8 February 1919, page 2045: *'On 5 November 1918, this officer set a fine example of determination and devotion to duty. In pouring rain and at a height of seldom over 200 feet, he carried out a reconnaissance of the Army front, locating the enemy forces by drawing their rifle fire and machine gun fire. The information thus obtained proved of the utmost value'.* Sanderson stayed on in the Royal Air Force, making the service his career – and a distinguished career it was. He married in 1923, Hazel Evelyn Daly by whom he had two daughters. Sanderson was posted to various locations around the world, usually to areas of political or military uncertainty. He was in Ireland through the troubles of 1919 to 1922; the North West Frontier of India 1924-1929; Palestine 1938-1940; Malta 1940-1941 and Egypt 1942-1943. Sanderson's appointments included Director of Administrative Planning and Chairman of the Joint Planning Staff 1943-1945; AOC Burma 1946-1947; Air Officer i/c Administration of Air Command, Far East 1947-1948; AOC Malaya 1948-1949; Director-General of Personnel, Air Ministry 1949-1952 and, finally, C-in-C Far East Air Forces 1952-1954. He was knighted in 1953 (KBE) having already been created CBE in 1942 and CB in 1948. Sir Clifford Sanderson retired in February 1955, taking up residence at 24 Hovedene, Hove, East Sussex. He died on 28 January 1976 at the age of seventy-seven.

The bald, précised, citations that appear in the *London Gazette* in support of an announcement of a decoration, often underplay the merit of the award. A perfect example is the abbreviated official version of the events leading to the award of the DFC to Sanderson (see above). Compare this brief summary with the detail of the original recommendations, penned personally by Sanderson's Commanding Officer in his anxiety to get his pilot what he regarded as his just reward – not the DFC he was actually awarded but rather a well merited 'gallantry' DSO. The report also incidently gives a graphic account of the agonies and terror suffered by an army in retreat.

CONFIDENTIAL

C.C. 22nd Wing
R.A.F.

Temp. Lieut. Alfred Clifford Sanderson

I beg to recommend the above named officer for the immediate award of the D.F.C.

On 10-10-18 Lt. Sanderson, on low bombing dropped four bombs on an A.A. battery in a wood.

On 17-10-18, Lt. Sanderson, escorted by three other pilots, went out to make a low reconnaissance of the battle line. In spite of very thick weather, and heavy fire from the ground, he succeeded in sketching in, bit by bit, the line reached by our troops. This would be very difficult at any time in an unstable machine like a Camel, and to do it at tree-top level, (as it was impossible to see the ground above 100 ft.) and under heavy fire from the ground, was a very fine performance indeed.

Also this line was most accurate, and was confirmed by the situation report that night.

On 31-10-18 Lt. Sanderson, on a line patrol with Lt. Palk, saw four horse transport vehicles on the CATILLON-MEZIER ROAD. He therefore dived and fired at them, scattering the drivers in all directions and thereby stopping their progress. He was then fired on by seven machine guns from the ground, so, in company with Lt. Palk, dived right down at one, firing about 250 rounds into it and silencing it altogether. He then returned home with gun trouble.

On 4-11-18, Lt. Sanderson led Lts. Palk and Dowler on a low bombing attack on some transport South of LANDRECIES-MAROILLES ROAD. He bombed these from about 250 feet and then climbed into the clouds. On emerging, over Sheet 57 ^ 13, he found about two companies of infantry retiring in extended order. He led Lt. Palk and Dowler down on to them, and attacked them from tree-top level with machine gun fire, scattered them in all directions, and completely broke up their hitherto orderly retirement.

In the afternoon of 4-11-18 he led four other pilots in a low bombing attack on German batteries on the three roads entering PRISCHES from the S.W. They all dropped their bombs from a low height, two being observed to burst along the road alongside the limbers, and two just off the road. They then attacked these guns with machine gun fire, shot horses, made the men bolt for cover into the ditches and houses, and caused a complete panic.

Lt. Lazenby, who had not dropped his bombs first time, dropped one bomb which was observed to fall in the midst of a heap of struggling men and horses. When Lt. Sanderson thought this lot of guns were finished, he led his formation up again and saw a column of horse transport about 100 yards long on the LE NOUVION – BEAUREPAIRE ROAD. He attacked this with his formation with machine gun fire, with most successful results. He panicked the men, shot horses, and brought the whole column to a standstill. Lt. Sanderson then led the others back as it was getting dusk.

On 5-11-18 Lt. Sanderson, escorted by Lts. Palk and Dowler, went out to do a low reconnaissance of the battle front. In spite of high wind, low clouds, and poor visibility at first, and pouring rain at the end, he managed accurately to locate the Germans on a considerable portion of the Army front, and brought back a concise and accurate report of movements, etc. To do this he had to fly very low, seldom over 200 ft., and located the Germans by drawing their fire. This would have been a good effort on a clear, calm day, but on a day like today, it was exceptionally fine.

Lt. Sanderson has proved himself a leader of the greatest dash and judgement, and has put up a really wonderful show in the last two days.

Added to this, his previous five months war service as an Artillery Pilot, has given him the art of making an accurate tactical reconnaissance, so that his reports are of real value.

On the majority of the occasions on which he has done low bombing, strafing, or reconnaissance, his machine has been fairly well peppered which signifies to the thorough way in which he carried out his missions. On every occasion on which he has seen a decent ground target he has attacked it, and attacked it properly, and done a great deal of damage.

He has set a magnificent example to the rest of the squadron. I believe his courage and leadership have been of great value and must have helped considerably towards the local success of the operations.

G Allen, Major
Commanding No. 46 Squadron, R.A.F.

In the Field.
5th November l918

Headquarters
22nd Wing R.A.F.

I wish to call your attention to my report in today's Squadron Record book of the low flying attack carried out by Lt. Sanderson, Lt. Dowler, and Lt. Palk, as I think that the performance is worthy of special mention.

In the Field. *G. Allen, Major*
8th November 1918 *Commanding No. 46 Squadron, R.A.F.*

CONFIDENTIAL
C.C. 22nd Wing.
R.A.F.

Temp. Lieut. Alfred Clifford Sanderson

On 5.11.18, I submitted a recommendation for the award of the D.F.C. to the above named officer. Since then he has put up two very fine shows.

On 8.11.18, Lt. Sanderson led a low flying attack on infantry, guns, and transport retiring N.E from AVESNES. He attacked one gun galloping along a road, and brought down the leading pair of horses. The remainder of the patrol reported that shortly afterwards, this gun was captured by our troops.

He then espied about one Company of Infantry in close formation and led an attack on them causing them very severe casualties, and completely panicking the survivors. He then led a third attack on a column of 4 guns and some horse transport on a road. He dived at these, killing drivers and horses, scattering the gunners, and causing complete confusion.

On 9.11.18 Lt. Sanderson led a low bombing attack on about 30 M.T. lorries on the roads W. of CHIMAY. Very successful results were observed, three direct hits on lorries, and three bombs on the road just alongside some lorries; but it is impossible definitely to state which pilot dropped these bombs, though two are believed to have been his. Lt. Sanderson then attacked with machine gun fire, and had one gun put out of action by a bullet which went through the belt and into the feed-block. However, he continued his attack with the other gun, and scattered the drivers all over the place, thus completing the panic started by the bombs. His fusee spring then broke and he had to cease fire and come home.

These attacks were carried out at a very low altitude down to the tree-tops, and under very heavy machine gun fire from the ground.

Lt. Sanderson has proved himself a leader of the greatest courage and dash. His previous experience as an artillery pilot enables him to grasp the tactical situation and act accordingly, and his reports have been proved to be most accurate. I cannot speak too highly of the absolutely fearless example he has shown to the rest of the squadron. His attacks, well backed up by several other pilots, must have had a considerable result on the success of the local operations on the ground.

As his previous exploits, which are set out in my previous letter of 5.11.18, have been capped by two such good shows as those of today and 8.11.18, the latter being really brilliant, I hope you will see your way to combining the two and recommending this young officer for the D.S.O.

In the Field.
9th November 1918.

G. Allen, Major
Commanding No. 46 Squadron R.A.F.

LIEUTENANT

HARRY KOVRIGIN LYTTON,

3/ROYAL IRISH RIFLES AND 16 SQUADRON, ROYAL FLYING CORPS

Born on 20 March 1890, the son of Mr and Mrs Lytton of 'Heathfield', Fairlawn Park, Chiswick, London. He was educated at St Paul's School, Hammersmith, London. Gazetted Second Lieutenant to the 3rd Reserve Battalion of the Royal Irish Rifles on 23 May 1915, he soon afterwards joined his regiment in Ireland. The 3rd Battalion of the RIR, then stationed in Portobello Barracks in the Irish capital, was actively and heavily involved in opposing the Sinn Fein Rebellion in Dublin during the Easter of 1916, having one officer killed and four wounded. Of other ranks, five were killed and twenty wounded. On 6 May 1916, the 3rd RIR left Dublin for Victoria Barracks, Belfast. Lytton now sought transfer to the RFC, which he achieved in early 1917. After completing observer training, he was sent as a probationary to 16 Squadron, arriving on 2 May 1917 – just four days before being shot down by Lothar von Richthofen! Although physically unhurt in the forced landing, subsequent events indicated that either Lytton was unhappy with his experience or that possibly 16 Squadron was unhappy with him. Whatever the truth, it is certain that he returned for duty with the Royal Irish Rifles on 19 May 1917. Oddly, Lytton had not finished with the flying service as he volunteered again after the war and was accepted for further training on 11 January 1919.

VICTORY NO 19

7 May 1917 Nieuport XVII (No. A6609) 29 Squadron 18.30 hours

The first of two victories on this day was against a 29 Squadron Nieuport Scout. The Squadron had sent out a patrol at 15.45 (British time). Observers reported one of their number shot down by a German aircraft near to Fresnes. Lothar von Richthofen's claim places his victim as falling west of Biache – Biache-St-Vaast is just two or so kilometres south of Fresnes-lès-Montauban.

SECOND LIEUTENANT

CECIL STANLEY GASKAIN,

4TH LONDON HOWITZER BRIGADE (AMMUNITION COLUMN) ROYAL FIELD ARTILLERY (TF) AND 29 SQUADRON, ROYAL FLYING CORPS

The son of hop factor Denis Hinton Gaskain and Mrs Gaskain of 'The Grange', Grove Park, Lee, London, Cecil was born in 1891. He was educated at Eastbourne College (1906-1909) where he proved himself a very able all-round athlete. Gaskain was gazetted to the 4th London Howitzer Brigade (Ammunition Column) Royal Field Artillery (Territorial Force) on 22 June 1915 with which unit he proceeded to France for the first time later in the same year. In early 1916 he was wounded and during the period of his recuperation in England, he applied for transfer to the RFC. On 10 November 1916, Gaskain was awarded the Aviators Certificate (No.3808) of the Royal Aero Club, after which he embarked upon his formal pilot training. Awarded his 'Wings', he was again sent out to France, this time to join 29 Squadron at the front. Gaskain's remains were never located and so he is commemorated on the Arras Memorial to the Missing, France. He was twenty-five years old.

VICTORY NO 20

7 May 1917 SE5 (No. A4850) 56 Squadron 20.30 hours

The subject of much controversy over the years, the resolution of the uncertainties surrounding this 'victory' remains as distant as ever! What is certain is that Captain Albert Ball DSO**, MC, a 20-year-old Flight Commander with over 40 victories to his credit, was on this Spring evening leading one of his last patrols with 56 Squadron before leaving for home. A hero in his own country and respected by his peers, Ball, despite his comparative youth, was a combat veteran of considerable experience and a formidable opponent for the very best the enemy could put forward. On the evening of 7 May 1917, members of his patrol had had a sequence of inconclusive skirmishes with a number of enemy aircraft and, as a consequence, had been split up, completely losing contact with each other. The sky was busy that evening, Sopwith Triplanes from 8 Squadron RNAS and Spads from 19 Squadron also being engaged at one time or another by the Jasta 11 pilots. Lothar von Richthofen sparred with at least one of the Triplanes before engaging two of the SE5s, one of which may well have been Ball's. Certainly Ball was last seen chasing a red Albatros Scout into a large bank of cloud. What happened after that last sighting remains a matter of speculation. It is possible – even probable – that Ball became disorientated in the cloud and came out of it too low to correct his dive before his machine ploughed into the ground. He lived

for a few minutes after the crash, dying in the arms of a young French woman, Madame Sieppe Coulon, who had hurried to the scene. The death of so significant a figure led, inevitably, to speculation regarding the circumstances surrounding his demise and, too often, the speculators invented their own scenarios – some commentators never letting the truth get in the way of a good story! There was also a reluctance on the British side to believe that Ball could have been bested in combat or even that he could have been guilty of a simple error of judgement.

Lothar von Richthofen had originally claimed a Triplane on this day and at this time – the claim clearly recorded as such in the Nachrichtenblatt. The fact is, however, that no Triplanes were lost on this evening. The news of Ball's death quickly reached Berlin and as the location of his wrecked SE5 was similar to that of Lothar's 'phantom' Triplane, it hardly took a quantum leap of imagination to link the two. The propaganda value to the German High Command was immense. Manfred von Richthofen had, in November 1916, bested the great British ace Major Lanoe Hawker VC DSO in combat and now the Red Baron's brother Lothar had destroyed the current leading British ace, Albert Ball. Whatever the truth of the matter, Lothar was formally credited with the victory over Albert Ball by the German Air Service. Certainly Lothar von Richthofen knew he had been in a fight that day, his Albatros had been hit and with his engine giving him trouble, he had been forced to land although he was himself unhurt.

CAPTAIN
ALBERT BALL
VC (POSTHUMOUSLY AWARDED), DSO AND 2 BARS, MC, MID, LÉGION D'HONNEUR (FRANCE), ORDER OF ST GEORGE, 4TH CLASS (RUSSIA) 2/7TH SHERWOOD FORESTERS (THE ROBIN HOODS) (TF) AND 56 SQUADRON, ROYAL FLYING CORPS

The son of Alderman Albert Ball JP and Mrs Harriet Mary Ball of Sedgley House, The Park, Nottingham, Albert was born on 14 August 1896. He was educated at Nottingham High School and at Trent College. Volunteering immediately war broke out, he first enlisted as a private soldier in the 2/7th Battalion of the Sherwood Foresters – The Robin Hoods. Two months later, on 28 October 1914, Ball was gazetted Second Lieutenant into his own battalion. Keen to fly, Ball would frequently make the round trip by motorcycle from his camp in Luton to Hendon aerodrome until, eventually, he was awarded the Aviators Certificate of the Royal Aero Club (No.1898) on 15 October 1915. Transfer to the Royal Flying Corps and an intensive course of further training followed his successful acquisition of a

Albert Ball at London Colney, April 1917.

'ticket'. His training completed, Ball was first sent to the front on 18 February 1916, joining 13 Squadron to fly reconnaissance machines. Ball's subsequent prowess is well documented elsewhere, the chronicle of his brilliance perhaps best illustrated by the honours showered upon his young and slight shoulders – Military Cross, *London Gazette* of 27 June 1916: *'For conspicuous skill and gallantry on many occasions, notably when, after failing to destroy an enemy kite balloon with bombs, he returned for a fresh supply, went back and brought it down in flames. He has done great execution among the enemy aeroplanes. On one occasion he attacked six in one fight, forced down two and drove the others off. This occured several miles over the enemy lines'*. The first of his DSOs came with the announcement in the *London Gazette* of 22 September 1916, that he had been created a Companion of the Order: *'For conspicuous gallantry and skill. Observing seven enemy machines in formation, he immediately attacked one of them, and shot it down at fifteen yards range. The remaining machines retired. Immediately afterwards, seeing five more machines, he attacked one at about ten yards' range, and shot it down, flames coming out of the fuselage. He then attacked another of the machines which had been firing at him, and shot it down into a village, where it landed on top of a house. He then went to the nearest aerodrome for more ammunition, and, returning, attacked three more machines, causing them to dive and get out of control. Being then short of petrol, he came home. His own machine was badly shot about in these fights'*. The same *Gazette* announced the award of a Bar to his DSO for subsequent acts of gallantry: '......*When on escort duty in a bombing raid, he saw four enemy machines in formation; he dived on to them and broke up their formation, and then shot down the nearest one, which fell on its nose. He came down to 500 feet to make certain it was wrecked. On another occasion, observing twelve enemy machines in formation, he dived in among them and fired a drum into the nearest machine, which went down out of control. Several more hostile machines then approached, and he fired three more drums at them, driving down another out of control. He then returned, crossing the lines at a low altitude, with his machine very much damaged'*. The by then Lieutenant Ball was invested with the insignia of the DSO by King George V at Buckingham Palace on 18 November 1916. Shortly afterwards, he was promoted to Captain and a second Bar to his DSO was announced in the *London Gazette* of 25 November 1916: '......*He attacked three hostile machines and brought one down, displaying great courage. He brought down eight hostile machines in a short period and forced many others to land'*. Still only twenty years of age, Ball was presented with

Albert Ball is buried with full military honours afforded by the Imperial German Army; British POWs are also in attendance.

the honorary freedom of his native city, Nottingham. In August 1916, the Tsar of Russia had conferred upon him the Order of St George. After his death, the President of France added the Cross of the Chevalier of the Legion of Honour to his many awards. Ball became the first British officer to receive the Medal and Diploma of the Aero Club of America. He had also been Mentioned in Despatches on a number of occasions but the ultimate accolade was presented posthumously, the award of the Victoria Cross being announced in the *London Gazette* of 3 June 1917: *'For most conspicuous and consistent bravery, from 25 April to 6 May 1917, during which period Captain Ball took part in twenty-six combats in the air and destroyed eleven hostile aeroplanes, drove down two out of control and forced several others to land. Flying alone, on one occasion he fought six hostile machines, twice he fought five and once four. When leading two other British planes he attacked an enemy formation of eight – on each of these occasions he brought down at least one enemy plane, and several times his plane was badly damaged On returning with a damaged plane he had always to be restrained from immediately going out in another'*. Albert Ball was buried by the German Air Service with full Military Honours in Annoeullin Communal Cemetery, German Extension, France (Fr. 1279). He was twenty years old.

VICTORY NO 21

9 May 1917 Bristol F2b (No. A7110) 48 Squadron 18.30 hours

At 16.25 in the afternoon, the beleaguered 48 Squadron put up a patrol of Bristol Fighters to cover Arras. It was still less than a month since Jasta 11 had subjected the new British fighter plane to, literally, its baptism of fire. Now they were again attacked by the red Albatroses and one of their number was hit early in the fight by the deputy Staffelführer, Lothar von Richthofen. Both crew members were wounded in the attack north-east of Fampoux but still, the pilot, Second Lieutenant W T Price, managed to get the Bristol down – albeit in a crash-landing – into the British lines, his skill and pluck earning him a Military Cross. Price and his wounded observer, Second Lieutenant C G Claye, were taken off to the nearest Aid Station.

SECOND LIEUTENANT

WILLIAM THOMAS PRICE

CBE (1960), MC, 13/ROYAL WARWICKSHIRE REGIMENT AND 48 SQUADRON, ROYAL FLYING CORPS

The son of Mr and Mrs Price of 12 Ridbourne Avenue, Finchley, London, William was born on 15 November 1895. He was educated at Christ College, London and at Reading University where he gained a BSc. After leaving university, Price almost immediately received a commission in the Royal Warwickshire Regiment, being gazetted to the 13th (Reserve) Battalion on 26 August 1915. Keen to join the RFC, Price learnt to fly and was awarded the Aviators Certificate (No. 4121) of the Royal Aero Club on 28 November 1916. Following formal training, he was given his 'Wings' and sent out to the front with 48 Squadron. The announcement of the award of his Military Cross appeared in the *London Gazette* of 18 July 1917, page 7241: *'For conspicuous gallantry and devotion to duty. His machine being disabled by hostile fire, and his gun out of action, he managed by skilful handling to effect a safe landing, thus saving the machine and his passenger from capture. He has previously done fine work against hostile aircraft'.* Although wounded in the action with Lothar von Richthofen, he was, after recovery, able to continue combat flying. Indeed, even after leaving the RAF at the end of the war, he flew for a joy-riding aeroplane company, giving rides to paying passengers over the Blackpool sands! Turning next to more serious pursuits, Price was appointed as a lecturer in dairy husbandry at the Staffordshire Farm Institute from 1920 to 1922, before going on to lecture on estate management at the Harper Agricultural College from 1922 to 1924. He married for the first time in 1923, Fanny Louise Dale. Price next took up a technical appointment with the Wiltshire County Council before accepting the post of Organiser of Agricultural Education, a position he held from 1926 to 1946 when he became Principal of Harper Adams Agricultural College until his retirement in 1962. Price's contribution to British agriculture was formally acknowledged by the award of the CBE in 1960. His first wife having died in 1964, Price married secondly Mrs Beryl E Drew in 1965. His distinctions included the David Black Award (for the greatest contribution to the British pig industry) in 1961. Price was also a broadcaster for the BBC, commenting on agricultural matters generally, as well as writing books and numerous articles on his specialist subject of 'pigs'. He lived latterly at 'Eversleigh', 2 Clarendon Place, Leamington Spa, Warwickshire. William Thomas Price died on 17 January 1982, at the age of eighty-six.

SECOND LIEUTENANT

CHARLES GEOFFREY CLAYE,

5/SHERWOOD FORESTERS (TF) AND 48 SQUADRON, ROYAL FLYING CORPS

The only son of rolling stock manufacturer Wentworth Ernest Claye and Mrs Claye of 'Lenton House', Lenton, Nottinghamshire, Charles was born on 14 February 1895. He was educated at Charterhouse (1909-1913)

where he became a member of the OTC. After leaving school, he trained as a draughtsman with the family firm, Clayson Ltd, Railway Wagon Works, Long Eaton, Nottinghamshire. Volunteering for service when the war came, he was gazetted Second Lieutenant to the 2/5th Battalion of the Sherwood Foresters (Notts and Derbyshire Regiment) (TF) on 7 October 1914. After a long period in the UK, he was sent out to France to join the First Line of the 5th Battalion of his regiment in August 1916. On 8 September 1916, he was involved in a 'D' Company raid on the German trenches which, unfortunately, had to be aborted when the raiders ran into a strong German working party in no-man's land. Claye next successfully applied for transfer to the RFC, which occurred in early March 1917. Having completed his training as an observer in the new Bristol Fighter, he was sent out as a probationary on 18 April 1917, helping to reinforce the badly depleted 48 Squadron. Wounded in the action with Lothar von Richthofen, Claye returned to England to recuperate. Recovering his fitness by January 1918, he acted as an instructor in aerial navigation and bomb dropping until he returned to France as an observer with 99 Squadron on 18 April 1918 – exactly one year to the day after he had first gone to France to join 48 Squadron. On 5 July 1918, seven 99 Squadron DH 9s, led by Captain W D Thom DFC with Claye acting as his observer, mounted an early morning bombing raid. The original target was to have been Kaiserslauten but excessive cloud cover led to a change to Saarbrücken. Eight EAs attacking from the front and rear were successfully driven off with two of them being sent down. In the fight, Claye was killed in the air, his pilot, Thom, being wounded in the arm. Despite his wounds, Captain Thom successfully piloted their DH 9 back to base. Charles Geoffrey Claye is buried in Charmes Cemetery, France. He was twenty-three.

VICTORY NO 22

10 May 1917 Sopwith Pup (No. A7303) 66 Squadron 07.50 hours

66 Squadron was on an early morning Offensive Patrol between Douai and Brebières when it was attacked by Jasta 11. Two of the Pups went down under the guns of the German aces, one – flown by Second Lieutenant D J Sheehan – fell to Lothar von Richthofen south of Vitry, the second to Leutnant Karl Allmenröder, the German pilot's eleventh victory. When Lothar returned to his base, he learned that he could add the Knight's Cross with Swords of the Hohenzollern House Order to the First and Second Class Iron Crosses he already held.

SECOND LIEUTENANT
DANIEL JOSEPH SHEEHAN,
66 SQUADRON, ROYAL FLYING CORPS

The eldest son of Captain Daniel Desmond Sheehan, Member of Parliament for mid-Cork and Mrs Sheehan of 3 Osborne Mansions, Northumberland Street, London and Cork, Ireland, Daniel was born on 14 November 1894. He was educated at Christian College, Cork and Mount St Joseph's College, Roscrea. An exceptional sportsman, he played rugby for Munster for two seasons and was considered the best wing three-quarter in Ireland. After leaving school in 1912, he joined the Ocean Training Ship, *Medway*, as a cadet, winning first prizes for navigation and general seamanship. Next he transferred to HMS *Hibernia* as a midshipman, RNR, with the view of obtaining a permanent commission in the Royal Navy. Following service in the North Sea with the 3rd Battle Squadron, he transferred to the Royal Naval Air Service, gaining the Aviators Certificate (No. 1340) of the Royal Aero Club on 19 June 1915. After further training, he was awarded his 'Wings' and sent to join an RNAS Squadron in France. Unfortunately, he was wounded and injured shortly after arriving and was considered unfit for further service with the RNAS. After recovering his health, he was allowed to transfer to the RFC, being gazetted Second Lieutenant on 7 April 1917 and appointed Flying Officer on 27 April 1917. Sheehan spent some time as an instructor at Oxford before accompanying 66 Squadron to France in May 1917. Daniel's younger brother, Michael, an observer with 13 Squadron, Royal Air Force, was also to be killed in action on 1 October 1918. Daniel Sheehan is buried in Cabaret-Rouge British Cemetery, Souchez, France (Fr. 924). He was 23 years old.

VICTORY NO 23

11 May 1917 Bristol F2b (No. A7111) 48 Squadron 17.10 hours

Lothar von Richthofen inflicted yet more grief on the beleaguered 48 Squadron. The Bristol Fighters were on an Offensive Patrol to the south of Arras when Jasta 11 struck. First to go down, out of control, was the F2b flown by Lieutenant W O B Winkler, the machine crashing at Izel, the occupants taken prisoner. Five minutes later Karl Allmenröder accounted for another of the Brisfits over Beaumont. During their debreifing following their return from captivity in Germany, Winkler said that they had been attacked by seven enemy aircraft while their own formation of eight was split into four groups of two. *'The machine with me was hit and I endeavoured to protect him and was then shot in the engine and forced to land'.* Moore, the observer, also reported*: 'Escorting RE8s, (we were) attacked by seven enemy aircraft while in formation.... Engine hit and controls shot away. Crashed out of control and aircraft wrecked but we were not wounded'.*

Second Lieutenant W O B Winkler, Royal Garrison Artillery and 48 Squadron, RFC (on left) with his elder brother, Captain E R Winkler MC, Royal New Zealand Field Artillery.

SECOND LIEUTENANT
WILLIAM OTTO BRASH WINKLER,
MID, LOWLAND (CITY OF EDINBURGH) BATTERY, ROYAL GARRISON ARTILLERY (TF) AND 48 SQUADRON, ROYAL FLYING CORPS

The younger son of Mr and Mrs Winkler of 9 Ettrick Road, Edinburgh, William was born on 7 July 1895. He was educated at Merchiston Castle School, Edinburgh (1903-1912). After leaving school, he joined the family's manufacturing furrier business in the Scottish capital. A keen volunteer, he joined, pre-war, the Lothian and Border Horse Yeomanry as a trooper. When war came, young Winkler had, for those days, a rare skill that the Army could use – he could drive a motor vehicle. As a consequence of his driving ability, he was soon transferred to the Army Service Corps (Private, M2/049508). Winkler was gazetted Second Lieutenant to the Royal Garrison Artillery on

1 March 1915, going to France for the first time on 27 July 1915. Following a period with the BEF, a successful application for transfer to the RFC took effect from 28 August 1916. Having completed his pilot training, he was awarded his 'Wings' on 19 February 1917 and eventually sent out to strengthen the depleted 48 Squadron on 8 April 1917. William Winkler enjoyed a brief but extremely productive period as a Bristol Fighter pilot, claiming no less than six victories between 12 April and 2 May – so becoming an ace himself. In later life, Winkler would ruefully recall that after his battle with Lothar von Richthofen, his Brisfit fell no more than 300 yards from the British lines. Unfortunately, however, it did actually come to rest just 50 yards *inside* the German lines! He was kept a prisoner in Strohen, Germany, where he acted as adjutant to the 'escapes committee'. His outstanding work in that capacity was formally acknowedged by a Mention in Despatches, the announcment of which appeared in the *London Gazette* of 16 December 1919, *'...for valuable services whilst in captivity'*. Repatriated on 30 December 1918, he was finally placed on the Unemployed List on 22 February 1919. Returning to his native city, Winkler went back to the fur business, married and had two sons, the family living at 13 Lochlanton Crescent, Edinburgh. Retaining his interest in the volunteer movement, Winkler became a founder and active member of 603 (City of Edinburgh) Squadron, Royal Air Force Volunteer Reserve until he resigned his commission on 9 December 1929. William Winkler died in Edinburgh on 24 November 1952 at fifty-seven years of age.

Winkler's MID Certificate, signed by the then Secretary of State for Air, Winston Churchill.

The War of 1914-1918.

Royal Air Force

Lieutenant William Otto Brash Winkler (R.G.A).

was mentioned in the London Gazette

dated 16th December 1919.

for gallant and distinguished services.

I have it in command from the King to record His Majesty's high appreciation of the services rendered.

Winston S. Churchill

Secretary of State for Air

Air Ministry,
Kingsway,
London, W.C.2.

SECOND LIEUTENANT

ERNEST STANLEY MOORE,

48 SQUADRON, ROYAL FLYING CORPS

Born in 1890, Ernest was the son of Mr and Mrs Moore of 24 Elm Avenue, Garden City, Hull, Yorkshire. A professional engineer, Moore was employed by the Post Office before the war. He was gazetted Second Lieutenant to the RFC on 5 August 1916, going on to train as an observer before qualifying, on probation, on 9 March 1917. Moore was sent to join 48 Squadron in England on 27 February 1917 and accompanied the Squadron to France in the following month. In less than two months at the front, Moore was involved in a number of victories against enemy aircraft before he was himself shot down by Lothar von Richthofen. Repatriated on the last day of 1918, he finally left the Royal Air Force on 5 March 1919, taking up a position as Assistant Surveyor in Port Harcourt, Nigeria.

VICTORY NO 24

13 May 1917 BE2e (No. 7130) 13 Squadron 11.35 hours

At 09.30 hours a 13 Squadron BE2e set out on an artillery observation sortie over the 17th Corps front. The RFC crew Thompson and Rawlins, an odd mixture of youth and maturity, met Lothar von Richthofen over Arleux Wood, west of Fresnoy, and soon afterwards suffered the same fate as had the occupants of twenty-three other machines before them. Fortunately, their BE2e fell inside British lines and the pair were able to scramble clear before incoming shells reduced the two-seater to an unsalvageable wreck. The morning was hazy, so much so that Lothar was obliged to follow his victim down to make sure of his victory and in doing so, he became disorientated, losing his position in the murk and low cloud. Turning and climbing, Lothar had started in the general direction of home when he was fired upon by a number of ground batteries. Suddenly there was a sickening thump and he felt intense pain in his left hip. Looking down, he saw a red stain spreading down his flying suit. Gritting his teeth, he flew his machine into German territory before putting down in a field and promptly passing out. When next he regained consciousness, he found himself laying in a bed in a Douai hospital. Wounded for the first time – this would not be the only occasion when the 13th day of a month would prove unlucky for Lothar von Richthofen.

SECOND LIEUTENANT

FRANK THOMPSON,

13 SQUADRON, ROYAL FLYING CORPS

The son of Mr and Mrs Thompson of 31 Highfield Road, Chertsey, Surrey, Frank was born on 12 April 1900, which made him seriously underage for active service! Thompson was gazetted as a Second Lieutenant to the RFC on 26 September 1916. He then went on to qualify as a pilot and was awarded his 'Wings' (and appointed a Flying Officer) on 13 April 1917, the day following his seventeenth birthday. Happily, the youthful Frank Thompson survived not only Lothar von Richthofen's attentions but also lived to see the war out, spending much of his remaining service as a flying instructor in England.

LIEUTENANT

ARTHUR CHARLES CHAMPION RAWLINS,

ARMY SERVICE CORPS AND 13 SQUADRON, ROYAL FLYING CORPS

Whilst the pilot of the BE that became Lothar von Richthofen's 24th victory was easily the youngest of the German ace's victims, the observer in the same machine was quite definitely the oldest. Born on 25 July 1877, Arthur was the son of Mr and Mrs Rawlins of

89 Overhill Road, Dulwich, London. Rawlins, an interesting 'character', was variously described as a 'buyer' and a 'speculator' when he lived in the gold and diamond fields of South Africa during the last years of the nineteenth century. He was fluent in French and 'fair' in Dutch – the latter useful no doubt when he was dealing with the Boer settlers. During this period, Rawlins met and married his wife and they set up home in Piet Relief in the Transvaal. He then fought alongside the Imperial forces during the last two years of the South African war in 1901 and 1902. After this war he returned to Europe for a while, selling 'outdoor ware' around Belgium – his fluent French doubtless serving him well in the Walloon areas of that country. He again returned to South Africa, this time working for Frankel and Company in Johannesburg from 1910 to 1912, before becoming self-employed once more back in Piet Relief from 1912 to 1913. In 1914 he returned to England, securing a position with Lever Brothers of Liverpool. When the war came Rawlins, like most of the male staff of Lever Brothers, 'joined up' and his obvious talents and experience soon earned him a commission in the Army Service Corps. Not content to sit out the war in comparative safety, he volunteered for the RFC and, surprisingly in view of his thirty-nine years, he was accepted. He was trained as an observer and sent out to join 13 Squadron as a probationary on 16 April 1917. Surviving the Lothar von Richthofen incident, Rawlins resumed at the front until July 1917 when he was returned to England to take up duties as an instructor. After a period in the UK he again returned to France in 1917, this time serving with 2 Squadron. Because of illness, Rawlins was invalided to England on 15 December 1918 before finally leaving the service on 30 January 1919, taking with him the rank of Honorary Lieutenant.

Lothar's wound, although not life-threatening, kept him out of action (literally) for five months. In the meantime there was some consolation having reached the requisite number of aerial combat victories, the Kaiser could now award him the highest accolade in his gift, the Orde Pour le Mérite, which was formally announced on 14 May 1917. In Lothar's absence, Karl Allmenröder assumed the role of acting commander of Jasta 11, a position he retained until the return from leave of Manfred von Richthofen on 15 June 1917. Shortly afterwards, on 26 June 1917, Manfred was promoted to command JGI whereupon Allmenröder took over again at Jasta 11. This time Karl Allmenröder's tenure lasted just one day as he was killed in action on 27 June and so command of Jasta 11 passed to Kurt Wolff. The sequence of changes in the command of Jasta 11 continued when Wolff was wounded on 11 July 1917 and Wilhelm Reinhard took over. Reinhard lasted until 4 September before he, too, was wounded. Wolff who, in the meantime, had recovered and been put in temporary charge of Jasta 29, was again brought back to take over at Jasta 11. The poisoned chalice that was the command of Jasta 11 passed on yet again when Kurt Wolff was killed in action four days after his re-appointment on 15 September 1917. By this time Lothar von Richthofen was ready to return to combat and took command of Jasta 11 in his own right on 25 September 1917.

Lothar's Jasta 11 was, of course, one of four units, which, along with Jastas 4, 6 and 10, comprised Manfred von Richthofen's command – JGI, the 'Flying Circus'. By now Manfred had, physically at least, recovered from the wounds he sustained on 6 July 1917 and was back in charge, albeit a changed man – stress and injury had taken their toll. As Lothar arrived, so Manfred left to enjoy a lengthy leave of absence which would continue until 24 October. Manfred's victory count at this time was 62, a figure which left Lothar's not inconsiderable total of 24 far behind. Lothar's administrative duties curtailed the amount of time he could devote to combat flying as he was forced to spend more and more time flying a desk! A watershed in the fortunes of the German Air Service occured with the arrival of the new Fokker F1 Triplane, a machine which both von Richthofen brothers would adopt from October 1917. In the following month Jasta 11 was operating further north on the German 4th Armee Front and Lothar, in his new Triplane, began 'scoring' again.

VICTORY NO 25

9 November 1917 Bristol F2b (?) -?- 10.30 hours

Lothar von Richthofen claimed his first victory flying his new Fokker Triplane on 9 November, the victim being described in the Jasta 11 records as a 'Bristol Fighter', downed north-west of Zonnebeke at 10.30 hours. Unfortunately, however, there was no corresponding candidate that could possibly qualify for the dubious distinction. Certainly there were no Bristol Fighters lost on the day. As Lothar's 'victim' was said by him to have fallen into the British lines, was this perhaps yet another example of an undamaged machine hurriedly being guided down and out of the firing line (literally) by its anxious pilot, the ensuing rapid and precipitous descent being falsely interpreted by the aggressor as being a direct consequence of his attack?

VICTORY NO 26

23 November 1917 Bristol F2b (No. B1116) 11 Squadron 14.00 hours

On 22 November 1917, JGI, including Jasta 11, moved its base and its centre of activity southwards down the line to Avesnes-le-Sec near Cambrai. Just one day later the German flyers were up and looking to intercept intruders into their new territory. Two hours into the afternoon, Lothar von Richthofen fastened onto an 11 Squadron Bristol Fighter and sent it crashing down into the British lines west of Seranvillers. The Squadron machines had taken off at 12.35 (British time) on a reconnaissance sortie – B1116 was last seen over Cambrai.

SECOND LIEUTENANT
ERLAND DAURIA PERNEY,
11 SQUADRON, ROYAL FLYING CORPS

The son of Schools Inspector Frank E Perney and his wife, Margaret C Perney, of 32 Flatt Avenue, Hamilton, Ontario, Canada, Erland was born in 1895. He was educated in Ottawa, where he enjoyed a reputation as an outstanding athlete, particularly as a rower. As stroke of the New Edinburgh Canoe Club war canoe, he helped to win the half-mile championship of Canada in 1915. A keen pre-war volunteer, he held the rank of Second Lieutenant in the Queen's University 72nd Battery of Canadian Field Artillery. After the completion of his education, he obtained a position with the Health of Animals Branch of the Canadian Department of Agriculture in the Canadian capital. Screened and approved as a likely candidate for the RFC by the ubiquitous Lord Innes-Ker, Perney was sent to England aboard the SS *Southwind* on 31 October 1916. He trained first in Montrose in Scotland, going on next to Catterick in Yorkshire before finally completing his familiarisation course with the Bristol Fighter at Northolt some time later. Awarded his 'Wings', Perney was posted to 11 Squadron in France on 17 August 1917, with which unit he served for just over two months before meeting his death. Perney's body was never found and so he is commemorated on the Arras Memorial to the Missing, France. He was 22.

LIEUTENANT
EWAN JOHN BLACKLEDGE,
1/KING'S LIVERPOOL REGIMENT AND 11 SQUADRON, ROYAL FLYING CORPS

The son of James and Lucy Blackledge of Rose Hill, Lydiate near Liverpool, Ewan was born in 1897. He was gazetted Second Lieutenant to the 1st Battalion of the King's Liverpool Regiment on 24 November 1915, going out to reinforce his sorely tried unit in the Somme trenches on 16 July 1916. Blackledge was eventually accepted for observer training with the RFC and had only been at the front for a short period when he was killed. His remains were never recovered and he is commemorated on the Arras Memorial to the Missing, France. He was twenty years old.

With the onset of winter and adverse flying conditions, activity in the air lessened considerably. An auspicious time, it transpired, for Lothar to return to Germany for treatment to an inflammation of the middle ear. Coincidently, Lothar's brother Manfred, the eponymous Red Baron, was at home on leave at the same time and both men were invited to accompany the German delegation to the Russo-German peace negotiations at Brest-Litovsk. While they were there, the brothers were given the opportunity to take time off to go stag hunting – a change of quarry, at least, for both of them! They returned to Berlin on 20 January 1918 before going on to the family home at Schweidnitz. Manfred left for the front at the beginning of February with Lothar following him to France on 16 February.

VICTORY NO 27

11 March 1918 Bristol 2b (No. A7227) 48 Squadron 13.10 hours

Lothar soon took up were he left off, continuing his apparent one-man crusade against the Bristol Fighter! A 48 Squadron machine was again on the receiving end, this time one that was part of an Offensive Patrol that had started at 11.40 en route for St Quentin and back. The combat took place north-east of Presnoy le Petit at 13.10 and, fortunately, the German ace could do no more than shoot-up the Brisfit, the two-man crew escaping harm. The pilot, Second Lieutenant W L Thomas, managed to get the damaged machine down safely enough at 13.20 although the Brisfit later had to be taken to No. 2 ASD for extensive repair.

SECOND LIEUTENANT
WYNNE LLEWELLYN THOMAS,
48 SQUADRON, ROYAL FLYING CORPS

Wynne Thomas was accepted for officer cadet training on 14 May 1917, passing through the various stages at Winchester, at Oxford and at Hendon before being gazetted Second Lieutenant on 2 August 1917. On 22 August 1917, he satisfied the examiners at Hendon and gained the Aviators Certificate of the Royal Aero Club (No.5150). Formal training completed, he was awarded his 'Wings' on 14 October 1917 and sent for further training on Bristol Fighters. Finally, on 19 January 1918, he was sent to join 22 Squadron at the front. Shortly afterwards, Thomas was transferred to 48 Squadron and was heavily involved in the fighting that preceded and followed the German Spring Offensive. Although he survived Lothar von Richthofen's attack on 11 March 1918, he was not so lucky on the 24th of the following month when, flying his Brisfit low over enemy lines, he was hit by rifle fire from the ground and brought down – fortunately on the British side of the trenches. Wynne Thomas spent the next six months recovering in a London hospital, returning to duty in November 1918 just as the war ended. He was sent to France again on 19 December 1918 but his health broke down and he was hospitalised in the January following. Wynne Thomas was allowed to leave the RAF on 25 April 1919, returning to live with his mother at 'The Redlands', Handsworth, Birmingham.

CORPORAL
J H Bowler
(NO. 52874) 48 SQUADRON, ROYAL FLYING CORPS

Bowler joined the RFC on 8 February 1917 and, having successfully trained as an observer, was promoted to Corporal a year later on 7 February 1918. Unhurt in the clash with Lothar von Richthofen, Corporal Bowler lived to fight again! On 5 September 1918, Bowler – by then a Sergeant Observer with 57 Squadron, Royal Air Force (DH 4s) – was wounded during an aerial combat.

VICTORY NO 28
12 March 1918 Bristol 2b (No. B1247) 62 Squadron 11.00 hours

62 Squadron sent out an ill-fated Offensive Patrol at 09.30, its course a line through Cambrai-Caudry-Le Catelet. The British formation was attacked by a veritable cloud of JGI machines, losing four of their number – one to Manfred von Richthofen, one to Werner Steinhäuser and two to Lothar von Richthofen. Lothar's first – probably B1247 – was claimed at 11.00 at Maretz. The British machine was flown by the patrol leader, Captain D S Kennedy MC, a man of comparative maturity and an experienced pilot. Kennedy and his observer, Lieutenant H G Gill, were both killed.

CAPTAIN
Douglas Stewart Kennedy
MC, 62 SQUADRON, ROYAL FLYING CORPS

Born on 8 September 1887, Douglas was the son of James S and Mary F Kennedy of 'St Katherine's', Broughty Ferry, Forfarshire. After completing his early education in Scotland, he pursued engineering studies at Leeds University. From university, he

served a pupilage with an engineering company, following which he gained a position as an assistant engineer with the Madras and Southern Mahratta Railway in India, being responsible for 110 miles of main line. He was elected an associate member of the Institute of Civil Engineers in January 1915. Kennedy married and he and his wife, Kathleen Mary, bought 'Craigmore', a house in their home town of Broughty Ferry. As the war dragged on, Kennedy gave up his work in India and returned home to volunteer for service with the Royal Flying Corps, being gazetted Second Lieutenant on 17 June 1916. Awarded his 'Wings' on 15 November 1916, he was afterwards sent to France where he enjoyed success as a pilot and eventually as a Flight Commander. Serving first with 11 Squadron, he and observer 2AM J F Carr, were fortunate to survive a dogfight over Arras, their FE2b becoming Wilhelm Frankl's 18th victory on 6 April 1917. Subsequently he was awarded the Military Cross, the announcement of which appeared in the *London Gazette* of 18 July 1917 (page 7234), *'For conspicuous gallantry and devotion to duty. While on a close patrol he attacked three hostile scouts and succeeded in dispersing them. A second formation of four enemy machines then attacked but were also dispersed, two of them being driven down. The results of these combats were largely due to his skill and determination'.* Douglas Stewart Kennedy MC is buried in Honnechy British Cemetery, France (Fr. 660). He was thirty-one years old.

LIEUTENANT
HUGH GODDARD GILL,
10/WEST YORKSHIRE REGIMENT AND 62 SQUADRON, ROYAL FLYING CORPS

Born at Tiruvennananllur, South Arcot, Madras Presidency, India in 1889, Hugh was the son of Edward Irwin and Fanny Amy Gill of 10 Frien Park, North Finchley, London. Gill was gazetted Second Lieutenant to the 13th (Reserve) Battalion of the West Yorkshire Regiment on 12 October 1915, before subsequently being sent to reinforce the 10th Battalion of his regiment which had virtually ceased to exist after its involvement on the first day of the Battle of the Somme on 1 July 1916. After a period in the trenches, Hugh Gill successfully sought transfer to the RFC and having completed the necessary training, he was sent out to France with 62 Squadron in January 1918. Sharing both a relative maturity of years and the common experience of living in India, he and Douglas Kennedy were an obvious 'pairing' as a Brisfit crew. Both lie side by side in Honnechy British Cemetery, France (Fr. 660). Gill was twenty-eight years old.

VICTORY NO 29
12 March 1918 Bristol 2b (No. B1250) 62 Squadron 11.10 hours

The running fight continued, with the 62 Squadron machines desperately fighting their way back to the safety of the British lines. Lothar claimed his second victim ten minutes after the first, at 11.10 over Clary, south of Caudry. This time the crew, Lieutenants Fenton and Boyce, survived the crash but were taken prisoner. In post-war debriefings after their return from captivity, both gave their versions of the event. Boyce said that they were attacked by six enemy aircraft and although they were hit in the petrol tank by machine-gun fire, they themselves escaped injury. He also said there was no time to burn the machine when they landed. Fenton's version differered slightly in that he said that after attempting to help another pilot in his Flight, he was attacked by four enemy aircraft – *'our engine stopped and we landed amongst (enemy) troops'.*

SECOND LIEUTENANT

CYRIL BOYD FENTON,

62 SQUADRON, ROYAL FLYING CORPS

Born on 11 April 1897, Cyril was the son of Mr and Mrs G A Fenton of Melbourne, Australia. He was gazetted Second Lieutenant to the General List on 4 September 1916 with immediate attachment to the Royal Flying Corps. Fenton was awarded the Aviators Certificate (No. 4360) of the Royal Aero Club on 30 November 1916 and following further training was appointed a Flying Officer on 16 January 1917. Seven days after the award of his 'Wings', he was involved in a flying accident, receiving injuries that kept him sidelined for some months. He was finally sent out to join the newly arrived 62 Squadron in France on 29 January 1918. Fenton was repatriated on 17 December 1918 and remained with the Royal Air Force until he was finally placed on the Unemployed List on 1 February 1920.

LIEUTENANT

HENRY BASIL PRIDDEN BOYCE,

SASKATCHEWAN REGIMENT AND 62 SQUADRON, ROYAL FLYING CORPS

Of Spanish ancestry, Boyce was living in Battleford, in his native Saskatchewan when war broke out. He was amongst the very first to enlist, joining the Saskatchewan Light Horse in August 1914. His volunteer unit was quickly absorbed into the Fort Garry Horse and it was with that regiment that Boyce set sail for England in the September following. As part of the CEF's 2nd Brigade, Boyce's unit trained first on Salisbury Plain before going into barracks at Tidworth prior to their departure for the front. Before that happened, however, Boyce responded to a call for volunteer replacements for the Royal Canadian Dragoons and arrived in France in time to be involved in the Battle of Festubert on 15 May 1915. Although surviving that particular piece of nastiness, he was wounded later whilst on listening post duty in no-man's land in August 1915. After treatment in an American hospital, he served for a period with the Military Police at Le Havre before returning to full duty with his regiment. The Canadian Dragoons were held in reserve throughout the Battle of the Somme and not until the German retirement to the Hindenburg Line in early 1917, did he again see action. Boyce was part of a successful cavalry charge into a German position boasting 5 field pieces and 10 machine guns – surprisingly, the Canadians did not lose a man! Boyce was picked out as potential 'officer material' and sent to England shortly before the Canadian assault on Vimy Ridge. After first receiving his commission in the Saskatchewan Regiment on 1 July 1917, he was then seconded to the RFC on 13 October 1917 and, following the appropriate training, was posted to 62 Squadron. Recalling his experiences after the war, Boyce said that he saw his Flight Commander, Captain Kennedy, go down in flames before a red plane dived from above straight towards them from the front, forcing his pilot, Fenton, to take wild evasive action. Despite their petrol tank being holed and other damage to the Brisfit, they made a comparatively smooth landing 20 miles behind the German lines, near to Le Cateau. They were instantly surrounded by German troops and consequently unable to set fire to their machine. Questions were fired at them in French before a black motor car arrived to take them into captivity, a German officer standing on the running board and rather theatrically pressing a revolver into Boyce's back. Manfred von Richthofen himself enquired as to their well-being, expressing his regret at not being able to entertain them in his Mess before they were hauled away to spend the rest of the war at Holzminden. Repatriated on 14 December 1918, Boyce returned to Canada as soon as he could, taking up a position in the Judical Department of Saskatchewan. He served again in the Second World War, this time as a legal officer (with the rank of Captain) in Regina, Saskatchewan. Henry Boyce died in 1975, after a full and active life.

On the following day (the 13th of the month!) Lothar von Richthofen was again wounded, this time in a fight with Bristol Fighters from 62 Squadron and Camels from 73 Squadron. The Bristols had been stalking several German fighters for some time but had been unable to manoeuvre themselves into a good position to attack. Just as the leader, Captain G F Hughes, decided to give it up and return to base, he saw two of his crews take it upon themselves to have a go at the enemy. However, the aggressors had not seen reinforcements in the form of several Fokker Triplanes heading for them at the same height. With no option but to go to the aid of the two errant Bristols, Hughes and the rest of his planes dived into the fray. Lothar von Richthofen singled out Hughes and closed in but Hughes's observer, Captain H Claye, cooly took careful aim and opened fire as the Fokker tore into them. The top wing of the Triplane began to shed fabric and then the whole centre section peeled away, causing Lothar to lose control. At that moment, Hughes and Claye were engaged by Manfred von Richthofen and had their hands full for several minutes before they managed to extricate themselves from what was an extremely fraught situation. Lothar in the meantime, had crashed, receiving injuries which kept him out of action until the following July. His jaw was badly broken and to his great and evident discomfort, was kept wired-up for months. Hughes, of course, claimed the Triplane but so too did Captain A H Orlebar (who later captained Britain's Schneider Trophy Team). Orlebar, flying a 73 Squadron Camel, also described his 'kill' as shedding most of its top wing; certainly both British pilots appear to have been credited with this one victory.

Lothar was still in hospital when news of his brother's death reached him on 21 April 1918.

VICTORY NO 30

25 July 1918 Camel 73 Squadron 19.50 hours

Lothar von Richthofen returned to take over his command of Jasta 11 on 19 July 1918 and, following a brief period of re-establishment, soon settled into the familiar routine by gaining his thirtieth victory six days later. As chance would have it, his opponents on this day were the same as those that had almost done for him on 13 March – the Camels of 73 Squadon. The RFC machines had taken off at 18.00 hours on an Offensive Patrol to the Fismes area. They had reached their objective when they were engaged by enemy scouts, losing three Camels in the ensuing dogfight. Lieutenant R F Lewis (No. D9398) as well as Second Lieutenants W A Armstrong (No. D1794) and K S Laurie (No. B7874) were shot down – only Laurie survived to be taken as a prisoner of war. The authors have to admit that despite their best efforts, they are unable to state with any degree of certainty which of the three fell under Lothar von Richthofen's guns. His was the only claim made by Jasta 11 and it is likely that one of the other 73 Squadron Camels was shot down over French territory by Karl Bolle of Jasta 2 at Fère-en-Tardenois. 43 Squadron machines were also in a fight in the area and they, too, lost three Camels – probably to Jasta 2.

Lothar was flying a borrowed Fokker DVII (244/18) for this victory – notable not only because it was his thirtieth but also because it was JGI's 500th!

Some records incorrectly time Lothar von Richthofen's 30th victory as occurring at '07.50' – probably a confusion between '7.50 pm' and the '19.50' of the twenty-four hour clock.

VICTORY NOs 31 & 32

1 August 1918 Spad VII 13.10 hours • 1 August 1918 Spad VII

By this time the war on the ground was going badly for the German Army but still the Imperial German Air Service was a force to be reckoned with, claiming six Spads on this first day of August. Lothar von Richthofen registered two victories, both against Frenchmen. Unfortunately, the Jasta 11 records do not give precise locations for the combats and an examination of the relevant French records reveals only that two pilots were said to be lost on this day – Adjutant-chef J Raszewski of Spa. 96 and Caporal Georges Perrin of Spa. 73 (who had joined his Escadrille only six days earlier). Both units were part of Groupe de Combat 19 and both men were flying Spad VIIs. Groupe de Combat 19 was centred on Pierre-Morains, south-west of Châlons.

VICTORY NO 33

8 August 1918 DH 9 49 Squadron 17.30 hours

8 August 1918 – the first day of the Battle of Amiens – a black day for the German Army but not, personally, for Lothar von Richthofen who achieved a hat-trick of victories. As the war began to go badly for the Germans and the old certainties eroded, so it became more and more difficult to keep up the old administrative standards. With

the fluidity of the front lines, it was often no longer possible to identify wreckage and so record the details of the occupants – there were more urgent and pressing problems to contend with. Three years after the war ended, Lothar von Richthofen published his recollections and identified this, his thirty-third victory, as a 'two-seater', one of a number in a bombing formation. The bridges over the Canal du Nord were the prime RAF targets of the day with several DH4 and DH9 squadrons being particularly active. Jasta 11 had recently moved to Ennemain airfield, ten kilometres south of Péronne, just east of the canal. Lothar recalled how 49 Squadron DH9s passed over his aerodrome after dropping their bombs and how he and Erich Löwenhardt chased after them. Lothar caught up with one of the British machines and a short struggle ensued before his opponent went down in flames. In fact two of the 49 Squadron machines, 'C6110' and 'C2152', were shot down with the crew of 'C6110' being taken prisoner. However, in view of Lothar's description of the sorry fate of the machine under his assault, quote – *'down in flames'* – it seems on the face of it that the occupants of 'C2152', Lieutenant G S Ramsay and Second Lieutenant W N Hartley, (both of whom were killed) were the victims on this occasion.

Lieutenant C B H Lefroy, 43 Squadron, Royal Air Force

Confusingly, however, a 43 Squadron Camel (F5919) flown by Lieutenant C B H Lefroy is often credited with the dubious distinction of being Lothar von Richthofen's 33rd victory and certainly the time and location of the Sopwith's destruction are not too awry. 43 Squadron, tasked with a Special Mission (ground attack) had taken off at 16.00 led by Captain C F King MC DFC. Forty-five minutes into their mission (16.45), they ran into seven or eight Fokker biplanes west of Péronne. In the ensuing fight, King himself claimed one Fokker 'out of control' and witnessed yet another break up in the air. As, afterwards, none of the British survivors made a claim for the Fokker that had broken up, the Squadron CO, not unreasonably, awarded it jointly to the two men of his patrol – Lefroy and Lieutenant P W R Arundel – who failed to return.

As we know from Lothar's own account of the action, Erich Löwenhardt of Jasta 10 was in the immediate vicinity of the engagement and, indeed, claimed a Camel at roughly the same time as Lothar's claim. So the problem is, did Lothar and Löwenhardt actually shoot down the two 43 Squadron Camels and was – three years later – Lothar's memory at fault when he described his victim as a two-seater?

In the final analysis, it is beyond the arrogance of the authors to contradict the man himself and we opt, therefore, for the two-seater.

LIEUTENANT GEORGE STRACHAN RAMSAY, 49 SQUADRON, ROYAL AIR FORCE

Born on 18 October 1892, George was the son of Peter and Annie Ramsay of 'Elmbank', 72 Norse Road, Scotstoun, Glasgow. After leaving school in 1909, he secured a position as a trainee draughtsman with the shipbuilders and engineers, Brown & Company of Clydebank. The first five years of his apprenticeship were dedicated to practical marine engineering, following which he was appointed as a fully fledged draughtsman to the Drawing Office. After only two years, he was promoted to Manager's Assistant and had spent a further year in that capacity when he decided to volunteer his services to the RFC. Strachan was gazetted as a Second Lieutenant on 27 September 1917 and, two days later, reported to 3 Training Squadron at Farnborough. Awarded his 'Wings' by the begining of 1918, he was first sent to 110 Squadron then still at Rendcombe in England. By the time he was finally sent out to join 49 Squadron in France on 22 June 1918, he had accumulated 75 hours flying time. George Strachan Ramsay's remains were never recovered for burial and so he is commemorated on the Arras Memorial to the Missing, France. He was twenty-seven years old.

SECOND LIEUTENANT

WALTER NOEL HARTLEY,

49 SQUADRON, ROYAL AIR FORCE

The son of Robert and Margaret Jean Hartley of Park Farm, Capenhurst, Wirral, Cheshire, Walter was born on 22 December 1899. He was educated at the Collegiate School, Shaw Street, Liverpool, near to his father's Auction Rooms in Erskine Street on the fringe of the city centre. Shortly after leaving school and as soon as he was old enough, he volunteered for the RFC, being accepted for officer cadet training on 29 December 1917. Hartley was gazetted Second Lieutenant to the Royal Air Force on 18 May 1918 and sent out to 49 Squadron as a probationary observer on 6 June 1918. Like those of his pilot, his remains were never found and he is commemorated on the Arras Memorial to the Missing, France. He was still only eighteen years old.

VICTORY NO 34

8 August 1918 SE5a (No. B151) 60 Squadron 17.45 hours

The second of his victories on this day also occurred in the late afternoon when SE5s from 60 Squadron were engaged in the Foucaucourt-Wancourt area at about 16.40 British time. One SE5, piloted by an American, Second Lieutenant J G Hall, came down in the German lines near Estrées. (Ernst Udet also claimed an SE5 at 17.30 but this was over Barleux, eight kilometres to the east of Lothar von Richthofen's claim.) In his published recollections in 1921, Lothar recalled that after a desperate low-level fight, the RAF pilot seemed to attempt a landing in a hollow or small valley, but he was going too fast and the machine cracked up and disintegrated into splinters as he touched down.

SECOND LIEUTENANT

JAMES GRANTLEY HALL,

60 SQUADRON, ROYAL AIR FORCE

Born in West Dennis, Mass. on 8 January 1896, James was the son of Charles Edwin and Edith J Hall of 52 Summer Street, Malden, Massachusetts, United States of America. He was educated at the Medford and Malden High Schools and at Burdett Business College. A runner of some note, he won numerous athletic prizes and, in January 1913, was awarded a Silver Medal by the Humane Society for bravery when attempting to save the life of a friend following a skating accident. As well as attending Business College, James worked part-time in his father's automobile business, Chas E Hall & Sons, 40 Summer Street, Malden. In 1917, Grantley tried to join the US Air Service straight from College but was refused entry because he failed the height requirement by half an inch! Nothing daunted, he enlisted in the Royal Flying Corps in Boston during July 1917 and shortly afterwards was sent to Toronto, Canada, for training. He trained at several places in Canada and later in Texas. He was gazetted Second Lieutenant to the Royal Flying Corps on 12 December 1917 and attached to 92 Squadron in England with effect from 16 January 1918. After a final course at the School of Gunnery in May 1918, he was finally sent out to join 60 Squadron in France on 6 June 1918. One source credits Grantley with three victories during the two months of his active service at the front. Originally buried one and a half kilometres south of Maricourt, his body was moved, after the war, to the Somme American Cemetery, Bony, France. He was 22 years of age.

VICTORY NO 35

8 August 1918 SE5a (No. D6962) 1 Squadron 18.50 hours

Identifying von Richthofen's third victim of the day also presents some problems. In the early evening he and the rest of Jasta 11 had landed to refuel and rearm and in so doing, Lothar damaged his Fokker DVII by colliding with a tent! Nothing daunted, the Staffenführer borrowed Leutnant Erich Just's DVII and took off again with four others of his Jasta. Above the front lines, which had changed their configuration drastically during the course of the day, the Germans were engaged by ten British machines. Von Richthofen first made a wide turn in order to evaluate the situation before picking out one of the enemy at the rear of the formation, which he then attacked with immediate and devastating results – the British machine hurtling straight into the ground. The unfortunate victim of this attack was most probably a 1 Squadron SE5a flown by Captain K C Mills, an ace with five victories of his own. At 16.45, and for the second time that day, the RAF Squadron took off from their base tasked with the low level bombing of a bridge – probably on the Canal du Nord. Mills, the leader, dropped his bombs and then was seen to engage five Fokker DVIIs before he disappeared from sight.

CAPTAIN
KENNETH CHARLES MILLS,
1 SQUADRON, ROYAL AIR FORCE

Born on 26 March 1899, Kenneth was the elder son of Charles and Kate Mills of 'Croylands', South Side, Wimbledon Common, London. He was educated at Rugby (1913-1917), from where he joined the Royal Flying Corps during his last term in February 1917. Mills was gazetted Second Lieutenant on 10 May 1917 and awarded his 'Wings' on the 17th of the following month. He served as a ferry pilot from September 1917 until February 1918 when he was sent to join 1 Squadron at the front. Mills enjoyed some considerable success, gaining five victories between 21 April and 7 May 1918 when he was wounded during the action which yielded him his fifth victory. After recovering from his injuries, he was promoted to Captain and Flight Commander and returned to the front,this time to join 1 Squadron, on 4 August 1918. The circumstances of his last flight were described in a letter to his parents from one of the officers under his command: *'The Squadron was stationed at Fienvillers, south-west of Doullens, and the aeroplanes of Captain Mills' Flight were detailed to drop bombs on a bridge at Péronne and on any of the enemy seen on the ground. On returning safely the first time, they went out again to complete the destruction of the bridge. They dropped their bombs, but then met a formation of five Fokkers, when the clouds were very thick and low, and after the fight which ensued Captain Mills was not seen again'*. Kenneth Mills' body was never found and so he is commemorated on the Arras Memorial to the Missing, France. He was still only 19 years old.

VICTORY NO 36

9 August 1918 DH9 (No. D5666) 107 Squadron 07.30 hours

While the battles on the ground continued to rage, there was also intense activity in the air and after his three victories on the previous day, Lothar von Richthofen claimed a further two on this, the second day of the Battle of Amiens. Although his victories were more than eleven hours apart, both were from the same RAF Squadron. DH9s from 107 Squadron, taking off at intervals and escorted by Camels from 54 Squadron, had been ordered to bomb the Brise Bridge (Pont lès Brise) over the Canal du Nord by Marchélepot, south of Péronne. A combined force from both Jasta 11 and Jasta 27 engaged the DH9s with dire consequences for the British bombing planes. In all, five of the DH9s fell to German scouts with Lothar von Richthofen registering his victory as falling at Villers Carbonnel, just to the west of the targeted bridge and alongside the Amiens to St Quentin Road.

CAPTAIN WILLIAM HENRY DORÉ, SASKATCHEWAN REGIMENT AND 107 SQUADRON, ROYAL AIR FORCE

The son of building contractor Henry James Doré and Mrs Janet C Doré, Bill was born on 29 April 1892 at Arichat, Cape Breton, Nova Scotia, Canada. He was educated at local Public and High Schools before securing a position with the Canadian Bank of Commerce on 20 December 1909. Doré enlisted in January 1915 from the Winnipeg branch of the bank into the 44th Canadian Battalion, being gazetted Second Lieutenant on 1 June 1915. He transferred to the RFC in England in November 1915 and learnt to fly – satisfying the examiners on 10 February 1916 who, as a consequence, awarded him the Aviators Certificate (No. 2445) of the Royal Aero Club on the same day. Doré first served in France with No. 1 Squadron, joining that unit in April 1916. On 2 January 1917, Doré married nineteen-year-old Norah Helen Reeves of 28 Church Road, Moseley, Birmingham. In the Spring of 1917, by now an experienced pilot and promoted to the rank of Captain, Doré was posted to Toronto, Canada, to serve as 87 Training Squadron's OC. Later in 1917 he transferred to Fort Worth, Texas, as an instructor before again returning to England. In May 1918, he was sent to join the newly formed 107 Squadron at Lake Down, Salisbury, as a Flight Commander. Two weeks later, on 3 June, the Squadron landed in France. Described as *'the best DH9 pilot in France'*, Captain Doré imposed a strict and exacting training regime on the largely inexperienced crews, sometimes leading them down to a height of less than 500 feet above the enemy trenches to *'test their nerve!'* 107 Squadron became officially operational on 25 June 1918, serving under 13th Wing, 3rd Brigade, RAF. Doré himself enjoyed some success over the enemy when he, and his observer of the day, were responsible for sending down an Albatros 'Out of Control' on 11 July 1918. The Squadron was constantly involved in bombing raids against the enemy and on 8 August word came through that every effort must be made to destroy Brie Bridge. The first raid was made in a blinding rainstorm which perhaps helped to protect the bombers from the predatory attentions of the German Jastas. On the following day, Brie Bridge was again the target with each Flight raiding separately. It was said that those who saw Captain Doré going down in flames could hardly credit it, for not only was he a brilliant pilot but seemed to have led a charmed life. Shortly after the war ended, a letter from the Adjutant General's office in Ottawa, addressed to Doré's mother, then living at 1039 California Drive, Burlingame, California, gave the following information – *'Captain Doré left the aerodrome at 5.08am......with Second Lieut J A Wallace (sic) in a de Havilland 9 No.5666. A formation of eight machines left the ground with him......Wallace was reported killed by a message dropped over our lines from hostile aircraft. Capt Doré's machine was seen by other pilots to go down in flames'*. Bill Doré's body was never found and so he is commemorated on the Arras Memorial to the Missing, France. He was aged 26.

SECOND LIEUTENANT

JOHN EWING WALLACE,

107 SQUADRON, ROYAL AIR FORCE

Born in 1899, John was the son of the Reverend John Ewing Wallace and Margaret Anderson Wallace of 25 Blackett Place, Edinburgh. He was educated at Glasgow High School and at the University of Edinburgh where he became a member of the OTC. In August 1917, as soon as he was old enough, Wallace gave up his university place and entered the RFC as a cadet. He was gazetted Second Lieutenant into the newly formed Royal Air Force in April 1918. Wallace's remains were not recovered or identified and, like his pilot, he is commemorated on the Arras Memorial to the Missing, France. He was still only eighteen years old.

VICTORY NO 37

9 August 1918 DH9 (No. F6066) 107 Squadron 18.40 hours

In the late afternoon, 107 Squadron set out on another bombing raid on the bridges over the Canal du Nord. They were again opposed by elements of JGI, including Lothar von Richthofen and Jasta 11. Von Richthofen picked out a crew that had themselves claimed two Fokkers shot down on the earlier morning raid. The luck enjoyed by the British pair ran out in this encounter as the German ace sent them down to crash near to Foucaucourt. The formal German record – the Nachrichtenblatt – lists both of Lothar von Richthofen's victories as being 'DH12s', although no such type existed at that time. Furthermore, 'F6066', flown by yet another of the Squadron's flight commanders, was 107 Squadron's only loss on this evening raid.

CAPTAIN

ALEXANDER JOHN MAYO,

107 SQUADRON, ROYAL AIR FORCE

Born on 6 July 1895, Alex was the son of Mr and Mrs Mayo of 'Avebury House', St Peter Street, Winchester. After leaving school, Mayo secured a pupilage under Mr W V Anderson, associate member of the Institute of Civil Engineers and was himself eventually admitted as a student of the Institution in December 1915. At his own request, he was allowed to suspend his pupilage in order to offer his services to the RFC. Mayo was gazetted Second Lieutenant to the RFC (SR) on 13 December 1915, going on to gain the Aviators Certificate (No. 2484) of the Royal Aero Club on 19 February 1916. After completing his formal training, he first experienced operational flying with 5 Squadron, a unit he joined in France on 21 June 1916. Mayo returned to the UK for rest, recuperation and a spell as an instructor in March 1917, before again going out to France for a second tour of operations on 17 January 1918. Six months later he was briefly posted to 136 Squadron in England before going back yet again to France for the third and last time, joining 107 Squadron as a Flight Commander ('B' Flight) on 1 August 1918 – just eight days before he was killed. Mayo had successfully completed the first raid on 9 August but his luck ran out on the second when he fell under the guns of Lothar von Richthofen. Alexander Mayo is buried in Heath Cemetery, Harbonnières, France (Fr. 526). He was 23.

SECOND LIEUTENANT

JOSEPH WESSON JONES,

107 SQUADRON, ROYAL AIR FORCE

The son of Mr and Mrs Joseph Jones of 153 Stoney Lane, Sparkbrook, Birmingham, Joseph Junior was born on 10 April 1918. Educated locally, Jones afterwards studied engineering and chemistry before securing a post as a technical clerk in the City of Birmingham Gas Works. Gazetted Second

Right: Lothar's Fokker DVII with yellow nose and checkerboard rear wings and elevators.

Below right: A DH9 day bomber similar to the 98 Squadron machine shot down by Lothar for his 38th victory.

Lieutenant to the RFC on 13 April 1917, he completed his training and was appointed a Flying Officer on 18 May 1917. Still underage for overseas active service, he was kept in the UK until 14 July 1918 when he was sent out to join 107 Squadron in France. Remarkably, the morning raid on Brie Bridge was Joseph Jones's first operational flight and yet he still managed to claim *'two Hun machines!'* His success, however, was short lived – in every sense. Unlike those of his pilot's, his remains were never recovered and hence he is commemorated on the Arras Memorial to the Missing, France. He was nineteen years old.

VICTORY NO 38

11 August 1918 DH9 (No. D3097) 98 Squadron 08.30 hours

A formation of DH9s from 98 Squadron left their base at Blangermont at 06.30 on a bombing raid against targets at Cléry-sur-Somme, to the north-west of Péronne. An hour later they ran into elements of JGI from both Jastas 4 and 11. Two of the DH9s were shot down, one by the brilliant Ernst Udet of Jasta 4 – his 52nd victory – the other by Lothar von Richthofen.

SECOND LIEUTENANT BRIAN CHARLES GEARY, 98 SQUADRON, ROYAL AIR FORCE

The son of James Page and Ellen Geary of London, Brian was born in 1899. He was educated at the Central Foundation School, London, at Kimbolton Grammar School, Huntingdon (1911-1914) and at Finsbury Engineering College. Following the completion of his training course at Finsbury College, Geary was employed in the manufacture of munitions until he joined the RFC, being gazetted Second Lieutenant to the General List on 10 January 1918. Geary trained at Hastings, Oxford and Thetford prior to being appointed a Flying Officer on 10 June 1918. Shortly before he left to join 98 Squadron on 13 July 1918, Geary visited Kimbolton Grammar and insisted upon purchasing the entire contents of the school's tuck shop for distribution amongst the boys! In a letter to his mother, the 98 Squadron Adjutant, Lieutenant R Mungo Park, wrote, *'....As his machine was seen to fall to pieces we are afraid there is no doubt that he was killed............ His death must have been quite instantaneous'.* Brian Geary's body was never found and he is commemorated on the Arras Memorial to the Missing, France. He was nineteen years old.

SECOND LIEUTENANT EDWARD HENRY EDGELL, 98 SQUADRON, ROYAL AIR FORCE

Born on 1 July 1899, Edward was the son of scientific instrument maker Albert Edward Edgell and his wife, Esther, of 'Holne Chase', Arundel Road, Littlehampton, Sussex. Educated locally, he joined his father's firm, A Edgell & Company of 26 Norfolk Road, Littlehampton, after leaving school in 1913. As soon as he was old enough to be accepted, he volunteered for service with the RFC and was initially sent to Halton Park to commence his training in October 1917. Completing his training at Eastchurch on 1 June 1918, he was sent to France as a probationary observer on 14 July 1918. He lasted less than a month. His remains were never identified and so, like his pilot, he is commemorated on the Arras Memorial to the Missing, France. And like his pilot, Edward Edgell was nineteen years old.

VICTORY NO 39

12 August 1918 Sopwith Camel (No. D9668) 209 Squadron 09.30 hours

Lothar von Richthofen's last two combat victories were achieved in the same dogfight and within minutes of each other. 209 Squadron, who had been involved in brother Manfred's last action in April, were out on an early sortie over the battle front above Péronne when they became embroiled with the Fokker D VIIs of Jasta 11. The Germans claimed four of the Camels as victories whereas, in fact, one of the four actually managed to nurse his damaged machine back to base. The first of Lothar's two victories was most probably, although not certainly, against the Camel flown by Second Lieutenant K M Walker which went down in flames. The less likely candidate was newcomer Lieutenant D K Leed (B7471) who was in combat for the first time.

SECOND LIEUTENANT
KENNETH MACKENZIE WALKER,
3/WILTSHIRE REGIMENT ATTACHED 209 SQUADRON, ROYAL AIR FORCE

Born in 1894, Kenneth was the son of John Franklin Walker and Rita Walker of Rua Joad de Dens No.1, Villa, Nova de Gaya, Portugal. He was gazetted Second Lieutenant to the 3rd Reserve Battalion of the Wiltshire Regiment on 5 August 1916 before eventually transferring to the RFC. A very useful Camel pilot, Walker had had a share in five victories during July and August, three of them with his Flight Commander Captain J K Summers, who would also be shot down by Lothar von Richthofen in this, the German ace's last combat. Walker's remains were never found and he is commemorated on the Arras Memorial to the Missing, France. He was 24.

VICTORY NO 40
12 August 1918 Sopwith Camel (No. D9668) 209 Squadron 09.30 hours

The fortieth and last of Lothar von Richthofen's victories was against a worthy opponent – a Flight Commander (as the streamers trailing in the slipstream of his Camel testified) and an ace with eight victories of his own – Captain J K Summers MC. Von Richthofen described the streamers in his 'claim' and even mentioned them to Summers himself after the Englishman was brought to see him as a prisoner that very afternoon. Oddly, although Lothar could be quite specific about such a minor detail, he was convinced, albeit mistakenly, that he had shot down not 'Camels' but two 'Dolphins'!

CAPTAIN (LATER GROUP CAPTAIN)
JOHN KENNETH SUMMERS
MC, MID, 209 SQUADRON, ROYAL AIR FORCE

Born on 22 December 1894, John was the son of Mr and Mrs Summers of 76 Stanhope Avenue, Church End, Finchley, London N3. He was educated at Denstone College (1908-1912) and at Birmingham University (1912-1914). Summers was gazetted Second Lieutenant to the New Army battalions of the Royal Warwickshire Regiment on 25

January 1915. Almost immediately, he successfully applied for transfer to the RFC which occured during the April following. In May he joined 3 Squadron as an observer and after five months of operational flying he returned to Castle Bromwich to train as a pilot. Summers gained the Aviators Certificate (No. 2154) of the Royal Aero Club on 13 December 1915 and was awarded his 'Wings' early in the new year. Summers returned to France to rejoin 3 Squadron in June 1917, serving with that unit until October during which time he was both Mentioned in Despatches and awarded the Military Cross, the announcement of which appeared somewhat belatedly in the *London Gazette* of 18 July 1918, page 7246 – *'For conspicuous gallantry and devotion to duty. He has continuously performed valuable work in co-operating with artillery. He has on many occasions flown at a very low altitude in order to give information to the infantry, which has proved of the utmost value'*. Summers acted as a liaison officer with 1st Brigade HQ for a period before briefly returning to his Squadron. A transfer to the Home Establishment for some well deserved rest was followed by a posting to 209 Squadron as a Flight Commander in June 1918. Summers proved himself a very successful Camel pilot, gaining eight victories between 23 June and 11 August 1918 – the day before he was shot down himself. Taken prisoner, he was shown handsome hospitality by the pilots of the Richthofen Circus before being taken away to a camp. Repatriated just in time for Christmas on 23 December 1918, Summers decided to make the RAF his career and was given a permanent commission in August 1919. He served with 45 Squadron in Iraq in 1925, taking command of the Squadron and being promoted Squadron Leader in the following year. His subsequent career included appointments at HQ, Air Defence of Great Britain and with Bomber Command. In 1940 he became CO of the Blenheim Operational Training Unit. His last posting was to Rhodesia where he formed the Combined Air Observers'

Left: Lieutenant Field Eugene Kindley (12 victories) of the US 148th Aero Squadron.

School. J K Summers retired in 1943 and stayed in Rhodesia, taking up farming.

The day following Lothar's 39th and 40th victories was, portentiously for the ace, the 13th of the month of August! He was, of course, acutely aware of the bad luck that day of the month had in the past generated for him. He could, no doubt, have fully justified a day on the ground, attending to pressing administrative duties. Determined, however, not to give in to terdekaphobia, he took off in his Fokker DVII with others from the Staffel, to link up with aircraft of Jagdesgeschwader III, led and commanded by Hermann Göring's old friend, Bruno Loerzer.

Arriving over the front, von Richthofen spotted a two-seater and immediately dived to attack. Stealing a glance over his shoulder to confirm that his men were following him, Lothar was astonished to see, instead, a flight of six Camels closing in on his tail. Breaking off the attack on the two-seater, he rolled the Fokker over into an evasive dive. He realised he was too late, however, when a machine-gun bullet thudded into his leg. Using both hands to lift the injured limb off the rudder pedal, he contemplated using his parachute to bale out of the damaged machine. Deciding that he would not have sufficient strength to propel himself out of the cockpit, he steered the Fokker down to a rough landing onto the ravaged Somme battleground below.

The evidence suggests that his antagonists on this thirteenth day were Camels of the US 148th Aero Squadron, part of the 65th Wing of the Royal Air Force. The Flight was led by Lieutenant Field Eugene Kindley, a twenty-two year old from Pea Ridge, Arkansas. Kindley claimed a Fokker Triplane 'Out of Control' north of Roye at 1352 hours (1452 hours German time). It would seem from this relatively modest claim, that the Americans were too busy with von Richthofen's companions to follow the ace's full descent to a forced landing.

The Americans were as surprised as Lothar when they found themselves on his tail. Kindley's Flight had spotted the gaggle of Fokkers in the distance and, turning north, dived into a huge bank of cloud between them and the enemy. Eventually emerging on the other side, they found themselves virtually on top of a Fokker in the act of attacking an Allied two-seater. Opening fire immediately, Kindley saw his bullets striking home, forcing the enemy machine into an uncontrolled dive. There remained, however, the problem of von Richthofen's companions. In their first diving pass the Americans claimed three Fokkers shot down, with the possibility of a fourth! Lothar, however, was the only Jasta 11 casualty on this day, although Jasta 36 (one of JGIII's Jastas) did have a pilot wounded – he baled out over Bussy.

Lothar von Richthofen was Field Kindley's fourth of the twelve victories he would eventually achieve by the war's end. A distinguished ace, he was awarded the British DFC and the American DSC and Oak Leaf Cluster. Sadly, on 1 February 1920, by then a Captain and the Commander of the 94th Aero, he was killed in a flying accident back home in Texas. Lothar von Richthofen survived the war, of course, returning to a Germany heaving with political unrest and torn by riots and raging inflation. At first, he tried to settle to a life of farming but soon tired of this and got himself a middle ranking management job in industry. On 5 June 1919 he had married Doris, Countess von Keyserlingk, by whom he was to have a son and a daughter. Still restless and unsettled, he tried for work in the profession he knew best – flying. Eventually he was successful in securing a job as a civil pilot with Deutsche Luft-Reederei, mainly flying mail and passengers daily between Berlin and Hamburg. In June 1922, within days of its third anniversary, his marriage to the Countess von Keyserlingk was dissolved. Two weeks later, on 4 July 1922, he was

'A' Flight, US 148th Aero Squadron, left to right: Laurence Wyly, Louis W Rabe, Field Kindley, W B Knox and J O Creech.

approaching Hamburg on a routine flight when his engine failed. Lothar was piloting a converted LVG C VI, a former bomber aircraft that had been adapted for passenger and light cargo use. On this occasion he was carrying two passengers, the American silent screen film actress, Fern Andra and her business manager. He had made forced landings before and was probably not too alarmed at the prospect of another, but the terrain was rough and wooded and as he came in he clipped the top of a row of trees which tipped the machine nose down and over on to its back. Help was not long in coming and first, the two seriously injured passengers were helped from the wreck. The rescuers turned next to Lothar, carefully extricating him, still barely alive, from the smashed machine, only for him to die later in the ambulance carrying him to hospital.

Lothar's body was returned to the family home in Schweidnitz for burial alongside his father who had died shortly after the war ended. His old comrades in the Association of German Fighter Pilots attached the following words to their floral tribute: *'Now the brothers, upon whom all Germany once looked with pride, are united in Valhalla'*. Lothar Freiherr von Richthofen was twenty-seven years old.

Now Lothar's remains lie alongside his brothers Manfred and Bolko at Südfriedhof, Wiesbaden.

BIBLIOGRAPHY

A Contemptible Little Flying Corps	I McInnes & J Webb, London Stamp Exchange
Above the Lines	Franks/Bailey/Guest, Grub Street, 1993
Above the Trenches	Shores/Franks/Guest, Grub Street, 1990
Above the Trenches Supplement	Shores/Franks/Guest, Grub Street, 1996
Activities of the British Community in Argentina During the Great War	
Alumni Felstedienses, 1890-1950	
Balliol College War Record 2 Volumes	
Bank of Montreal – Memorial of the Great War	
Before Endeavours Fade	Rose Coombs, MBE, After the Battle, 1983
Bloody April	Alan Morris, Jarrolds, 1967
Book of Remembrance and War Record of Mill Hill School, 1914-19	
Bradfield College Register	
British Roll of Honour	
Burke's Landed Gentry	
Burke's Landed Gentry – Irish Family Records	
Charterhouse College Register	
Cheltenham College Register	
City and Guilds College Register	
City of Coventry, Roll of the Fallen	
Clifton College Register	
Cross of Sacrifice, Volumes I and II	SD & DB Jarvis, Roberts Medals Ltd
Croydon and the Great War	edited by Ald H Keatley Moore and WC Berwick Sayers, Croydon 1920
Das Letzte Mal an Der Front, Juli-August 1918	Lothar von Richthofen (ed G Dickhuth-Harrach, Munich 1921) Translated by Jan Hayzlett
Dean Close School Register	
Deeds That Thrill the Empire Volumes 1 to 5	
Denstone College Register	
Downside and the War 1914-19	compiled by Dom Lucius Graham, OSB, Hudson and Kearns, 1925
Dublin University, Trinity College War List	
Dulwich College War Record, 1914-19	
Durham University, 1914-18	
Eastbourne College Register	
Edinburgh Academy Register 1824-1914 (and War Supplement)	
Etonians Who Fought in the Great War MCMXIV-MCMXIX	
Fettes College Register	
Flying Fury	JTB McCudden, Aviation Book Club
Fokker, The Man and the Aircraft	Hegener/Robertson, Harleyford Publications, 1961
Germany's First Air Force 1914-1918	Peter Kilduff, Arms & Armour Press, 1991
Greenbank School, Liverpool, Register	
Harrow School Register	
High in the Empty Blue	Alex Revell, Flying Machines Press, 1995
History of the Queen's Royal Regiment, Vol VII	Colonel HC Wylly, Gale & Polden Ltd, 1925
History of the Royal Irish Rifles, Volume II	Cyril Falls, Gale & Polden, Aldershot 1925
Immelmann, The Eagle of Lille	Franz Immelmann, Hamilton Ltd, 1935
In Memoriam, Royal Grammar School, Newcastle on Tyne	
Into the Blue	Captain Norman Macmillan MC, AFC, Duckworth, London 1929
Kelly's Handbook to the Titled, Landed and Official Classes	
Kelvinside Academy Roll of Honor	Haileybury Register
Kimbolton School Register	HA Jones MC, Vintage Aviation Library (reprint) 1987
King of Air Fighters	IRA Jones, DSO, MC, DFC, MM, Thackwell Publishing (reprint) 1986
King William's College Register	
Letters from the Front, 1914-1919 Two Volumes	The Canadian Bank of Commerce, 1920
Leys School Register	
List of British Officers Taken Prisoner in the Various Theatres of War, 1914-1918	London Stamp Exchange (reprint) 1919
Liverpool College Magazines	
Malvern College Register	
Manchester University Roll of Service	
Manfred von Richthofen, The Man and the Aircraft He Flew	David Baker, Outline Press, 1990

Marlborough College Register

Merchiston Castle School Register

Naval Eight — EG Johnstone, Arms and Armour Press, 1972

No 1 Squadron — Michael Shaw, Ian Allan Ltd, 1986

Officers Died in the Great War — JB Hayward (reprint) 1990

Officers of the Durham Light Infantry — Malcolm McGregor

Oundle Memorials of the Great War, 1914-1919

Over the Front — Franks/Bailey, Grub Street 1992

Record of Service of Solicitors and Articled Clerks, 1914-1918

Richthofen – Beyond the Legend of the Red Baron — Peter Kilduff, Arms and Armour Press, 1993

Richthofen, The Red Knight of Germany — Vigilant (Claude Sykes) Hamilton

Roll of Honour and War List, 1914-18, of University College School, Hampstead

Royal Air Force 1918 — Edited by C Cole, Kimber & Co, 1968

Royal Flying Corps, 1915-16 — Edited by C Cole, Kimber & Co, 1969

Royal Flying Corps, Honours, Decorations, Medals Etc

Rugby School Register

Sherborne Register

Shetland's Roll of Honour

Soldiers Died in the Great War — JB Hayward & Sons (reprint) 1989

Squadron Histories, RFC, RNAS and RAF, Since 1912 — Peter Lewis, Putnam & Co, 1968

St Lawrence College Register

Stoneyhurst War Record

The Air Defence of Britain, 1914-1918 — C Cole/EF Cheesman, Bodley Head, 1984

The Barrovian (King William's College)

The Ceylon Roll of Honour and Record of Service in the Great War

The Combat Records of Hermann Goring — Frank Olynyk, Over the Front, Vol 10 No 3

The Connaught Rangers, Volume III

The Court Journal 1917

The Distinguished Service Order, 1886-1923 — JB Hayward & Sons (reprint) 1978

The Graphic

The History of 60 Squadron RAF — Group Captain AJL Scott, Wm Heinimann, 1920

The History of the King's Regiment (Liverpool) 1914-19 3 Volumes — Everard Wyrell, Edward Arnold & Co, 1918-35

The House of Commons Book of Remembrance 1914-18 — E W Moss-Blundell, Elkins, Mathews & Marrot, 1931

The Illustrated London News

The Inns of Court OTC During the Great War

The Institution of Civil Engineers, Memorial Volume The Great War 1914-1919

The London Cyclist Battalion — Published for the 25th London (Cyclist) OCA, Forster, Groom & Co, London 1932

The Manchester Grammar School Book of Remembrance

The Manchester University Roll of Honour

The Red Airfighter — Manfred von Richthofen, Greenhill (reprint) 1990

The Red Knight of Germany — Floyd Gibbons, Cassell & Co

The Roll of Honour of the Institution of Electrical Engineers

The Roll of Honour, Volumes I to V — The Marquis de Ruvigny, The Standardart Book Co

The Royal Berkshire Regiment — FL Petrie, The Barracks, Reading 1925

The Scottish Pictorial

The Sphere

The Times

The Victoria Cross, 1856-1920 — JB Hayward & Sons (reprint) 1985

The War in the Air, Official History of the War, Volumes I to VI — HA Jones, Clarenden Press, 1937

The Watsonian War Record, 1914-1918

The Worcestershire Regiment in the Great War — Captain H FitzM Stacke, MC, GT Cheshire & Sons Ltd, Kidderminster 1929

The Zeebrugge Raid — Philip Warner, William Kimber, London 1978

Tonbridge School and the Great War of 1914-1919

Trenchard, Man of Vision — Andrew Boyle, Collins, London 1962

Univ College London, Univ College Hospital & Medical Record, A Record 1914-19

University of Edinburgh Record of Honour, 1914-1919

University of Liverpool Roll of Service, 1914-1918

University of London OTC Roll of War Service, 1914-1919

Uppingham School Roll

Von Richthofen and the Flying Circus — Harleyford Ltd, 1958

Wellington College Year Book

Wellington Register

Who Downed the Aces in WWI? — Norman Franks, Grub Street, 1996

INDEX